HIGH COMMAND:
The Genius of Generalship from Antiquity to Alamein

The sword is the key of heaven and hell
Arab proverb

JOHN LAFFIN

BARNES
&NOBLE
B O O K S
NEW YORK

Originally published as *Links of Leadership*.

Copyright © 1966, 1995 by John Laffin
All rights reserved.

This edition published by Barnes & Noble, Inc.,
by arrangement with John Laffin.

1995 Barnes & Noble Books

ISBN 1-56619-792-9

Printed and bound in the United States of America

M 9 8 7 6 5 4 3 2 1

Author's Note

◆◆

BELIEVE that every victorious military commander has in-
erited something of his ability, perhaps without realizing it,
m his professional predecessors. Great generals are the links in
` chain of leadership, while the chain itself is made up of their
lective experience, transmitted from one commander to the
t by the reading, study, and appreciation of history. Many
litary leaders are mentioned in this book, but relatively few can
discussed at length, and they have been chosen because they
: the most representative or the most outstanding of their era.
ch of these generals is shown against the background of his
atest battle.

In places throughout the book I have used the term *chain of
nmand*; this possibly needs explanation. In the Armed Forces
: expression 'chain of command' is a formal term referring to
: structure of command, to the channel through which orders
: passed from the Supreme Command to subordinate com-
nders, or for any intermediate distance along this channel. It
vers the whole progressive sequence of implementing a decision
command, and equally it refers to the passing back of results
information from the lower to the higher echelons. However, in
netaphorical sense the term adequately fits the chain of leader-
p which is the subject of this book.

Acknowledgments

————— ◆◆◆ —————

M Y sources for this book begin with the Old Testament and e
with my own war experiences and conversations with sen
military commanders. Among classical and ancient writers I ha
referred to Tacitus, Procopius, Herodotus, Pausanias, Thucydid
Socrates (as quoted by others), Polyaenus, Plutarch, Polybi
Livy, Aelius Aristides, Aristotle, Velleius Paterculus, Strabo, a
to the works of anonymous monkish chroniclers of later times.

A full list of the 500 or so books which I found helpful wo
make tedious reading, so for the bibliography I have selected th
which were of most use and which I found most interesting. I
debt to all these historians is great, but individually I have nobo
to thank but my wife, whose labours on my behalf are beyo
recompense, and the publisher's readers, who made some valua
suggestions.

I am grateful to various publishers and authors for permissi
to quote from copyright material, in particular to Faber a
Faber, Ltd, in relation to writings by Sir Basil Liddell Hart and
Cassell and Co., Ltd, for permitting me to draw from my o
book, *Jackboot*, for material about certain Prussian and Germ
commanders.

Contents

Maps and Plans

CHAPTER ONE

---◈·◈---

The Hunger for Glory

'NOBODY who has systematically studied military science can
learn much in war.' So said General Gerhard von Scharn-
st, founder of the German General Staff.

This blunt statement, apparently inviting challenge, meant that
arnhorst believed that a leader who had studied battles and
rfare of the past would find actual conflict merely a natural and
urprising consequence of his research.

I intend to take Scharnhorst's claim even farther. I believe that
distinct linking of leadership or chain or command can be
arly seen in the grand canvas of warfare throughout recorded
tory and that some links in this chain are so strong and so en-
ring that each great commander can be shown to be in the debt
outstanding soldiers of the past. Generally, they all owe some-
ng to Gideon, victor over the Midianites about 1200 B.C. and
David, conqueror of Goliath about 1000 B.C. More specifically
ltiades, who won the battle of Marathon in 491 B.C., also won
battle of Alamein in 1942; the English bowmen who won
écy in 1346 also won Waterloo in 1815; Hannibal, the victor
Cannae in 216 B.C., was also victorious at Austerlitz in 1805;
poleon Bonaparte, who dominated the battle of Austerlitz and
o died in 1821, ruled the field at Solferino in 1859; Sabutai,
Mongol general who annihilated the Hungarian armies in
41, was responsible for the Prussian victories against the French
1870. Montgomery or MacArthur or von Rundstedt, who won
ttles during the war of 1939–45, might well win others a cen-
y or so hence. These are merely samples; other links in the
in will become evident.

Scharnhorst could have added that no commander or milita
historian sufficiently dedicated to his profession could possib
be surprised about any development in warfare, whether it co
cerns strategy and tactics, methods and weapons, equipment ar
uniforms, discipline and morale, civilian and political attitude
The outcome of a war and usually of a battle is crystal clear
to anybody willing to spend fifteen years or more in close study
three thousand years of warfare and high command.

Training by the study of history has not yet reached full d
velopment except in Germany, and cannot do so until Gener
Staffs realize that every military eventuality can be foretold l
close study of the past—and 'the past' means every moment
historical time up till yesterday.

No great commander is a copyist—those commanders wl
have slavishly copied an earlier general have nearly always fail
dismally—and the last impression I want to give is that one w
can be fought on the methods of a previous one. The circu
stances of war and the conditions under which the fighting tak
place are never repeated, but the essence of major tactics has n
changed so greatly as some writers would have us believe. Tl
methods of their application have altered—this is the point.
essence the general tactical principles used by Britain up to tl
time of the Second World War can be traced back directly to tho
of the Romans, while those of Germany prove an equally clo
descent from the tactics of Alexander the Great. The chain
command, when studied, is as clear and positive as this.

A commander might be isolated in time from other co
manders, but he achieves a unity with them by the historical r
sponsibility they have shared. Most great leaders have, througho
history, studied the campaigns of their predecessors, profiting l
their mistakes, capitalizing on their successes. The writings
many commanders show clearly that they have been close studen
of earlier great captains. A few, it is true, have been so egotistic
as to go their way without reference to history, but of these m
only one or two were successful, for another ingredient in tl
amalgam that makes a commander great is the readiness and tl
ability to profit from the experiences of others.

Charles James in his *Military Dictionary* of 1810 pointed o
that:

the best modern generals have never lost sight of the brillia
examples that they have been left; they have never ceased
call into practice the tactics of the ancients, as far as tl

difference of arms and a change of manners would allow. To those who peruse the histories of the 17th and 18th centuries and read over the actions of the most celebrated generals this observation will appear peculiarly apposite. It is justified in the uniform conduct of the great Condé, Prince Eugène, Turenne, Marlborough, Marshal Saxe and Frederick the Great. . . . Impressed as it were by the result of cumulative reflection they overlook immediate occurrences, *plunge into futurity and snatch out of the womb of time the ultimate issue of events*[1] . . .
Thus in the extensive field of modern and ancient military history everyone may find the particular kind and degree of instruction to which he is ambitious of arriving.

General de Gaulle was always acutely aware of the chain of mmand. He has no place in the battles recounted in this book, it since his ideas and ideals have been largely Napoleonic he s an assured place in the chain of command.
Writing in 1934, in *The Army of the Future*, he said:

Whatever the time and place there is a sort of philosophy of command, as unchangeable as human nature. It is the true lesson of military history. When Charles XII wept at the recital of Alexander's exploits, when Napoleon pored over Frederick the Great's campaigns, when Foch taught Napoleon's methods, it was because they were impregnated by the feeling of this permanence.

Gaulle himself was so 'impregnated' by this feeling that he t himself destined to lead France back to Napoleonic greatness.
One of Britain's most outstanding military writers, Colonel F. R. Henderson, wrote in 1905, in *The Science of War*:[2]

It can scarcely be denied that an intimate acquaintance with the processes of war, even though purely theoretical, is useful. . . . Military history offers a more comprehensive view of those processes than even active service. . . . The art of war is crystallized in a few great principles and it is the study of military history alone that makes such principles so familiar that to apply them . . . becomes a matter of instinct. . . .
Study of the campaigns of famous predecessors must be active and not passive. . . . We may take it that in soldiering there is more to be learned from the history of great campaigns than from manoeuvres of the training ground. For instance, a man thoroughly penetrated with the spirit of Napoleon's warfare would hardly fail to make his enemy's com-

[1] Author's italics.
[2] The book was published two years after the author's death.

munications his first objective; and if Wellington's tacti
methods had become a second nature to him it would be strai
if he were seduced into delivering a purely frontal attack.
Again, the study of military history results in the accumu
tion of facts and the knowledge of facts, however acquired, c
stitutes experience. The product of habit, which, as being
powerful in moments of excitement or danger, plays an ev
even more important part in warfare than in any other pha
of human affairs.

A nation loses wars and battles when its commanders have i
been acutely conscious enough of the chain of command, perha
because they were too dull, too vain, or too lazy. All the gr
military lapses in any nation's history can be easily explained
this principle, up to the cancerous decay of military leadership
France since 1870.

This is not to say that France has lost all military greatne
Given the right leadership, her soldiers could still fight. The Fig
ing French showed this against the Germans at Bir Hachei
Libya, in 1942 and even more spectacularly in the dogged defer
of the entrenched camp of Dien Bien Phu, North Vietna
1953–54. Communist General Vo Nguyen Giap wrote that "c
combatants fought with remarkable heroism and stubbornnes
before being encircled and forced into defeat. The French I
peditionary Force suffered 140,000 casualties in Indochina.

Every nation is apt to lose sight of the comparative standing
its own military leaders. To the German Frederick stands out i
equalled; to the Scandinavian, Gustavus; to the Frenchm:
Napoleon; to the Austrian, Prince Eugène or the Archdr
Charles; to the Englishman, Marlborough or Wellington. O
when the great leaders are studied in the perspective provided
the others can the place of each be adequately gauged. To
Englishman it probably seems outrageous to suggest that Prii
Eugène was equal as a general to Marlborough. But the pro
exists. Alone he conducted more successful campaigns, won m
victories, and performed more first-class work than Marlborou,
At Blenheim, Oudenarde, and Malplaquet he carried half
burden and won half the fame. But if a people as a whole tends
believe that its own commanders are the best, the great co
mander does not underestimate his foreign counterpart.

As a starting-point we could go back to the battle of Megid
1479 B.C., the first great clash known to us between the pasto
and agricultural civilizations, but this would be an inconveni

ginning, since information about the battle is partly conjecture,
d in any case it was relatively little known and therefore had no
eat influence on the chain of command.

Therefore we shall start with Gideon, one of the first great
ptains, and discuss the general theory of the linking of leader-
ip before progressing to the ten great battles described at length
this book, to the tumultuous centuries that separated these
ttles, and to the scores of colourful, dynamic, and enterprising
ilitary commanders whose writings, words, and actions prove
e existence of an intangible but powerful and enduring philo-
phy of command. The great captains held up as examples in
is book were not merely generals and commanders-in-chief; they
ere military craftsmen, superb artists of war.

A military force, to be effective, must live with the desire for
ttle, and its commanders must be hungry for 'glory'—what-
er that might mean to them individually. The great captains
ho live in this book had that hunger—Miltiades to Montgomery,
ey all had it.

The chain of command is not formed with links of even length
' even strength. It is an untidy chain, better looked at in per-
ective and better appreciated in long lengths. If we were to
udy only a brief period—say, a mere century—the links might
ot even appear to be joined.

To the sceptical I would be the first to admit that breaks exist
this chain; for example, the links were twisted and snapped by
e clumsy brutal imbeciles—there were outstandingly some ex-
ptions—who conducted the First World War. But, somehow or
her, the great captains who followed these periods of military
cay always managed to pick up the pieces and weld the chain
to shape. And so it will always be.

It is extraordinary how few observers and historians have
othered to give a description of the field *after* a battle, yet the
ying embers of conflict are often the most vivid and are always
e most tragic and poignant. Perhaps many historians believe
at the glory ends with the victory and prefer not to disturb
eir readers with the sordid details of the cleaning up. These
etails will be found in this book, at least in respect to some of the
attles, for, human and inhuman, they restore war to a proper
erspective and help rub the superficial gilt from the glory.

Yet mere acts of heroism or mere scenes of carnage do not
stify a battle's being called great any more than they necessarily
ake a battle important. Therefore the greatest of all cavalry

battles, Dorylaeum, A.D. 1097, finds no place in this book, wh
the only mention I can give of the Swiss piling up the rampart
ten thousand dead at St Jacob's, 1444, is here and now. So w
the vain charge of Talbot, representing the dying chivalry, agai
cannon and earthworks at Châtillon-sur-Seine, 1475.

As General Pierre Bosquet, watching the charge of the Li
Brigade, said, "It is magnificent, but it is not war."

For war is an art, not a trade.[3]

[3] At this point it might be as well to distinguish between strategy and tac
for the terms are sometimes carelessly used to mean the same thing,
most writers on war have their own definitions. The best simple definitio
that strategy forms the plans of war and brings troops to the battlefield, wh
tactics employs them and their weapons. To put it another way, tactics is
application in the field of the strategy evolved at the War Office or at h
quarters.

CHAPTER TWO

❖

Gideon started it

GIDEON went forth to battle because the Israelites, having
suffered for several years under the incursions of the Midi-
es, had finally decided that their very existence depended on
'ing off the invaders. The Midianites, "like a multitude of
sts, with camels as innumerable as the sands of the seashore",
hed their camp in the eastern part of the Plain of Esdraelon.[1]
re their stock devoured the Israelites' crops.

Vith his army Gideon advanced towards the plain and reached
hills near by. The only water available to the Israelites was at
foot of these hills and very close to the enemy. Most of the
elites were unskilled and untrained and, heedless of the proxi-
y of the enemy, drank deeply and carelessly. Guerrilla-like,
few veterans kept their weapon in one hand and their eyes
ards the enemy while they scooped up water with their other
d.

Most modern people, brought up on mechanized warfare, are
ware of the high state of the military art in the centuries be-
: Christ and, for that matter, in the early centuries *after* Christ.
: battles of this period were not mere wild tooth-and-nail
wls between savages, but were fought by well-equipped,
-accoutred soldiers, many of them professionals.

jideon chose his proven men—300 of them—for combat, for
ealized that his army as a whole was unfit for a pitched battle.
eon was a very early military propagandist; he saw to it that

This was near the modern El Afule—where, in 1917, General Allenby's
sh, Australian, and New Zealand horsemen cut Turkish communications.

stories spread to the Midianites about the remarkable porte
and omens that marked the rise of the Israelites' new leader, a
the stories fell on receptive minds.

Gideon's tactics were simple—he had to create panic in
enemy's ranks, and to this end he planned a night attack,
ambitious operation with a small, relatively inexperienced for
He formed his 300 men into three companies and sent other, l
worthy troops to hold fords across the Jordan.

He then issued to each of his 300 men a trumpet, a pitcl
and a torch—which must have seemed strange weapons to
men. However, if Gideon was the commander he appears to ha
been he probably took them into his confidence. Born to lead
ship, Gideon now made a personal reconnaissance with his t
man-runner, and learned that the Midianite outpost men w
nervous and edgy and that no enemy patrols were active.

He returned to his camp, gave battle orders and the passwe
"The sword of the Lord and of Gideon", a somewhat presur
tuous but confident appropriation of the Almighty's aid t
Cromwell, Napoleon, and Montgomery, among others, were
emulate.

The men lit their torches and hid them in the pitchers, she
their trumpets, grasped spears and swords. To strict timetable
companies moved off, quietly and well led, to their prede
mined positions around the enemy's camp.

About midnight—at which time the Midianites were in
habit of changing their watch—Gideon gave his signal. His
men blew their trumpets and waved their torches. The result v
instantaneous and spectacular as panic swept the Midianite car
In the darkness tribe fought tribe, tents and encampments w
wrecked, what discipline there was broke down. The Israeli
did not need to fight; they merely stood and watched while
Midianites fled. Gideon was too able a commander to leave
victory at that. Relentlessly he pursued and relentlessly he
tacked until the victory was complete in every sense.

The principles on which Gideon acted and the faithfulness w
which they were recorded established lessons for many gr
captains who came after him. These principles, which he put i
effect, are still entirely valid:

> Quality is better than quantity. A small force of well-chos
> trained, and steady men is better than a semi-train
> uncertain mass.

Attention to detail and sound staff work helps greatly towards victory.

It is important for a commander to make a personal pre-battle reconnaissance.

Enemy morale can be destroyed by a surprise night attack.

Action of the component parts of an army should be thoroughly co-ordinated.

An enemy can be softened up by stories of his opponent's 'invincibility'.

A commander must hold absolute command and must never be hampered by possibility of dispute with joint-commanders.

Choose the most suitable weapons for the action in hand.

The commander's own dominant personality and confidence will inspire confidence in his army and increase its morale.

Victory can only be complete when the pursuit is pushed to the limit and the enemy destroyed as well as demoralized. The enemy's retreat must be hampered by prior blocking of escape routes.

Troops in attack and pursuit should travel lightly.

Guile often succeeds where strength of arms could only fail.

Plans should be simple, especially for night actions.

A general must know the capabilities and limitations of his army.

Many great captains evolved maxims of their own based on [G]ideon's victory, and some were published—without a word of [cr]edit as to their original source—and were usually acted upon. [M]any of the earlier great captains and some of the later ones had [ce]rtainly not read the Bible, but a large number had heard the [st]ory and must have been consciously or subconsciously im-[pr]essed by it. The tactics of Gideon recur again and again, right [up] to Alamein.[2]

[2] Gideon was an enterprising commander in his own right, but it is tan-[ta]lizing to speculate on the possibility that his ruse was partly influenced by [m]emories of Joshua's trumpets at Jericho.

The Israelites established one principle, however, which wɑ rarely afterwards practised. Gideon was not what we should cɑ today a 'steady and safe' commander; in short, he was not med ocre. Thirty centuries of warfare have shown that few con manders whose abilities are limited to steadiness and safety wi battles or wars. War itself is neither steady, safe, nor predictabl₁ and therefore the original, imaginative general is the best con mander to have. Unfortunately, he often appears only after a lon series of defeats, rather as if somebody had said, "Well, we'v tried all the sound men, now let's give that eccentric Scipio a go. It is one of Napoleon's marks of military greatness that he chos few of his marshals for their 'soundness' but most of them fo their dash.

About two centuries after Gideon another Israelite army face₁ an army of Philistines. As their chosen representative the Phili stines sent forth Goliath, a well-armed giant of a man with a coɑ of mail said to weigh 5000 shekels of brass—a confident, veteraɪ soldier, scoffing at his opponent, the young David. David nimble but quite unarmoured and armed only with a sling, picke₁ up a stone and fired it at Goliath "and smote the Philistine an₁ slew him". Then, with a borrowed sword, he cut off the biɡ man's head.

Stones were hardly new as weapons—they must have beeɪ among the very first weapons man used—but in his fight Davi₁ formally introduced the missile into warfare, and showed that th₁ best way to overcome an enemy is not to rush at him with swor₁ or spear or to protect oneself with enveloping armour, but to kil him with an accurate bullet from a distance. Thus he established one of the first tactical principles of war. By cutting off Goliath's head David showed that for a victory to be complete the enemy must not only be felled but destroyed and his comrades demora- lized. The Prussian Clausewitz (1780–1831), the greatest philo- sopher of war, restated with startling clarity the principle illus- trated by David's victory.

One of the major links of leadership is that the great captains have realized that tactics and developmental innovations must be *thought out in advance*, as Gideon and David showed. We can begin with Epaminondas and his 'oblique order' in the fourth century B.C. and end with Guderian's panzers in 1940 and the Polaris submarines of the nineteen-sixties, and in the intervening centuries we can point, successively, to Hannibal's grasp of sur- prise tactics, Claudius Nero's use of interior lines, Scipio's use

planned reserve, all in the third century B.C., English longbow
d-off tactics at Crécy, 1346, Gustavus' 'combinations' in
Cromwell's use of battle discipline as a tactical weapon in the
enteenth century, Marlborough's ingenuity of manoeuvre early
the eighteenth century, Frederick's oblique attacking order
ing the middle years of the same century. Late in the eigh-
1th century and progressively through the nineteenth and
ntieth centuries we have Napoleon's rapid concentrations
tactical ambushes, Wellington's mastery of the defensive-
nsive, Moore's astonishing British light infantry, so spartan in
ir toughness, Scharnhorst's Prussian military machine, Moltke's
sso-German General Staff war-by-rail-and-telegraph system,
enby's bluff and deception, the will-o'-the-wisp tactics practised
Africa by the German Colonel von Lettow-Vorbeck 1914–18,
ntgomery's attitude of 'change the plan to fit the situation' in
nineteen-forties. These men won victories very largely because
y looked ahead, and, even more significantly, they *looked*
·k and saw that their predecessors had looked ahead.

Vhile battle was limited to sheer muscular action of men and
ses the leader's skill lay in keeping his forces in such a rela-
to the enemy, the field, and the sun as to be able to use his
1y rapier-style—cut, thrust, and parry. Resolution was para-
unt, for the determined soldier, company, or army could para-
the enemy with fear. Hence the commander had to inspire his
ordinates with enthusiasm and so increase their drive.

very leader had a direct view over the whole field of the en-
;ement; it is astonishing how frequently both commanders in
action managed to find a windmill or a tower of some sort, a
nsion roof or a mound from which to observe and direct battle.
en enough the commander could give orders without needing
ermediaries, and could by his presence and personal conduct
uence the behaviour of his men. Tactics depended on a quick
and quick reactions. Hannibal won his victories because he
both, backed by outstanding personal example.

n contrast to this in one way only has high command changed
ough the centuries—the commander's duties have become
re complex. But we shall see at the end of this book that even
his respect warfare is turning full circle.

deally, military command at any level is a rich compound of
ny ingredients. Foresight and anticipation. Leadership and
mple. Direction and control. Decision and daring. It pre-
poses superior knowledge and ability, and it is nearly always

accompanied by loneliness, which increases in proportion
rank. Few men reach high command, and of those who do few
still relish it, for with it comes awful responsibility. Fortunate
for the peace of mind of those who hold high command, by tl
time they have attained it most are also attuned to it.

Socrates (470–399 B.C.), himself a soldier for several year
was one of the first to summarize the qualities required by
general. His assessment, as quoted by others, made an impre
sion on many commanders up to as recent a leader as Wave
who quoted Socrates' sayings as a foreword to one of his ow
books.

> The general must know how to get his men their rations an
> every other kind of stores needed in war. He must have i
> agination to originate plans, practical sense and energy to s
> them through. He must be observant, untiring, shrewd, kind
> and cruel, simple and crafty, a watchman and robber, lavi
> and miserly, generous and stingy, rash and conservative. A
> these and many other qualities, natural and acquired, he mu
> have. He should also, as a matter of course, know his tactic
> for a disorderly mob is no more an army than a heap of buil
> ing materials is a house.

Socrates was giving a blueprint for the most complex, challen
ing, and frighteningly responsible job known to man.[3] Most
the great captains of history can be measured against it.

There are always those who fail when put to a sharp or ir
mense test, though not necessarily because of their own deficie
cies; for defeat may be the result solely of insufficient strength
relation to the power of the enemy. Napoleon did not fail the te
at Waterloo, despite his defeat; Hannibal did not fail in any w
at Zama, 202 B.C., although Scipio defeated him decisively. H
brother, Hasdrubal, was killed and had his army decimated at tl
Metaurus, 207 B.C., but he did everything that a great con
mander could do. History has known victorious commanders wl
had smaller quantities of the ingredients of high command tha
did the men they vanquished; on the day of the test circumstanc
simply happened to fall their way. Hindenburg won the battle
Tannenberg in 1914, not so much by superior skill, as becau
he happened to get hold of a copy of the Russian field cipher.

Command, and especially high command, calls for the abili

---

[3] Nockhern de Schorn in his *Idées Raisonnées sur un Système Génér*
wrote that the life of man is not sufficient for the acquirement and full posse
sion of the science of war in all its parts and branches.

how compassion on one occasion and ruthlessness on another.
io Africanus showed both on practically the same day in 209
He terrorized New Carthage by sacking the town and then
aved kindly to the Spanish hostages he found there and loaded
n with presents. This had a profound influence on winning
goodwill of the people.

ympathy and understanding are vital qualities in a com-
nder, and only through them can he gain real co-operation.
itrary control will stand up for a time, but, being no more
n voice control, it breaks down sooner or later, as it did for
ler.

ome soldiers have originated tactics which have echoed down
centuries. A prime example is the Athenian Xenophon, the
atest rearguard commander in history. After the defeat of
us the Younger by Artaxerxes at Cunaxa in 401 B.C. Xeno-
n commanded the rearguard of the Ten Thousand in their
rch to the Euxine. He carried out this controlled and disci-
ed retreat for fourteen months and marched more than 4000
es. He was the originator of all rearguard tactics, and no simi-
action in modern times reveals any tactic not employed by
nophon. Modern rearguard actions directly attributable to the
nophon method include: Moreau's rearguard offensive against
suing Austrians in 1796; the gallant rearguard actions by
John Moore's troops at the defile of Constantino and at Cal-
ellos in 1809 to check the French; Ney's protection of Mas-
a's retreat from the line of Torres Vedras in 1811; the holding
El Bodon heights and village by Wellington to cover his with-
wal in 1811; Ney's superb rearguard actions during the French
eat from Moscow in 1812; Lee's use of two brigades and
ty guns to cover his retreat from Sharpsburg in 1862; John-
n's series of actions to delay Sherman's advance, 1864; the
ering of the First Austrian Corps at Müchengratz in 1866; the
ited infantry, artillery, and cavalry rearguard defence during
retreat from Mons in 1914; Townshend's covering of his re-
it from Ctesiphon in 1915; Rommel's splendid delaying
ions against Montgomery after Alamein in 1942.

he outstanding military pioneer of the seventeenth century,
stavus Adolphus, the creator of the first 'modern army', re-
led that he prized the teaching of Xenophon. The *Cyropaedia*,
nophon's book, was for Gustavus his military Bible, as it was
the great captains of the ancient world.

A study of Gustavus's tactical formations clearly shows that

they were adapted from the Roman legion and its manoeuverab[
maniples.

Not all leaders have learnt from the successes or failures
their predecessors. At the battle of Pydna (Macedonia) in 168 B[
Perseus, commanding the Macedonians, apparently had no co[
ception of the tactics employed by Alexander the Great, who h[
built the Macedonian and Hellenistic empires. Alexander w[
his greatest victory, Arbela, in 331 B.C. by taking advantage of
big gap in the Persian front. At Pydna it was the Roman lead[
Aemilus Paullus, who clearly had learned how to exploit such [
opportunity. When several small gaps appeared in the Maced
nian phalanx of pikemen Paullus quickly ordered units of [
force to infiltrate these gaps, thus leading to the collapse of t
Macedonian army, with the loss of 20,000 killed. Had Ale
ander's front become full of holes he would have pushed forwa
all his cavalry and light infantry against the Romans—who, as
happened, were badly shaken at that moment—and under the
protection would have reformed his front of pikemen. Perseu[
failure to apply Alexandrian tactics destroyed the empire
Alexander, 155 years after his death.

Again and again one finds contemporary historians referri[
to 'new strategy', 'new tactics', 'new methods'. There a
'new types of generals', and 'revolutionary advances in mobili[
mechanization, and military engineering'. They even talk
'new principles of war'. Strictly speaking, there are not even a[
new weapons, for no entirely new weapon has much influenc
the course of any war; the decisive weapon in a war has alwa
been known in a previous war, although it might have then be[
in only a crude form. There was nothing new about the Germ[
rocket bombs of the Second World War; rockets as military p[
jectiles had been invented by Sir William Congreve almost 1[
years earlier. The atom bomb was new only in its vastly increas[
destructiveness.

Frederick the Great has been credited—and not only by Pr[
sian and German historians—with having invented the obliq[
order of battle, discussed in the account of the battle of Leuth[
(Chapter Twelve). But Frederick, an educated man, had re[
about the battle of Leuctra, which took place in 371 B.C., wh[
Epaminondas with 6000 Thebans defeated 11000 Spartans by t[
oblique battle-order.

Alexander the Great's army provided other lessons for Fr[
erick, two thousand years later. Alexander's army not only had

ajor and basic cavalry and phalanx, but many lightly equipped
its, archers, javelin-men, slingers, horsemen. This swarm of
egulars foraged for the main body and protected it while on the
arch and in battle co-operated with it.

Frederick copied these tactics, using Pandours, Croats, and
rolese riflemen. True guerrillas, they spread in all frontal direc-
ns, adding weight to the more deliberately moving profes-
nals they protected. As the mass neared the enemy the light
ldiers would usually edge round the flanks to the rear. When the
emy was defeated they would harass his withdrawal and hold
ptured ground. Sometimes they would swarm—and 'swarm'
ally is the word—around the enemy's flanks, not giving battle,
t acutely embarrassing him. If their own army was beaten they
uld provide a difficult-to-get-at rearguard.

Hitler the would-be Great used truck-borne infantry, motor-
cle infantry, and motorized artillery in just the same way. Their
ctics were irregular and were based on opportunism, mobility,
d independence just as were those of the Greeks, and the earlier
ussians.

"Hitler has organized a brand-new kind of private army", wrote
newspaper correspondent in 1936. Private armies were not new
en when the Emperor Augustus came to power, but in 27 B.C.
organized one of the most efficient private armies—the Prae-
rian Guard. During the last years of the Roman Republic
any commanders had raised special bodyguards—*cohortes
aetoriae*, so named because the general's camp headquarters
is called the *praetorium*. When Augustus restored the republic
kept these guards and organized them into nine cohorts, each
1000 men. The whole principle underlying the formation, re-
ntion, and use of the Praetorian Guard was copied by Hitler,
th his Brownshirts and S.S., though both these organizations
sumed larger proportions and wider duties than did the Prae-
rian Guard. The Life Guards of Britain were a very similar
rmation to the Praetorian Guard, although they were not used
support a military autocracy as the Praetorian Guard was.

Caesar (102–44 B.C.) left a considerable contribution to military
adership, though in the intervening years he has become larger
an life. Fine leader and efficient soldier that he was, he does not
ual Napoleon, Gustavus Adolphus, or Frederick the Great as
all-round leader.

He was certainly the soul of his army, and in this he equals, for
ample, Alexander and Hannibal in ancient times and General

Moore (of Light Division fame), the Americans Sherman a
Lee, von Lettow-Vorbeck, Montgomery, and Rommel of m
recent times. Caesar was constantly interested in his soldiers' w
being, though the Roman historian Suetonius notes that
valued his soldiers neither for their personal character nor th
fortune, but solely for their prowess. In this he was like Welli
ton, who did not give a damn for his soldiers as human beings.
later historian, Mommsen, said that Caesar treated his soldi
"as men who are entitled to demand and were able to end
the truth". Montgomery certainly emulated Caesar in t
respect. When Caesar and Montgomery were with their men
feat never entered their head.

Caesar had four great qualities as a leader of armies. His c
fidence in his own genius was immense, and he was an c
standing organizer: he had a true conception of war in his o
era, and was thus able to visualize a grand strategy clearly:
could foresee his enemy's intentions: he had that streak of au
city and bold self-confidence that made him immune to
fears and apprehensions that beset lesser leaders and tied th
down.

Alexander, Hannibal, and Scipio had much the same qualit
but Alexander and Hannibal had actually hammered into sha
the type of army that fitted their own genius. Scipio and Cae
inherited their army system, though Caesar improved on w
was left to him.

Many generals have followed Caesar in having faith in th
own genius, and even if that genius was nothing more than a
perbolic term for extreme thoroughness the faith they had in
served its purpose. Since most great generals studied Caesar a
his campaigns at some time of their earlier military career it
reasonable to suppose that they were influenced by him.
modern times Cromwell, Marlborough, Napoleon, Masséna (c
of Napolean's marshals), Frederick, Gustavus, Clive, Sherm
Wellington, Moltke, "Gordon of Khartoum", Kitchener, Eis
hower, Patton, MacArthur, Montgomery, the Australians M
ash and Morshead—all these men, though of differing statu
had great faith in their own genius.

Most of them, and others, had Caesarian audacity, too. Cl
of those who inherited this are Charles XII of Sweden; Freder
the Great; the Englishmen Marlborough, Wolfe, Clive, Be
ford, Elles; the Frenchmen Soult and Ney; the American Sl
man; the German general Guderian; and Morshead.

CHAPTER THREE

———————◇◆◇———————

The Moral Element and
Mobility

N Napoleon, perhaps more than in any other military commander, can be clearly seen the result of intensive study of military history, of which he is the arch-advocate. Many generals have learned from their own mistakes; Napoleon tried to void making his mistakes; he learned from the mistakes and from the triumphs of others. His only major mistakes occurred when he had no lessons from history to guide him. Had an earlier commander made a disastrous march to Moscow Napoleon would never have done so. Napoleon was familiar with every great battle ever fought, and though no battle can ever be a copy of an earlier one, he applied the strategy and tactics of his military forbears to his own campaigns.

"Read, re-read the history of the eighty-eight campaigns of Alexander, Hannibal, Caesar, Gustavus, Turenne, Eugène, and Frederick," Napoleon said emphatically.

His debt to these previous great captains and to others is discussed in detail elsewhere in this book. But what did he find in the history of the campaigns of Alexander, Hannibal, and Julius Caesar? He found a record of marches and manoeuvres and of the general principles of attack and defence, but all this was mechanical and elementary. What he found most valuable was a complete study of human nature under war conditions—details of men under discipline, affected by fear, hunger, lack of confidence, over-confidence by distrust, shock, patriotism, political

interests, the oppression of responsibility, physical, emotio
mental, moral, and sexual stress.

He was no imitator; no great general can be, for no campa
or battle can have its exact prototype in history. But from hist
Napoleon learned the vast value of the moral element, and
use of this knowledge became instinctive. He was able to w
on the minds and emotions of his own men and of his enemie
at long distance and close range—with a subtlety and skill t
few generals have equalled and none have surpassed.

A great general, as distinct from merely a competent one, c
penetrate his opponent's brain—and his study of history as m
as his own ability has helped him to do this. All the great c
tains had this faculty. By getting into his opponent's brain Mi
ades defeated Datis, Arminius defeated Varus, Cromwell
feated the Royalists, Turenne, Frederick, and Napoleon defea
all and sundry, and Montgomery defeated Rommel.

War is, or should be, more of a struggle between two hum
intelligences than between two masses of armed men.[1]

"It is to be ignorant and blind", wrote Hannibal's Greci
biographer, "in the science of commanding armies, to thi
that a general has anything more important to do than to ap
himself to learning the inclinations and the character of his a
versary." He ascribes Hannibal's astonishing victories to I
observance of this maxim.

When Napoleon's baggage was captured during the retro
from Moscow the Russians found among his private pape
biographies of all the Russian generals opposed to him.

Wellington closely studied the French marshals, so that on o
occasion when facing Soult he was able to observe that So
"is a very cautious commander" and based his tactics on this fa

Up till 1815 at least the French made a more careful study
military history in all its facets than any other nation. All milita
papers, records, and correspondence since 1661 in the time
Louvois were kept in the War Department in Paris and with su
splendid system that anything could be referred to in a momer
When the expedition which sailed for Bantry Bay in 1796 w
fitted out it was done entirely from papers found in the W
Department; they had been there since 1689, the year in whic
action took place between the French and English fleets in th

---

[1] As Liddell Hart pointed out in 1929 in *Thoughts on War*, "the profounde
truth of war is that the issue of battles is usually decided in the minds of tl
opposing commanders, not in the bodies of their men."

. From these papers, which were in such immaculate order
v might have been placed there the day before, detailed in-
ctions were given to every senior officer.

he British have never had such a fine system, which perhaps
vhy they 'always lose at the beginning', even if it does not
lain why 'they always win in the end'.[2]

ll the generals of the American Civil War paid close atten-
. to the moral aspect of war, and the Southern General Lee
cially so. He studied his opponent, knew his peculiarities,
adapted himself to them. His military secretary revealed
he had "one method with McLellan, another with Pope,
ther with Hooker, and yet another with Grant".

: is no puzzle to realize that the Russian Skobeleff (or Skobe-
was the first European general to master the problem of the
nsive. As he said, he "knew the American War by heart",
in his successful assault on the Turkish redoubts at Plevna in
7 he followed the plan of the American generals on both
s when attempting to carry such positions. He followed up the
ulting column with fresh troops without waiting for the first
e repulsed. But the Americans had learned these methods
n the British; there is a strong similarity between the tactics of
American Civil War and those taught in the British *Field
rcises*. And the British had learned from Napoleon, who
er kept a reserve 'for tomorrow'.

he blitzkrieg—the lightning war—is another supposedly new
hod of warfare. The word is new, but the tactics are ancient.
: keynote of all reforms had been 'increase of mobility',
all the more enlightened leaders strove for it. This is evident
any study of men like Gustavus, Cromwell, Marlborough,
derick and Napoleon. From the advent of mechanization
ility has been pushed to what I should be inclined to call the
t, did not history show that there is no apparent limit.

he real break-through with mobility arrived in Europe with
Mongols in the twelfth and thirteenth centuries. With armies
quality, highly mobile, the Mongols' tactics were flexible in
cution, and their moves were made with clockwork precision.
y combined fire and shock tactics—disorganizing the enemy

In August or September 1794 the British Army occupied ground near Bois
uc that had been occupied by the Duke of Cumberland in 1747, and a
ch was made for records of that campaign, but nothing could be found, not
. a sketch map. Marlborough had operated over the same country for
ral weeks during 1703, but to have expected to find records would have
futile.

by fire and then charging him with relentless, ordered spe
while they sought out soft spots.

When necessary the Mongol horse-archers would ride
close as possible to the enemy and then go to ground to give cov
ing fire while other horsemen, armed with lance or swo
charged the enemy. If necessary they could withdraw to the p
tection of their covering-fire position. This leap-frogging proc
would go on until the enemy was overcome.

The Germans based their mechanized and armoured tac
precisely upon those of the Mongols. Light armour or motori
infantry would test the enemy's defence, and if they found
strong would take reasonable cover and engage the enemy wl
the heavy tanks or bombers came up.[3]

Deceit too is supposed to be something fairly new in v
although it is something that the enemy uses, but never ones
never the side on which God is fighting. There is nothing r
about deception. Gideon used it effectively. Polyaenus mad
collection of more than 900 stratagems for the use of Ror
emperors in the war against Parthia in the second century A
Verus and Antonius thought that no deceit was too bad to se
as a good precedent for the conduct of war, and every sold
from private to field-marshal, at some time or another makes
of deception, even if only in order to survive. In ancient tir
deceit was fairly straightforward. A besieging general would o
the defenders of a town safe conduct if they laid down their ar
then, as they filed weaponless out of the gates, they would
slaughtered. Today, with increased intellectualism, deceit is m
more complex and subtle, and ranges from unfounded atro
stories—"the Germans are throwing babies on to bayonets
to letters allegedly found on dead enemy soldiers purporting
tell of their despair and their bestialities. Faked photographs
hundreds of different subjects were a deceit-refinement used
the Second World War.

The chain of command has impressed itself into strategy
well as into tactics, but tactics are given much greater wei
than strategy in this book because they are more usually the p
vince of individual commanders, while strategy is the busines
what we might term the 'base staff'.

However, it is necessary to refer to the so-called strategy
'indirect approach'. Alexander showed by his overthrow

---

[3] A fuller account of these tactics will be found in Chapters Eight, Twe
one, and Twenty-two.

rsia and Scipio by his defeat of Carthage that when fighting a
ajor enemy supported by minor enemies it is more efficient to
ush the minor ones first and individually than to attack the
ajor power. The Romans and the Macedonians built their
mpires on this system, and later Napoleon followed it assi-
ously. The British Empire was built on the same pattern, and
e United States climbed to positive power in much the same
ay. In a way the strategy was used against Nazi Germany, when
r satellite limbs were hacked off one by one—Libya, Tunisia,
cily, Italy, Holland, the Eastern countries, and so on. It might
ell be argued that since Germany had buffers in all directions
e could not be directly attacked except by air, but I believe that,
matter what her geographical position might have been, the
rategy of indirect approach would have been the only feasible
ay of defeating her. That Germany could not be knocked out
the smashing, continual blows from the air appears to prove
is belief.

Of the roughly 300 campaigns of the 30 major wars covered
the period of this book, in only 6, up to 1939, was a decisive
sult achieved by a direct strategic approach to the main army
the enemy. The most recent of them up to 1939 were Wagram,
09, Sadowa, 1866, and Sedan, 1870. Between 1939 and 1945
alingrad and Alamein were the only two purely military victories
hieved in this direct manner.

It would be possible to point to many wars and battles where
e result might well have been reversed had the senior com-
anders of the defeated side been more conscious of the chain of
mmand and had they "read" and "re-read" those eighty-
ht campaigns and others as well. Two modern examples will
sufficient.

Study of previous wars and campaigns would have helped
e Japanese in their war with Russia in 1904. Indeed, they had
udied recent campaigns, but they should have gone farther
ck, to Turenne, Marlborough, Napoleon, Sherman. Inanely,
e Japanese concentrated their strength and threw it straight at
e Russian Army. No Japanese general, it appeared, had intel-
gence enough to study a map or to reflect that the Russian
my, far, far removed from its bases, depended for its day-to-day
istence on the trans-Siberian railway. By cutting this single-line
ack the Japanese could quickly have strangled the Russians into
bmission. Instead they exhausted themselves in a series of
oody, stand-off brawls and were lucky to be able to make peace.

A decade later military command began to ebb towards i lowest watermark. The generals were given a blank cheque i lives, equipment, and money. Inevitably this led to extravaganc and it killed any sense of improvisation and enterprise. In ai case, these generals had never learned the supreme lesson of t study of military history—that the past enables a command to forecast the future. They had made no realistic plans in a vance.

Liddell Hart, in *Thoughts on War*, emphasized that "the are over two thousand years of experience to tell us that the on thing harder than getting a new idea into the military mind is get an old one out". This biting comment is unfortunately on too true—of second-class commanders. The Great Captains ha not been so inhibited, as Liddell Hart himself indirectly observe "Throughout military history the hallmark of the Great Captai has been that they stripped the art of war of the coils of custor that . . . like ivy drain the sap from the tree of commonsense."

During 1914–18 the generals apparently thought little nothing of mountains of butchered men. Manpower and shell-fi seemed inexhaustible, so blind force replaced surprise ar mobility. Very few leaders of the thousands who functioned 1914–18 were able to break through the doctrine of force and use their brains.[4]

If they had no outstanding mental capacity of their own the could have used or taken notice of the several accurate, detaile forecasts published in English and in their own time about t trend of war. As early as 1817 one of Napoleon's general Rogniat, in his *On the Art of War*, made some pertinent cor ments about the way war was bound to develop, as indeed it ha already developed in some of Napoleon's later campaigns.

Rogniat noted that it was wrong to place excessive relianc on artillery, and claimed that the number of guns should be inverse proportion to the excellence of the troops. If a cor mander relied chiefly on artillery, Rogniat reasoned, he was tie to the good roads, for only on them could he advance his gui and his munitions wagons. In the battle he mounted his guns t command the enemy's lines, so that the infantry merely supporte the guns. "Therefore the engagement merely degenerates into a artillery duel at long range, little or no pursuit is possible and th whole thing becomes a cruel game which wastes men's lives wit out results and leads to an endless prolongation of the war."

[4] They are named in Chapter Twenty.

he influence of history and of various great captains is shown the maxims published in the British Army's *Field Service ʒulations*. Their appearance here is to be commended, but it ns a pity that the originators of the maxims are not credited. Iere are some samples:

Moral qualities are the soul of victory. *Said by several com-nanders, Napoleon especially.*

There must exist unity of direction and control of the armed ɔrces. *Clausewitz.*

Impersonal, passive or weak command inevitably results in ɔss of morale, in want of resolution and ultimately in failure. *ʼound in military writings as far back as those of Caesar.*

The full power of an army can be exerted only when all its ·arts combine in action. *Napoleon.*

A commander [when acting on the offensive] must be clear n his own mind as to what he has to do in order to achieve ·is object and be determined to succeed in his task. His plan, ɔnceived in accordance with the principles of war [which is antamount to saying that the commander must be well read], nust be simple and based on the best information possible; it nust be understood by subordinates and carried through by hem with resolution. *Noted by dozens of great captains and nilitary writers.*

It is by superior fire-power and not by men's bodies that uccess is won. *Put into practice by the Biblical David, exer-ised at Crécy, stated by Mahomet (among others) in the fteenth century, and finally regurgitated, inter alios, by Churchill.*

In order to achieve victory a commander must sooner or ater assume the offensive. *This goes back to the Chinese ɣeneral Sun Tzŭ, the earliest known military commentator.*[5] Its ruth is so obvious that many great captains have not bothered ɔ re-state it, but have merely put the principle into practice. Iowever, Bernhardi, a leading German military thinker of the ast generation, said bluntly, "The offensive is the stronger orm of war and has even gained in superiority."[6]

The offensive is the stronger form of war." We shall see this strated by Miltiades at Marathon.

Ɉe wrote *The Art of War* five hundred years before Christ. See Appendix. ɪupporters of the defensive quote Clausewitz's statement—"The defensive ɪ of war is in itself stronger than the offensive", but fail to appreciate the ification of the phrase *in itself,* and apparently have not read a few lines ɪer where Clausewitz says that "We must make use of it [the defensive] as long as our weakness compels us to do so."

CHAPTER FOUR

---◇◦◇---

Unorthodoxy at Marathon

ARLY in the afternoon of a September day in the year 491 B.C.
n Athenian general, Miltiades, gave to his small but compact
y the command to prepare for battle. This was a momentous
er, for it led to the shaping of history, and the battle that
owed provided a model which many a general would follow
he centuries to come.[1]

Jo battle could better serve as a starting-point for a study of
links of leadership, because the victor was the weaker
nerically, because he had his opponent at a psychological
dvantage before the battle, because he dared to take the
iative, and because the fruit of the victory was the birth of
ope, from where most of the great generals of history were to
1e.

roperly to understand Marathon we must retreat briefly to
B.C., the year of the death of the Persian ruler Cambyses—
n the Persian Empire stretched from the borders of India to
Aegean Sea, from Nubia to the Black Sea, and from the
ian Ocean to the Caspian Sea. The Persians, in thirty violent,
orious years, had swallowed up four great kingdoms—Media,
ylonia (Chaldea), Lydia, and Egypt. Heir to this great
still unconsolidated empire was Hystaspes, but while he

I must admit that some historians claim the importance of Marathon to
xaggerated. Liddell Hart believes that the Greeks exaggerated it because of
impression the victory made on their imagination and that, through
, Europeans in all subsequent ages over-valued it. But he does admit that
reduction of its importance to juster proportions its strategical significance
creased".

procrastinated a pretender seized the throne, only to be killed Darius (521–483 B.C.), son of Hystaspes.

Darius assumed sovereignty and organized the empire, div ing it into twenty regions, each ruled by a capable governor. created a strong fleet to command the Eastern Mediterranean a built a system of roads to link the regions with his capital S —also known as Suster or Shúshan. One of the first rulers to the necessity for rapid communications, he established a post station and inns every 14 miles along his roads so that a m senger could cover the 1600 miles from Sardis to Susa in less th a week.

A thoughtful, thorough, systematic general, Darius put army on a divisional basis. Each division had 10,000 me formed into ten battalions of ten companies, each compa having ten sections. Most of his senior officers and garrison co manders were Persians or Medes, while his royal bodyguard—t 10,000 "Immortals"—was exclusively Persian. His cavalry t was wholly Persian. His organization must have been extrem efficient and was indeed an outstanding achievement of t epoch.

With an eye capable equally of appreciating the petty and t important, Darius set out to secure his empire from attack. Af a series of campaigns in the East he pushed his frontier beyo the Indus, using this great river and the mountains west of it li some great moat and wall. This task was relatively easy; securi the western frontier was difficult. Darius recognized that the g between the Caspian Sea and the Hindu Kush was a weakness his frontier, but this he could block if necessary. In practice weakest frontier was along the shores of the Aegean and t Sea of Marmara. Darius believed that, because the peoples either side of these seas were of kindred race and therefore like to help each other in adversity, he must force his frontier we ward until all the many Greek states were behind it.

About the year 512 B.C. he crossed the Bosphorus, sailed up t Danube a little way and made a foray north. Eventually he wi drew to Sardis, leaving behind his lieutenant, Megabazus, and powerful army to reduce Thrace from the Sea of Marmara to t Struma river. Megabazus tried to reduce Macedonia, too, a though he failed, its king, Alexander, acknowledged allegiance Darius.

This was the real beginning of a two hundred years' war tween Greece and Persia, the first recorded conflict betwe

rope and Asia. The historic struggle between East and West,
ll in progress, began at that point.

It is possible that at this date Darius had never heard of the
istence of insignificant Athens, although Athenians had cer-
nly found their way to some of the Persian dominions in Asia
nor to plead for armed assistance against their fellow-country-
en. Chief of the refugees was Hippias, the tyrannical ruler of
hens, who had been driven out in 510 B.C. The Athenians sent
voys to Sardis to urge the Persians not to take up the quarrel
the Athenian refugees, but Artaphernes, Darius's governor at
rdis, bluntly told the envoys that the Athenians must take back
ppias if they wanted to be secure.

While this crisis mounted the Ionian Greeks pleaded with
eral cities and states for help to regain their independence
m Persia. Athens and the city of Eretria in Euboea—the large
and off the coast of South-east Greece—were the only ones
give help. Twenty Athenian galleys and five Eretrian crossed
e Aegean Sea, and the troops they carried made a bold sur-
se attack on Sardis, capturing it from the domineering Arta-
ernes. The startled Persians rallied, and the small Greek
rce was forced back and then defeated before it reached the
ast.

Heredotus graphically describes Darius's reaction:

> When it was told to King Darius that Sardis had been taken
> and burnt by the Athenians and Ionians he took small heed of
> the Ionians . . . but he asked who, and what manner of men, the
> Athenians were. And when he had been told he called for his
> bow . . . let the arrow fly towards heaven . . . and said, "O
> Supreme God! Grant me that I may avenge myself on the
> Athenians". And when he had said this he appointed one of
> his servants to say to him every day as he sat at meat, "Sire,
> remember the Athenians".[2]

Darius's fury is understandable when we realize that dozens of
ngdoms were in his power—among them such powerful races as
e Syrians, Assyrians, Chaldees, Phoenicians, Babylonians,
rmenians, Palestinians, Bactrians, Phrygians, Parthians, Ly-
ans, Medes.[3] The Medes ranked next to native Persians in
nour, and the empire was frequently spoken of as that of the

---

[2] "Remember Pearl Harbor!"

[3] In one inscription which has survived Darius describes himself as "Darius
Great King, King of Kings, the King of the many-peopled countries, the
porter also of this great world".

Medes and Persians. It was to be a Mede whom Darius wc
choose to exact vengeance on the Athenians.

After he had completely reduced Ionia, Darius ordered
victorious forces to punish Athens and Eretria and to conq
European Greece. In 492 B.C. his son-in-law, Mardonius, redu
Thrace, compelled Alexander of Macedonia again to submit
Persia, and was about to advance into Greece when his fleet
wrecked by a storm off the Acte Peninsula, near Mount Atl
Darius ordered a larger army to be collected and sent to all
maritime cities of the Persian empire for ships to carry cava
and infantry across the Aegean. Heralds toured the Grecian ci
demanding submission to Persia. Nearly all the contine
Greeks and islanders submitted, but Athens and Sparta—
Greek warrior-state—spiritedly refused, and underlined tl
decision by beating the Persian envoys.

In the summer of 491 B.C.[4] the invasion army was assemble
the Aleian Plain of Cilicia and embarked on a fleet of 600 gall
and many transports. Darius placed command of the force joi
with Datis, a Median general, and to Artaphernes, a son of
governor of Sardis. Datis held the effectual command, with spe
instructions from Darius to take Athens and Eretria and
bring all the inhabitants away as slaves.

After some minor actions Artaphernes attacked Eretria,
which Athens had sent 4000 troops to help in the defence,
they heard in time that Eretria was to be betrayed by so
leading Eretrians and hastened back to defend their own c
Datis crossed to the Attic coast at Marathon, 25 miles no
east of Athens, where he drew up his galleys on the shelv
beach. His rear was entirely secure, for he held all the isla
and on many of them, especially Euboea, provisions and milit
stores.

Datis's decision to land at Marathon was largely influenced
the renegade Athenian Hippias, who was in touch with a group
would-be traitors in Athens—the powerful and noble Alcmae
dae family—who, to obtain pardon for the Athenian part in
Ionian revolt, were willing to take orders from the Persia
These traitors suggested that if the Athenian Army could
lured away from Athens while another Persian force was lan
at Phaleron, near Athens, to support the Alcmaeonidae, Ath
could be carried by revolt instead of by ruinous battle.

[4] 490 B.C. is the traditional date for the battle, but modern belief is that
correct year was 491 B.C.

Hippias had another reason for suggesting Marathon; 47 years
eviously he and his father had won an easy victory over their
henian enemies on that very plain.

But Hippias made a serious mistake in proposing Marathon as
battlefield, a mistake so serious that it gave the Athenians a
stinct psychological advantage, and one Miltiades was astute
ough to be aware of. Marathon itself was a region sacred to
ercules; the plain was the scene of the exploits of the Athenian
tional hero, Theseus. Also, according to old legends, on this
in the Athenians and the Heraclidae had beaten the invader,
rystheus. In short, the plain of Marathon was almost holy
ound for the Athenians, and men will fight especially hard for
eir own holy ground.

The Athenians sent a messenger to Sparta asking for help, and
o one to Plataea, on the Gulf of Corinth. It is doubtful if this
essenger's duty was to do more than give news of the invasion,
r Plataea was a weak state. Nevertheless, the Plataeans at
ce equipped and sent 1000 men to help the Athenians, a
nerous gesture to repay Athenian help to Plataea in a similar
sis a few years before.

The courier to Sparta covered the 150 miles in 48 hours,
riving on September 9th. The Spartans, the finest soldiers
 Greece, at once promised aid, but they had religious
ruples about moving before the night of the full moon on
ptember 19th–20th when a particular festival was held.
ey would send help the moment this festival was over they
id.

The Athenians took the Persian bait and probably realized
at it was a bait. They no more wanted battle in the city than the
itors did. About 10,000 strong, the army marched north from
hens, wheeled towards Marathon, and camped in the valley
 Avlona near the shrine of Hercules. The Persian Army was by
is time ashore, camping under the protection of the Great
arsh. South of the marsh lay the Plain of Marathon, cut practi-
lly in half by the Charadra river. On the southern flank of the
ain was the Little Marsh. The entire plain between the Great
arsh and the Little Marsh, and edged by the rugged limestone
lls which overlooked it on the west, covered no more than eight
uare miles.

The Persians had had time to occupy the passes leading from
e plain to Athens but had not done so, hence it was obvious
at they did not intend to make an overland march on Athens.

The wise course for the Greeks appeared to be a wait until
Spartans could join them, and for eight days the opposing arm
warily watched each other.

At this point news came through that Eretria had fal
through treachery and the inhabitants were bound for shipm
to the Persian Gulf as slaves. Artaphernes could now move
sea to Athens and capture the city while Datis held the Athen
Army impotent at Marathon.

A council of war, momentous as it happened, was summor
to the slope of Mount Agrieliki, overlooking the plain. The syst
of Athenian command is now obscure, but basically the army l
a polemarch or war-ruler who held command for a year—Ca
machus at the time of Marathon—under whom were ten gener
each a tribal leader and each holding tactical command fo
day at a time. On the day that the news arrived that A
phernes was embarking his troops the general of the day v
Miltiades, and it was he who dominated the council of w
Two of the eleven generals present were Themistocles,
future founder of the Athenian Navy and the victor of Salan
and Aristides, who later led the Athenian troops at the battle
Plataea.

Miltiades wanted an immediate attack on the Persians. T
idea was put to the vote, which resulted in five generals agai
Miltiades and four with him.

The five who did not favour battle based their objections
the Persians' numerical strength, which has been much deba
over the centuries. Between 100,000 and 150,000 sailed from
Persian bases, but Datis's effective strength at Marathon v
probably no more than 20,000.

Everything now depended on the vote Callimachus cast. He
dotus, who spoke to veterans of Marathon, records what M
ades said to the polemarch.

> It now rests with you, Callimachus, either to enslave Ath
> or, by ensuring her freedom, to win yourself immortality
> fame.... For never since the Athenians were a people w
> they in such danger as at this moment.... If Athens co
> victorious out of this contest she has it in her to become
> first city in Greece. Your vote is to decide whether we are
> join battle or not. If we do not bring on a battle presently so
> factious intrigue will disunite the Athenians and the city will
> betrayed.... But if we fight, before there is anything rotter
> the state of Athens, I believe that, provided the Gods give

ay and no favour, we are able to get the best of it in an en-
agement.[5]

part from indulging in this poetic extravagance Miltiades
t have pointed out, more practically, that as the Athenians
e occupying an unattackable position the Persians clearly had
ntention of attacking them. The obvious conclusion was that
y work was afoot.

allimachus voted for attack, and the other generals conceded
tiades their days of command to him.

Iiltiades was the right man on hand at the right moment.
tiades had been ruler of the Chersonese (the Gallipoli penin-
), but when the Persians extended their power to this region
tiades had been forced to submit to Darius, and he was one of
many tributary rulers who led contingents to serve in the
sian Army. He turned against Darius, who became bitterly
geful, and in 494 B.C. he sent a strong squadron of Phoenician
eys against the Chersonese. Knowing that resistance was hope-
, Miltiades loaded five galleys with treasure and escaped to
ens. His enemies there had him tried for tyrannical govern-
it of the Chersonese, but Miltiades rode high in public
our and was not convicted.

robably on September 21st Miltiades drew up the Athenian
ny and marched his 10,000 men in two parallel columns,
1 about half a mile in length, on to the plain, where he wheeled
n into line. The Persians at once deployed their army between
right bank of the Charadra and the Little Marsh, so that they
e parallel to the shore. On a mile front and with slightly less
1 a mile between them the armies stood and waited.

fearly all of the men on the battlefield had seen action and many
hem much action. The Persians and their supporting troops
e soldiers by trade, accustomed to pre-battle tension, to the
r of combat, and the inevitable post-battle pillage and rape.
ry free Greek was trained for military duty, and because of
incessant wars between the states few Greeks reached man-
d without having seen active service. The muster-roll of free
enians of military age never exceeded 30,000, and at the time
Marathon was probably only 20,000.

he Greeks, with fast-beating hearts, eyed the massive Persian
ny and murmured to one another about the odds. According

I am intrigued to know if Montgomery had read Herodotus at the time of
nein. "The Lord Mighty in Battle...";   "...we will hit the enemy for
.."; etc.

to old national custom the soldiers of each tribe went into ba
together—another psychological advantage—and, being clos
this way, they spoke freely and intimately as they waited
orders.

Miltiades or Callimachus reduced the Greek centre to f
ranks, lengthening his line and maintaining eight on the flank
that the Persian front would not overlap the Athenian line. C
machus led the right wing, the post of honour; the 1000 F
aeans were on the left. Miltiades was somewhere near the ce
at the head of his own tribal regiment, while Themistocles
Aristides led the centre.

Miltiades faced a serious tactical difficulty, one that must h
been obvious to every man in the Greek ranks. The bulk of
Persian infantry consisted of archers; the Athenians had
archers. The Persians had at least 1000 cavalry; the Athenians
no cavalry.

In fact, the entire effective Greek force was composed of h
lites—the heavy infantry—although there were some thousa
of irregular, lightly armed troops. But the Greeks, until the t
of Iphicrates, early in the fourth century B.C., did not use lig
armed soldiers in a pitched battle, keeping them for skirmi
or for pursuit of a broken enemy. Each regular soldier was
tended in the camp by one or more slaves, who were also lig
armed.

To compensate for Persian power and variety of weapons h
tiades had to depend on discipline, confidence, leadership—
unity.

In the Persian Army there was no common creed, langua
or race. It was a splendid but motley army—magnificent ho
men from the Khorassan steppes, archers from Ethiopia, swo
men from Egypt, the Indus, the Euphrates, and the O
mountain men from Afghanistan and Hyrcania. They were un
only as tried fighting men and by the example and drive of t
leaders.

At close quarters the Persian Army was a fascinating specta
for the troops of the various nationalities which comprised
wore different uniforms. The Persians and Medes wore felt
bans which they called tiaras, sleeved tunics of various colo
corslets of iron or steel made of rows of metal scales sewn
leather or linen. Their shields, or *gerrhes*, were made of wic
work, and on their right side they carried large bows, cane arro
and short darts.

The Assyrians were easily distinguished by their helms of brass
ail and by their tunics of flax, formed of about eighteen strips
woven flax, glued together one above the other. They could
sist quite a heavy blow from an edged weapon, but were easily
erced by a sword or spear. The Egyptians also wore these
nics. The Ethiopians, in skins of lions or leopards, used 600
ws of palm-wood and long cane arrows tipped with sharp
eces of stone and darts with the pointed horns of roebucks. The
dians in their arms and armour resembled the Greeks, while
e Phrygians used the shield and axe, the double edged *bipennis*,
ten combined with a hook or hammer.

The Greek hoplites wore a strong leather tunic, and sometimes
breastplate, a helm, shield, and greaves. The shield was gener-
ly round or elliptical but there was a variety of helms. The one
ost favoured was the 'Boeotian helm'—with deep head-piece
d with nose, neck, and cheek guards, the whole wrought into a
nple solid piece. Eventually all hoplites wore this helm.

The greaves of this period were of bronze—a development
ace the Homeric age, when they were of pewter. Made to indi-
dual measurements, they were fitted to the legs below the knee
d, because of the pliability of the metal, could be worn without
y clasp or fastening.

The hoplite or man-at-arms never went into action except in
s own proper place in the phalanx.[6] At different periods the num-
r of men comprising a phalanx varied greatly. In its earliest
rm it had no more than 200. During the Persian wars the num-
r rose to 5000; still later, in the wars of the Greeks with the
omans, the phalanx embodied an army 16,000 strong. Milti-
es used all his 11,000 men in one phalanx. The hoplites stood
mly pressed one against the other, shields partly covering one
other, spears protruding menacingly in front.[7] Thus equipped,
e phalanx usually advanced slowly and steadily into action.
iltiades could rely on such a powerful mass breaking the Persian
ont, but first of all he had to reach that front. He was in the

[6] Until Philip of Macedon reorganized the phalanx the Greek word 'phalanx'
licated no special unit of hoplites but merely the hoplite army, often quite
all, of a Greek state.
[7] The phalanx as evolved by Philip and used by him and by his son, Alex-
der, was a fearsome sight. The *sarissa*, the Macedonian spear, was much
nger than the earlier Greek spear—it measured up to 24 feet in fact. In
alanx formation the points of the front rank projected at least 16 feet in
vance of the line, while those of the second, third, fourth, fifth, and sixth
nks projected, respectively, about 13, 10, 7, 4, and 2 feet. At the head of
ch file protruded a layer of six points.

position of a modern leader trying to take a position with t[
bayonet without any covering fire. From about 250 yards fro
the Persian archers the Athenians must assault at the double b
fore too many arrows find their mark. But no phalanx a mile lor
however drilled and disciplined, however fit and athletic its mer
bers might be, could maintain its dressing. Disorder had to [
risked.

The initial hum died away. Sun glinting on their armour, t
Athenian troops waited while the army augurers prepared the
sacrifices and announced that the aspects were propitious f
victory. The trumpet sounded for action, and, chanting a batt
hymn, the Athenians moved towards the motionless Persiar
Behind the soldiers, on the mountain slopes, many civilians ha
gathered, apprehensive and excited, shouting support to the
troops. They might have been enjoying sports at a picnic,
they gathered under the cedars, pines, and olive-trees, with t
scent of myrtle and arbutus permeating the warm autumn a
Many of the men were armed with javelins, swords, and shield
and were ready to join in the battle if necessary.

The tragic poet Aeschylus, who fought at Marathon, recor
that the civilians said: "On, sons of the Greeks. Strike for t[
freedom of your country; strike for the freedom of your childr
and your wives—for the shrines of your fathers' gods and t[
sepulchres of your sires."

Right from the beginning the Athenian attack was faster tha
usual. Miltiades wanted to be close to the enemy before t
Asiatic cavalry could mount and manoeuvre against him.

Until the battles of Leuctra and Mantinea, more than a centu
after Marathon, there is no other instance of a Greek gener
deviating from the standard way of committing a phalanx
spearmen into action.

It seems likely that although the Greeks advertised their pr
jected attack, the Persians were not fully prepared to receive
Nevertheless, they waited confidently for the assault, reasonab
certain that the Greeks could not cross the zone beaten by arrow
and that their own cavalry would soon be attacking the enem
rear. Herodotus said that the Persians thought the Athenians "
set of madmen rushing upon certain destruction".

But the Athenians crossed the dangerous zone in good orde
and the front rank of the Persian Army was speared and trampl
underfoot. As was only to be expected in a long charge by a lor
line, the wings swept forward faster than the centre and t[

ek line became concave. At the weaker centre the Persians
ke the line and drove back the regiments led by Aristides and
emistocles. This spirited Persian defence turned into a
nter-attack, and the Athenian centre was chased back over
plain and into the valley, where the Greek leaders checked
retreat and re-formed their men.

he Persian success in the centre was partly their own un-
ng, for it drew their front into a convex shape, automatically
uced the length of the front, and presented the Greeks with
ks to attack. The Athenian wings brought about a double en-
opment and reduced many of the Persian regiments to panic.
s not possible to say for certain if Miltiades planned this
noeuvre.[8]

After great success on the flanks Miltiades linked his two wings
ether—a difficult movement during such a battle—and led the
enians against the Persian centre as Aristides and Themi-
cles also came back into the fight with their re-formed troops.

While the Persian archers in the rear kept up a hail of arrows
r the heads of their comrades the leading Persian infantry
ned forward many times, sometimes singly, sometimes in
ll groups, trying to force a break in the phalanx, but
st of these brave men had no chance to use their swords and
gers before being impaled on an enemy spear.

he apparent inaction of the Persian cavalry is puzzling. Orien-
cavalry has always taken an embarrassingly long time to pre-
e for a charge, but the battle at Marathon lasted some hours,
l the Persian horse could easily have harassed the Greek rear.
tainly the Greek line took up the entire breadth of the practi-
le ground of the plain, and the flanking marshes were wet at
time of year, but when the Greek centre was broken the
sian cavalry could have followed their own infantry through
breach. There is no historical evidence that this happened,
I think it is a reasonable assumption. It is also reasonable to
ume that although the horsemen were able to drive away part
the phalanx for a time, neither they nor their horses could
e the wall of spikes presented to them. The people of Mara-
n have told me firmly that this is what happened, and there
 often good ground for local belief, even two and a half thou-
d years after the event.

Miltiades, who had thorough first-hand knowledge of the

Three hundred years later Hannibal won Cannae by a deliberate double
elopment.

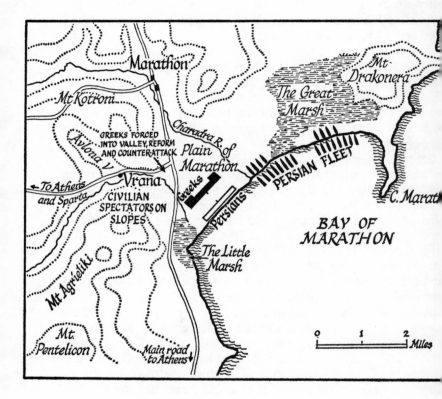

An army with its back close to the sea is at a tactical disadvantage compared with the opposing force. This was the position of the Persians at Marathon. Initially they were successful but their success was their undoing. They forced the Greek line to become concave, and in the centre actually drove the Greeks back. However, the troops from the centre, temporarily beaten, were able to regroup in safety in Avlona Valley. Also, the Persian pressure in the centre brought the Greek flanks wheeling inwards. The result was a double envelopment—that is, with the Greek wings folding around the Persians. Forced on the defensive and finally to breaking-point, the Persians had no room for manoeuvre and could only run for their ships. Three centuries later the situation at the battle of Cannae was very similar.

organization and capabilities of Persian armies—he had, after
served with them—obviously did not worry too much about
threat the Persian cavalry represented.[9]

Time was passing and evening was approaching. T
Greeks were tired, but they scented victory. Then, almost s
denly, the Persian Army broke and fled towards the boats.
fierce fight took place on the shore as the Persians struggled d
perately to get their galleys into the water. The Greeks l
more men here than during the main battle. Callimachus
killed, as well as Stenislaus, another general, and the scho
Cynaegeirus, who grasped the ornamental work on the stern o
galley and had his hand axed off.

Datis lost only seven ships, but he left behind at Marathon 64
dead soldiers of the Persian Army. The Athenians, according
the reliable testimony of Herodotus, lost only 192 men killed
loss as disproportionate as in any battle in history. The contr
is quite believable, for the Persians simply could not get to gr
with the Greeks, whose armour protected them from the arrows.

Soon after the battle 2000 Lacedaemonian spearmen fr
Sparta arrived. Starting immediately after the full moon, th
had marched the 150 miles in three days. They inspected
battlefield and the masses of enemy dead, praised the Atheni
for their victory, and departed.

Datis, still trying to achieve a victory, and in obedience to
signal flashed from a shield by someone on Mount Pentelic
sailed quickly for Athens, hoping to find it unprotected and
gain possession of it from Hippias' supporters. But Miltiad
leaving Aristides and his regiment on the field, led his Atheni
in a rapid night-march back to Athens. When the Persian fl
sailed into Piraeus harbour next morning Datis could clearly
on the heights the long spears of the troops who had beaten h
only hours before, and he made no attempt to land. The Persi
giant had been humbled by the Athenian dwarf; a vast empire
a tiny republic of 700 square miles.

It was customary for all Athenians slain in battle to be inter
in a public sepulchre near Athens, but everybody felt that a c
tinction should be made for the dead of Marathon, so they w
buried under a mound on the plain. The Greeks built ten mo
mental columns on the spot—one for each Athenian tribe—

[9] Some historians have doubted if the Persian cavalry was ashore that d
and suggest that it had been sent back to Euboea for forage, but Miltia
own tactics strongly indicate that the cavalry was present.

ich were engraved the names of the fallen. These columns,
ne of the first war memorials, existed for many centuries. At
: end of the first century A.D. the historian Pausanias read the
mes of the dead on the columns, which have long since
imbled into dust, although the mound remains.

Another monument was built in honour of Miltiades, and
merous memorials erected in Athens and elsewhere. The battle
s sculptured also on the Temple of Victory in the Acropolis.
en more importantly, the Athenians deified the spirits of the
:n who had fallen in the battle.

The gallant Plataeans, who had risked so much without pros-
:ts of reward, were made, in effect, honorary Athenian citizens,
d at all sacrifices in Athens the blessing of Heaven was asked
: the Athenians and the Plataeans jointly.

Greece never forgot Marathon. The significance of the battle
dured through the country's greatness and through her decline
d fall. Many much larger Greek-Persian battles followed
arathon—Artemisium, Salamis, Thermopylae, Plataea, Euryme-
n, but none has the significance of Marathon, which was a
tical day in history. Until this day the Persians had been in-
icible, and other races were paralyzed by their acceptance of
s invincibility. Marathon started a chain reaction which was to
pire the Greeks to beat back Xerxes, Darius's son and avenger,
d which led on men like Xenophon, Agesilaus, and Alexander
their Asiatic campaigns.

Strategy was in its infancy at this time, so the Persian strate-
al plan was startling in its inventiveness. Few generals were
ute enough in those times to evolve a triple plan of campaign
Datis did: to subdue Eretria and terrify the Athenians; to lure
army away from its natural object of defence; to encourage a
h column in the city scheduled for capture. Datis left a stra-
ical legacy no less than Miltiades' tactical one. Miltiades
ywed that a national army with high morale could defeat a
ger, heterogeneous army that had no national will; that a psy-
ological advantage was a military weapon.[10] He showed that
ld tactics could triumph over military disadvantages; that

---

[10] Examples of other battles where the victor had his opponent at a psycho-
ical disadvantages are Salamis, 480 B.C.; Aegospotami, 450 B.C.; Mantinea,
B.C.; Ipsus, 302 B.C.; Cannae, 216 B.C.; Metaurus, 207 B.C.; Zama, 202 B.C.;
ston, 1648; Dunbar, 1650; Blenheim, 1704; Oudenarde, 1708; Quebec, 1757;
oli, 1797; Austerlitz, 1805; Jena, 1806; Vicksburg, 1863; Königgrätz, 1886;
an, 1870; the battle for France 1940; Singapore 1941; the Australian defence
Tobruk, 1941; Alamein, 1942.

armour was vital against missiles and that disciplined obedie
to command could win the day. That day at Marathon Miltia
forged one of the first recorded links in the chain of command.

It is important to remember that the soldiers Miltiades
were tough and physically fit, for all Greeks had an almost
gious reverence for athleticism. I believe that Hannibal, m
later, was influenced by the remarkable strength and stamina
the Spartans when he insisted that his army be trained to l
physical fitness. His Spanish troops were especially sound in bc
Many subsequent commanders were aware of the need
strong, healthy bodies, but, oddly enough, few introduced reg
physical training, though the Turkish Janissaries, enlisted in l
hood, were well developed physically by planned exerci
Napoleon's army was remarkably tough, but this was due to
way the men were forced to live rather than to any system
exercises. The fittest soldiers in modern times have undoubte
been the Germans, New Zealanders, and Australians of
Second World War. The soldiers of all three races were outsta
ingly physically developed according to a predetermined
tem. Still, there was a distinct difference in the approach to fitr
between the Anzacs and the Germans. The Germans were fai
cally keen on *gesundheit*, and, like the Greeks, went at it v
religious fervour. They trained not only the body but the mine
well. The Anzacs simply happened to like to be fit; their appro
was systematic, but their attitude was casual, and since it
casual, it was not so necessary to devote so much attentior
making their minds fit. A casual mind is less likely to suffer fr
modern battle strain than an intense one.

————————◇•◇————————

CHAPTER FIVE

Claudius Nero's March
to the Metaurus

◥HE battle of the Metaurus in 207 B.C. has fascinated many a
scholar, historian, and commander, though possibly for dif-
ent reasons. Byron, who recognized a military feat when he
v one, commented that the "unequalled march" made by
ro[1] "deceived Hannibal and defeated Hasdrubal, thereby ac-
nplishing an achievement almost unrivalled in military annals".
fact, but for Nero's victory his imperial namesake might never
ve been able to reign at all.

The river which gave its name to the battle is today called the
etauro, and it reaches the Adriatic about midway between
mini and Ancona. We do not know exactly where the battle
ok place, but I believe, from a study of the ground and of
torical records, that it occurred along the ravine of S. Angelo,
ich joins the Metauro itself.

A battle between Hasdrubal's army and the Roman legions
s inevitable, but that it took place exactly where it did was
re chance. This was unusual in ancient times, when the place
battle was almost entirely predictable. The reason why Has-
ubal was brought to battle at the Metaurus and why he was
feated and killed there makes one of the most interesting battle
counts of history—as well as one of the most momentous. The
ks in the chain of command forged here have endured to
odern times.

[1] The consul, not the infamous emperor.

Immediately before the Second Punic War Rome was y and ambitious, but had two great powers to contend with the east Macedonia and in the south Carthage, a great city on the Gulf of Tunis by the Phoenicians in the ninth century B.

If Rome were to be secure she had to eliminate these po or at least she had to create unattackable frontiers—the called 'Alexandrian drive', named after the principle propou by the great Greek commander.

In Spain—the land approach to Carthage—there was such frontier, for the Ebro river was no barrier at all. Rome, the intriguer, was greedy for the Spanish silver-mines and Spa markets, and to strengthen her hold on them fostered into po a political party in Saguntum (now Sagunto, north of Valen This party attacked the Torboletae people, who were subject Carthage. Hannibal, in justifiable retaliation, attacked and t Saguntum, in 219 B.C., after an eight months' siege. The follow year Rome demanded the surrender of Hannibal, and when was refused war broke out.

Both sides welcomed the war. Hannibal, an astute n realised that Rome was not yet unified and that she was vul able, especially as the Gauls in Northern Italy were permane antagonistic to her. Hannibal, too, was a master of cavalry, wl was little understood by the Romans. Hannibal approached impending war somewhat impetuously, wanting to strike b and quickly to remove the Roman menace.

The Roman senators arrived at their decision with reaso deliberation. The Gauls had been beaten and colonies establis to control them; southern ports had been garrisoned, and c mand of the seas was in Roman hands. As Rome held Sicily could mount a direct attack against Carthage. With all these vantages the Roman senators were extremely confident, but often produces the unexpected, and while a nation can be eva ated its leaders cannot always be accurately measured. 1 Romans measured Hannibal short. Because of him the war which they were embarking would last sixteen years and be mendously costly. In the end, as we shall see, Hannibal's link the chain of leadership would pass to Rome, but nobody kn that in 218 B.C.

Hannibal was born in 247 B.C. and at the age of nine 1 Carthage with his father, the great Hamilcar Barca, for Spa Well educated, supremely fit, alertly intelligent, and simple in tastes, he was essentially a soldier from his early days. In 218 B.

he set out from New Carthage (now Cartagena) for the
, he planned to break up the Italian confederacy and force
e to make peace. Seeing himself as a liberator rather than
nqueror, he moved into France to what is now Perpignan
12,000 cavalry, 37 elephants, and 90,000 infantry. He
ed Avignon, forded the Rhône, and crossed the Maritime
, somewhere near the Little St Bernard Pass, losing many
is men to attacks by the mountain people. He reached the
is of Cisalpine Gaul with about 6000 cavalry and 20,000
try.

December 218 B.C. he tricked Tiberius Sempronius into
e, held him in the front, and sent half his cavalry to outflank
attack the Romans in the rear. The result was a rout, followed
nother in April the following year, when he deliberately
d himself between the armies of Servilius and Flaminius
practically annihilated Flaminius's army.

August 2nd, 216 B.C., near Cannae, he faced an immense
an army and drew his own force into crescent formation,
strong cavalry forces on each wing of his infantry line. He
d the Roman cavalry, calmly awaited the attack of the
an infantry, and allowed them to press back the Carthaginian
ent until it became concave. Naturally, the Romans became
confident. At the critical moment Hannibal ordered his
an infantry on the flanks to wheel rapidly inward, thus prac-
y sealing the Romans into a bag, which was finally closed
e cavalry. The Roman Army was smashed to pieces. They
70,000 infantry killed and practically all their cavalry.
ther 10,000 men not engaged in the battle were taken prisoner.
nibal had 5700 casualties.[2] One Roman who escaped the
hter was Scipio, later known as Scipio Africanus. A young
r at Cannae, Scipio became one of the great generals of
ry and defeated Hannibal at Zama.

is success was the most perfect tactical victory in history, and
not to be rivalled until Napoleon's victory at Austerlitz in
. The modern parallel is the Russian encirclement of the
an forces at Stalingrad.

nnae was a personal victory for Hannibal. Without detract-
from his brilliance it must be said that the Romans' own
y conception of war materially helped him. The Romans
practically no idea of tactics, and their generals, usually
en from political motives, had no imagination or foresight.

[2] These are the figures given by Polybius and are probably correct.

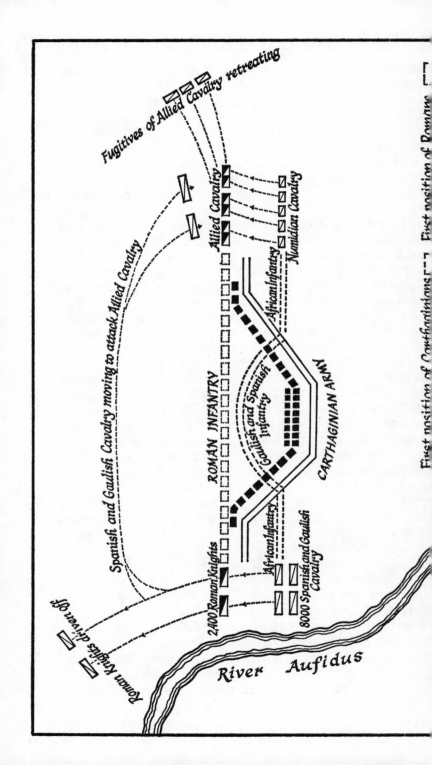

Fugitives of Allied Cavalry retreating

Spanish and Gaulish Cavalry moving to attack Allied Cavalry

Allied Cavalry

Numidian Cavalry

African Infantry

ROMAN INFANTRY

Gaulish and Spanish Infantry

CARTHAGINIAN ARMY

African Infantry

8000 Spanish and Gaulish Cavalry

2400 Roman Knights

Roman Knights driven off

River Aufidus

First position of Carthaginians ⌐ ⌐ First position of Roman

NNAE

This was a perfect tactical victory. Hannibal's army was
wn up in a bend of the river Aufidus, with the heavy Gallic
d Spanish cavalry on the left flank against the river. The
mans had great superiority of numbers in infantry, which
nnibal knew was efficient. Impressed by Roman use of arms, he
d given his African veterans the arms and weapons he had
tured from the Romans. On the left Hannibal's 8000 cavalry
ve the 2400 Roman knights from the field. The Numidian
alry contained the great mass of Roman cavalry on the right
til the Spanish and Gallic horsemen rode clear across the rear
the Roman lines and attacked the Roman cavalry from be-
d while the Numidians charged from the front. The Roman
rsemen were soon decisively beaten. The Roman infantry,
ted by the apparent ease with which they forced the Cartha-
ians back, were then caught in a bag—with African troops
eeling inwards and attacking the Romans in flank and the
rthaginian horse cutting off all escape to the rear. The Roman
feat was complete. Hannibal's handling of cavalry at Cannae
eminiscent of Alexander's tactics at Issus and Arbela.

The Romans depended purely on discipline, drill, and valour
useful formula against a rabble-like enemy, but not against go
troops brilliantly led. In 1870 and again in 1914 the French ma
precisely the same mistake as the Romans, believing that 1
valour and drill of their brightly uniformed soldiers would prev
against mechanized might.

Polybius said that

> of all that befell the Romans and Carthaginians, good or ba
> the cause was one man and one mind, Hannibal.... For s
> teen years he maintained the war with Rome in Italy, witho
> once releasing his army from service in the field, but keepi
> those vast numbers under control ... without any sign of d
> affection towards himself or towards one another ... thou
> he had troops who were not even of the same race.

This in itself was a great feat of leadership. Many nations
later years kept their soldiers in the field for longer periods—t
Dorsetshire Regiment of the British Army once spent more tha
thirty years in India—but Hannibal's army spent longer cut c
from their homelands than any other in history.

Hannibal's one material weakness was that he had no sieg
train, and his only personal failing was that he was not as brillia
in assaulting a fortress-city as he was in the field. He could hav
taken Rome immediately after Cannae, but when he delayed
was too late, and though he took the greater part of Souther
Italy his war became a series of field engagements, marche
counter-marches.

In Spain Hannibal's brothers, Hasdrubal and Mago, wei
successful against the Roman forces there, and the only Roma
victory was the taking of Syracuse, a Sicilian city allied wit
Carthage, but even here the Syracusans held out for four year
until their city was betrayed to the enemy in 211 B.C. Scipi
Africanus was appointed to command the Roman armies i
Spain, and so able was his leadership that by the summer of 20
B.C. the whole of Spain had submitted to Rome.[3]

However, in the spring of 208 B.C. Hasdrubal had cleverly dis
entangled himself from the Roman forces and crossed the wester
Pyrenees, outwitting Scipio, who had hoped to catch him in
the eastern mountains. With strong Spanish infantry, Africa
troops, some elephants, and much money, he made for Auvergne

[3] General Fuller believes that Scipio's continuous success was due to hi
"Hellenic open-mindedness". This is certainly true, for he had a mental elasticit
and tolerance that was certainly not an attribute of Romans at that time.

e he spent the winter and recruited large numbers of Gauls
ght with him against the Romans.

he Romans were now scared to death. With Hannibal on the
e in the South and Hasdrubal soon to be rampaging in the
th Rome would be crushed between them. The prospect of
such men campaigning around the hills of Rome was appal-
and the senators looked hurriedly for able leaders of their
. They recommended as consul Gaius Claudius Nero, a patri-
who had fought against Hannibal in Italy and against Has-
al in Spain. He had no great reputation in the sense of having
ing of victories to his credit, but the public elected him on
enators' recommendation.

noice of plebeian consul—Roman law stipulated that there
t be one patrician, one plebeian consul—was very difficult,
o many plebeian generals had already perished in the war.
elderly Marcus Livius was an obvious choice—Livius had
. consul in the year before the beginning of the war with
hage and had beaten the Illyrians. But after this success he
been unjustly accused and found guilty of peculation and un-
division of the spoils among his soldiers. Still bitter and re-
ul, he ironically mocked the senators when they asked him to
an army against the Carthaginians, especially as he and Nero
d each other, but eventually he swallowed his pride—as the
tors had already done—and consented.

asdrubal passed through the Alps without any of the diffi-
' his brother had experienced, using Hannibal's engineering
ks and recruiting men for his army in every settlement through
h he passed. In Liguria many trained soldiers joined him. He
sed the Po and for a time fruitlessly besieged Placentia,
h he had planned to use as a base.

ll this time the Romans worked frantically to get their six
es into shape. The fifteen legions were made up of 70,000
ans and about the same number of Italian allies. With
her 30,000 soldiers in Spain, Sicily, and Sardinia, Rome's
ary manpower was stretched to the limit, for she had already
well over 100,000 men during the war.

hree armies were sent north, one to threaten the restless
scans, one to check Hasdrubal's vanguard, and the main
e, under Livius's direct command, to move more slowly to
e. The 42,500 men of the three armies of the South were
er Nero, chosen to face Hannibal.

uck plays a big part in war, and Hasdrubal and Hannibal

now had some bad luck. Hasdrubal had sent a patrol of six w
a letter to Hannibal, telling him that he intended to cross
Apennines and would meet him in the district of Umbria, nor
east of Rome, the direction from which Rome could be best
tacked. The patrol expected to find Hannibal at Tarentum, whi
in fact, was a Roman stronghold. Hannibal had been in win
quarters in Bruttium in the south-west and had gone north
Canusium, near which the patrol must have passed in their le
and dangerous journey. The Carthaginians' quite heroic ride
hind enemy lines ended in disaster—they were captured by so
Roman foragers, and the vital letter they carried was sent on
Nero, not far away at Venusia. Hannibal had heard that
brother was in Italy, but could make no firm plans until he co
contact him. He did, however, know much about the Rom
movements because he had an efficient intelligence system. N
reacted to Hasdrubal's letter as one would expect from a gr
commander, as distinct from one of ordinary attainments.
had orders, as had all consuls, to keep within his own province
operate only on orders from Rome, and to make war only o
direct instruction from Rome. Nero, however, had the courage
act on his own initiative. He sent the captured letter to Rome,
gether with one of his own, reporting that while Hannibal
mained in doubtful inaction he intended to lead 6000 pick
infantry and 1000 cavalry north to reinforce the northern arm
He suggested that a legion at Capua should be moved to Ro
and that the troops in Rome should be moved to Narni. '
brothers, Nero realized, were within 200 miles of each other, a
if Rome were to be saved they must not meet. Hasdrubal at t
time was at Sena, south-east of the Metaurus.

With the fine eye of a quartermaster Nero sent messeng
ahead on his road of march with orders to local leaders to
that provisions, horses, mules, and carts were ready by the w
side for his soldiers to use.

After leaving camp Nero took another rather unusual step:
halted his army and told his 7000 chosen troops what he plann
to do. It seemed an audacious project, he said, but actually
was militarily sound. He was leading them to certain victory, a
they would get full credit for it. The reception they would rece
on the way to battle would prove how high their fortunes stood.

Meanwhile Nero's message to Rome had had the effect o
bomb thrown among pigeons. There was instant panic. Nero v
called irresponsible and rash; his action was labelled traitorc

had left his large army without proper leadership, and Hanni-
would push it aside and begin his ravages against Rome once
e. Two consuls had been lost in battle the previous year, now
o seemed bent on suicide, for if the speed and success with
ch Hasdrubal had crossed the Alps and moved down Italy was
indication, then he was an even better general than Hannibal.

city seethed with rumour, speculation, and terror. After so
y years of living under his shadow his very name frightened
Romans.

ut Nero was confident, and the districts through which he
ed along the Adriatic coast responded magnificently to his
. In the warm April sun farmers, traders, and their families
ked to the roadside in thousands, bringing food and drink,
ers and prayers. The army marched night and day, resting in
ys in the carts provided by the country people.

ivius and another leader, Porcius, had their camp near Sena,
half a mile from that of Hasdrubal. In collusion with Livius,
o timed his approach so that he would enter Livius's camp by
t—without any noisy reception—and so that the reinforce-
t would not be noticed he arranged for his officers and men
ouble up with men from Livius's army and to share their tents.
vas a masterly piece of deception, similar in effect to that
tised by Montgomery at Alamein.

ero arrived at Sena with considerably more than the 7000 men
et out with, for along the road he had enlisted many volun-
s, especially veterans of former campaigns.

ext morning Livius called a council of war, at which it was
posed that Nero's men be given time to rest after their gruelling
ch. According to Livy, Nero emphatically opposed the delay.
said,

Who is for giving time for my men to rest is for giving time
Hannibal to attack my men in camp in Apulia. He is for
ving time to Hannibal and Hasdrubal to discover my march
nd to manoeuvre for a junction . . . at their leisure. We must
ght instantly, while both the foe here and the foe in the South
re ignorant of our movements. We must destroy this Hasdru-
al, and I must be back in Apulia before Hannibal awakes from
is torpor.

is arguments prevailed, and it was decided to fight. The red
gn, the signal for immediate battle, was hoisted, and the
nan army was drawn up outside the camp.

Hasdrubal up to this point was equally anxious for battle, I
had not thought it wise to attack the Romans in their lines. Wh
they offered battle he too arrayed his troops. But, for all th
precautions, the Romans had been careless in one detail. One
Hasdrubal's patrols reported that the trumpet, which gave
signal to Roman legions, had sounded once in Porcius's camp I
twice in that of Livius—a strong hint that a third superior offi
was present. As Hasdrubal rode forward to observe the ene:
line he thought that their numbers seemed to have increas
Some of the horses, too, appeared out of condition, as if they l
made a strenuous forced march. He deduced that both cons
faced him.

Doubtful and apprehensive because he had not heard from
brother, concerned about the greater numbers of Romans
although, in fact, he outnumbered them—Hasdrubal decid
not to fight after all and ordered his troops back to can
Throughout the day both forces watched each other warily, I
when night fell Hasdrubal led his men out of camp, planning
retreat to the friendly region of Insubrian Gaul and to ma
further attempts to contact his brother.

He moved quietly up the Metaurus river valley towards 1
Via Flaminia, but he never did reach this road because
guides either deserted him or lost their way, and neither Hasd
bal nor his officers could find a ford across the river, so he had
halt for the night. The night's confusion did its inevitable e
work, and in the morning Hasdrubal found that many of
Gallic supporters were helplessly drunk and that even some
his own men had lost their sense of discipline and purpose.

His cavalry screen reported that the Romans were coming
steadily, and Hasdrubal knew that he could not continue his
treat; the Romans would simply walk over his army. He v
forced to prepare for battle. His dispositions were as sound
possible, considering that he was caught on ground he had 1
chosen. He put his Ligurians in the centre and protected a
heartened them with his ten elephants; he posted the Gau
with their long javelins, great broadswords, and big shiel
on high ground on the left flank, overlooking a ravine.
himself took charge of the Spaniards, his best troops, on the rig
flank.

These veterans, protected by helmets and shields and arm
with short cut-and-thrust swords, he could count on for desp
ate action. His front covered about five miles, but had big ga

ween the centre and flank forces. Hasdrubal's tactics were
nd. He hoped that the ravine and rough country on the
man side of it would delay the Romans in coming to grips
h the Gauls, who were undisciplined barbarians. With his
: Spanish troops he would smash the Roman left and try to roll
the Roman line. He could depend on the Ligurians at least to
d the centre.

'he Romans were capable troops, well led, but at this date
y had not reached the perfection of manoeuvre acquired a
tury later. The formation of a legion differed in various
iods, but at this time each legion had two main divisions of
ps—the *hastati* and the *principes*. Each legionary wore a
astplate of mail, bronze greaves, and a bronze helmet with a
ud crest of scarlet or black feathers—and very martial he
ked. He had a large oval shield and two javelins—one light
throwing, the other strong and with a four-foot iron blade for
isting and not usually for throwing. On his right thigh he
ried a short cut-and-thrust sword.

'he *hastati* formed the first ten ranks of the legion and the
icipes the second ten ranks, with about three feet between files
l between ranks—a vast difference from the phalanx system.
immediate battle-order each even-numbered rank took a
e and a half to the right, so that the legion assumed the quin-
x pattern and the troops looked rather like pieces on a
ughtboard. In this formation the men did not hinder one
ther's movements, and a battered front rank or one which had
wn its javelins could be moved to the rear without con-
on or disorder.

Vhen the Romans, in this formation, clashed with other well-
ned troops the fight was no mere hacking, untidy brawl, but a
ly orderly collection of single combats going on up and
vn the line. Unless many men fell the dressing of the lines re-
ined remarkably uniform.

'he third division of the legion was the triarii—a reserve of 600
erans—ready in an emergency to move to any part of the
on's front. Hastati, principes, and triarii were not arranged in
tinuous ranks but in maniples of 120 men each, which were
arated from each other and were themselves arranged in the
ncunx formation. Each legion also had some lightly ac-
tred skirmishers and a troup of 300 cavalry. Altogether, the
on was a hard-hitting, compact, practically self-contained unit,
n to a brigade group in some modern armies.

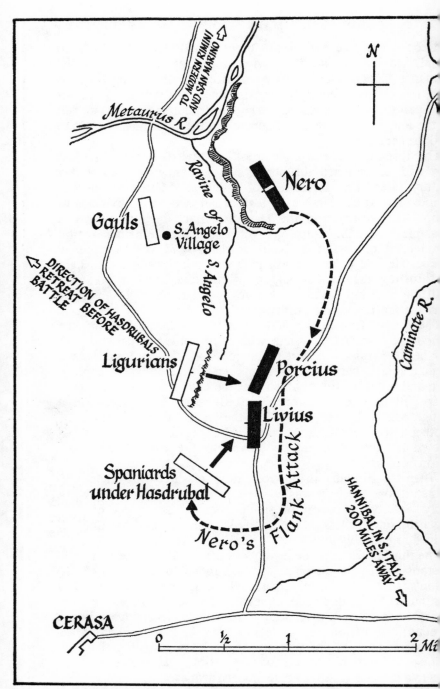

Based on a map from General J. F. C. Fuller's *Decisive Battles of the Western World* (Eyre and Spottiswoode, 1954–56).

IE METAURUS

After a magnificently organized and executed forced march
ero reached the Metaurus and joined with the forces of Livius
d Porcius to confront Hasdrubal's army. Hasdrubal hoped
at the Romans would not cross the very rough country to attack
Gauls, who were undisciplined and militarily weak, but he
uld have fared better had he allowed his Gauls to tie down
ero's force. Nero, seeing that he was wasted on the right flank,
arched about 2000 men across the rear of the Roman armies
attack Hasdrubal's Spaniards from the rear and from the
nk. Nero's fine tactical appreciation and his ability to make his
vn decisions defeated Hasdrubal at the Metaurus. It was mili-
ry command at its best.

The elephants took the initiative, and in their charge broke
Roman lines, causing gaps in several place. Despite this mi
setback the Romans under Livius and Porcius attacked de
minedly, to be met by stubborn resistance from the Ligurians a
Spaniards. They made no headway, and Hasdrubal, seeing t
Nero could not come to grips with the Gauls, urged his men
more fiercely. Livius himself must have wondered if he I
taken on more than he could handle.

Nero, on the Roman right, became very restive. His men w
struggling over very difficult ground, and the Gauls were
viously commanded by officers who had orders to refuse ba
and merely to keep the Roman right occupied. Acting once m
completely out of character for a Roman consul, Nero decic
to take a hand in the fight on his left. He moved some of
best troops—possibly 2000—in a rapid march along the rear
the Roman army. Livius and Porcius, had they looked rearwai
must have been astonished at this unorthodox manoeuvre. Th
with perfect surprise, Nero led his men in a violent charge on
flank and rear of Hasdrubal's force.[4] The impact and shock w
too great; the Spaniards and the Africans who fought w
them were thrown back on to the Ligurians and overwhelm
while the Gauls, at last brought to bay, were butchered in th
sands. The Carthaginians lost 10,000 dead in all, the Rom
2000.

As always, the battlefield was a shambles, made even wo
than usual in this case by the maddened elephants, now out
control and trumpeting around the battlefield. Most were kil
by their mahouts, who were equipped with a hammer and l
spike which was driven into the animal's spinal column.

Hasdrubal knew he had lost the battle, and probably had ti
to reflect that but for the surprise assault from the flank and r
he might well have fought a stand-off battle. He knew, too, that
a captive he would be treated with cruelty and contempt a
paraded in chains through the streets of Rome. As the son
Hamilcar and brother of Hannibal he could expect no mei
Sword in hand he charged into the middle of a cohort of Rom
—a force of 450 men—and died fighting.

Nero did not rest on his laurels, but again force-marched
troops, back to his lines in Apulia. He was facing Hannib
Carthaginians before they became aware that he had been abse
He took with him from the Metaurus a grisly trophy of his vict

[4] Marlborough did this at the battle of Ramillies in 1706.

asdrubal's head.[5] He had a rider throw it into Hannibal's
p, and a Carthaginian soldier hurried with it to his com-
der. Hannibal, who had not seen his brother for eleven years,
in his distress that he now recognized his country's destiny
that Rome would become mistress of the world. The battle of
Metaurus certainly ensured a further 200 years of Roman
tary conquest.

evertheless, the Romans still dared not attack Hannibal, even
gh the initiative had passed into their hands. Eventually he
recalled to Carthage to oppose Scipio, but was defeated by
at the battle of Zama (south-west of Carthage) in 202 B.C.
of the great turning-points in history, Zama established the
sputed authority of Rome over the Western Mediterranean
reduced Carthage to a mere defenceless mercantile town.
Carthage's road to ruin began on a lonely ravine in Italy.

olitical consequences apart, Nero's approach march was a
ndid military achievement, as outstanding as his decision to
e it in the first place. Marlborough might well have been in-
aced by it when he made his long, dynamic march from
ders to the Danube to win the battle of Blenheim in 1704.

Archduke Charles emulated Nero in 1796 when he marched
ng distance to defeat the French under Jourdan and then
e Moreau through the Black Forest and across the Rhine.
freed Germany from French invasion for a time, though not
nduringly as Nero had freed Rome. But if Nero's feat has
equalled it has not been surpassed.

t the battle itself his quick unorthodox decision to change
tion and attack on the flank had a profound influence on
tary thought, both in his time and many centuries later when
unts of his actions began to be read by commanders. Nero's
ribution to leadership has been one of the most enduring.

[5] This was a savage, barbarous act, but typically Roman at that time.

CHAPTER SIX

———◇◆◇———

Teutoburger Wald, the First
German Battle of Annihilation

JUDGED alone by its long-term consequences to Britain, the
battle of the Teutoburger Wald in the year A.D. 9 deserves a
special place in history, but, oddly enough, few Britons have ever
been aware of these consequences. In Victorian times the great
historian Arnold drew attention to them, and went so far as to say
that but for the German victory over the Romans "our German
ancestors would have been enslaved or exterminated along the
Oder and the Elbe; this island would never have borne the name
of England and we, this great English nation ... would have
been utterly cut off from existence."

Sir Edward Creasy, writing in 1851, claimed that Arminius,
the German victor at the Teutoburger Wald, "is far more truly
one of our national heroes than Caractacus and it was our own
primeval fatherland the brave German rescued when he slaugh-
ted the Roman legions ... in the marshy glens between the
Lippe and the Ems."

"An Englishman", said Creasy, "is entitled to claim a closer
degree of relationship with Arminius than can be claimed by any
German of modern Germany." Exploiting the theme mercilessly,
Creasy further referred to the English as "being the nearest heirs
to the glory of Arminius".

These historians and others have exaggerated the situation, for
if Arminius had not provided Britain with German ancestors
somebody else certainly would have done so. Arminius merely

happened to be the man on the spot. Still, his military achiev
ment cannot be denied, even if its glory was particularly savag
And Germans, despite Creasy's rather offhand reference to the
relationship with Arminius, have perpetuated his achievement.

The Germans had been involved with Rome since the end
the second century B.C. and initially had caused as great a par
in Rome as had the Gauls and Carthaginians. Finally, in 101 B
the brilliant but brutal general Marius, with the help of Catul
defeated them in the great battle of Vercellae.

Marius, seven times elected consul, made profound changes
Roman military organization, changes which influenced strate
and politics. About 104 B.C. Marius scrapped the old milit
system and opened the army to volunteers outside the properti
class, and later recruited men from the servant and even crimin
classes. More than this, he employed foreigners in Rome's arm
He reorganized the legion into cohorts, each cohort having
maniples of 200 men each. A maniple had 2 centuries of 100 m
each. All distinction between *hastati*, *principes*, and *triarii* disa
peared and the tactical unit grew from 120 to 600 soldiers. Sin
the legion had ten cohorts—four in the first line, three in t
second, and three in the third, the legion's strength rose fro
4500 to 6000 men. The legionary cavalry was done away with ar
foreign cavalry took their place. The legion was used in a diffe
ent way, too, for the spaces between cohorts was shortened un
the old phalanx order re-evolved itself.

The Roman Army was now a professional one, rather imbue
with a mercenary spirit—a fact which had a bearing on the c
cumstances which brought about the battle of the Teutoburg
Wald.

In earlier days the soldier had sworn allegiance to the Repu
lic; now he swore it to his general. If the army had well-educate
skilful generals the army was successful; when they were i
adequate discipline suffered. Julius Caesar inherited this milita
system and probably changed its basic structure little. Howeve
he increased the numbers of light infantry, bowmen, and slinge
and greatly improved cavalry, artillery, and engineers. Catapul
and *ballistae* were in close support to the infantry, and sometin
between Caesar's day and A.D. 9 each legion had an 'artiller
train of sixty *ballistae* and ten catapults—the equivalent of today
field guns and howitzers—to fire darts and stones.

Because of these developments the defensive became th
stronger form of war and the least expensive in casualties, a

ıgh at this date heavy casualties were accepted as a necessary
:omitant of war, and if generals were worried about them
˙ have left no evidence that this was so.

aesar made the Rhine the eastern frontier of Central and
thern Gaul, and to establish it as such conquered the Belgic
ɛs, most of which were of German origin, living roughly in
t is today's Belgium. In 57 B.C. Caesar defeated the Nervii
gained control of the left bank of the Rhine below Cologne,
a few years later had secured all the Rhine from Xanten to
ˋort. He bridged the Rhine south of Coblenz and made a ter-
ng demonstration against the semi-nomadic Germans to cow
n into submission.

hey were interesting people, fierce in battle, but with only the
blance of military organization. They carried short spears,
ı a narrow and small but sharp head. Most mounted men had
ield, but very few infantry possessed such a luxury. It might
ɛ been an impediment anyway, as the infantry moved rapidly
ıgh to fight with their own cavalry. Tacitus recorded, signi-
ıtly, that "on the field of battle it is disgraceful for a chief's
ıpanions not to equal him and that to aid him, protect him
by their own gallant actions add to his glory, were their most
ɛd engagements."

ʼith the help of the German General Staff both the Kaiser and
ɛr taught their followers the same creed 2000 years later.

ˌugustus, the first Roman emperor, had serious strategical
ɔlems connected with the area north of the Danube and east
west of the Rhine, and he decided to solve many of them by
ıing the Rhine frontier 200 to 250 miles eastward, first to the
ˌer and then to the Elbe. He would then have a roughly straight
ˌtier from Hamburg to Vienna, with a line of communications
ing these two centres via Prague and Leipzig. The great ad-
ːage of the new frontier would be to create a buffer that would
ːe it much harder for the Germans to attack Gaul, which
ˌustus viewed as a great supply centre.

apoleon in 1806 emulated Augustus's sound strategy when he
ˌted the Confederation of the Rhine as a similar buffer be-
ːn France and Austria and Prussia.

wo competent Roman generals—first Drusus, then his brother
ːrius—carried out Augustus's plan and pacified Germany to
ı an extent that the barbarians began to learn Roman ways.

he Romans' policy was to cause disputes and wars among the
ˌmans themselves, and all Roman generals and governors

were under orders to do just this when it was necessary to weak
resistance to Rome.

Arminius and his brother, sons of Sigimer, chief of the Cheru
tribe, were among those accorded Roman citizenship and ma
members of the equestrian order. Honours and wealth mea
nothing to Arminius, but they warped his brother, who turn
renegade, adopted the Roman name of Flavius, and fought f
the Romans in their wars against the Germans.

In A.D. 6 Publius Quinctilius Varus, former governor of Syr
and husband of a grand-niece of Augustus, was put in charge
Rome's Germanic region. The frontier was quiet, the garris
soldiers had become soft and lazy, and many of the Germans we
trusted. The ancient historian Strabo wrote, "Against these peo
mistrust was the surest defence, for those who were trusted
fected the most mischief." Varus did not learn this lesson u
too late.

The Romans were causing their own kind of mischief. Var
had some qualities, but he had neither morals nor principles a
was licentious and rapacious. In Syria this excited no comme
for there he lived in an immoral, debased cowardly communi
but somebody should have told him that he could not act this w
in Germany. The Germans, barbarians though some of them s
were, were decent and virtuous. Chastity was honoured and
spected. Varus treated the Germans as slaves and indulged
brutal orgies and was soon copied by his officers and men;
common German home was safe from outrage, and a sense
bitter resentment pervaded the Germanic tribes.

Some of the leading Germans had been carefully brainwash
by the Romans. Cleverly the Romans conferred rank and pri
leges on the younger members of prominent families. Varus
manded heavy taxes and tributes, and precious metals, mai
used among the Germans for making ornaments, were stead
drained away. If Varus had financial advisers with him they
Rome a disservice by not attempting to curb his greed.

Arminius, aged twenty-six, became the leader of a secret
sistance movement, which he fired with his own spirit and s
tained with his determination. But the Romans would not
easy to attack. Varus had about 14,000 Roman infantry, 10
Roman cavalry, and equivalent numbers of foreign infantry a
cavalry. Elsewhere in Germany were numerous detachmen
building roads, making bridges, and clearing ground.

Arminius had little respect for Varus as a general, but he b

:ofound respect indeed for Roman officers and men and their
tary prowess. A pitched battle, no matter how suddenly
ng on the Romans, could only lead to a slaughter of Germans.
Iobody who had yet defied the might of Rome had been suc-
ful. Some had had their minor triumphs—as had Vercin-
rix when he threatened Caesar at Alesia—but in the end all
succumbed.

ike Miltiades, who had fought with his enemies before he
ght against them, Arminius had seen action in Pannonia and
icum as a member of a Cheruscan contingent serving with
Romans. His familiarity with Roman tactics gave him an
ortunity to devise a way of beating them.

Ie complicated his own plans by falling in love with Thus-
la, daughter of a chieftain named Segestes, a collaborator, who
ped the girl from seeing Arminius. They eloped, and the
ous Segestes reported the elopement to Varus, giving him the
us information that Arminius was planning treason. He sug-
ed that he and his fellow-conspirators be chained. Varus be-
ed that Segestes' accusation was made in spite and refused to
eve it.

rminius and his comrades, frequently in Varus's company,
ived the Roman into believing that they respected and ad-
d him as a judge and orator. Also, they saw to it that the
mer of that year was quiet and uneventful and that Varus was
in peace. September arrived and Varus planned to move from
summer quarters near Minden to winter quarters at Aliso,
he upper Lippe river.

.t this point messages arrived to say that tribes near the Weser
the Ems had risen in open revolt. This was Arminius's
erly laid bait, for the 'revolt' was being carefully stage-
aged.

he Germans close to Varus pointed out that this rising must be
down at once and by him personally. They must have been
uasive, for Varus decided to return to winter camp at Aliso
vay of the rebellious area, but apparently he thought the rising
ld be easily crushed for he took with him the garrison's
ien and children. This was his first violation of Roman gen-
ship; his second was to clutter his column with a great train
aaggage-wagons and camp-followers. Perhaps he intended
old all these encumbrances back when he entered hostile ter-
y.

he first part of his journey lay through friendly country, but soon the track led away from firm, ground into marsh forests, and ravines. The engineers were constantly busy, fell trees, building small bridges, and laying planks for roadw through the marshes. All this time Arminius remained w Varus, and once again Segestes warned Varus that he was head into a trap. Still Varus ignored him.

Then, one evening, Arminius and his associates vanished fr the Roman camp. Next day reports came in that outpost tachments of soldiers had been overwhelmed and killed. Va apparently at last realized that Segestes' reports had been tr and he headed for the road which travelled through the Dö pass to Aliso. He was in a dangerous situation, but other Rom leaders had been in just such a predicament—Caesar and Drus for example—and had extricated themselves. Varus, unfor nately, was not the dedicated professional that these men were.

Varus's light infantry, the foreign auxiliaries, had now desert and the country was very difficult for normal Roman tactics. T day the Germans showered spears from the flanks into the str gling, disordered column. Under this harassing attack the Rom beat their way to the most open and firm place they could f and formed camp, barricading it and entrenching it. These g rison troops might have been soft but they were still Rom soldiers. Unfortunately they did not have the same sense of voted service to their Republic as had the men who served un Nero.

Next morning the Romans burned most of their wagons, wh were impeding their progress, and marched once more, to again harassed by spears from the forest. Probably every Rom soldier from Varus to legionary hoped the Germans would fo line-of-battle, but Arminius was too astute to court defeat l that. After a fairly secure night the column marched the n morning—right into a heavy rainstorm. Miserably wet a thoroughly apprehensive, the Romans approached a high, fores ridge, where Arminius had built tree barricades to make Romans' progress more difficult.

All wagons had to be abandoned now, and soldiers cluste around them, retrieving their belongings. Tired and discourag they reacted slowly to the orders of their officers. This co never have happened under a competent, strong commander. T column was near enough to chaos for Arminius to give the s nal for battle. He had detailed a party to spear the Roman hor and the wounded animals, throwing their riders, bolted throu

column, compounding the confusion. Numonius Vala, the
alry commander, abandoned the infantry, and with most of
other cavalry scrambled for safety. They did not find it. Un-
e to keep together and bogged in the mud, the Roman horse-
1 were slaughtered to a man.

arus ordered the column to counter-march in the hope of
ching the nearest Roman post on the Lippe, but this was only
indication of his panic. Such a movement was impossible.
us himself was wounded and committed suicide to escape
ture. Some reports say that all his leading officers also took
r own lives, but it would be more pleasant to believe the story
t one of his two chief aides died fighting.

he Roman column nevertheless held together for some time
ore the incessant German attacks broke it to pieces. Even then
Romans fought well wherever they could form an island of
stance. One group retreated to a mound, where they formed a
;, dug a pitiful trench, and resisted throughout the day and
at. Then, exhausted, hungry, thirsty, and wounded, they were
rwhelmed. Some fleeing Romans drowned in the swamps;
ers, throwing away their armour, escaped some distance be-
e they were picked off by the enemy. A few got away to carry
news of the bloody battle.[1]

he Germans spared nobody, for in those days it was rare to
w mercy to a fallen foe or respect for a brave enemy. The
mans, too, were reacting to years of oppression, and in many
es were bent on personal vengeance. The Romans who were
ed in the battle were fortunate; their end was swifter and less
nful than that of those who were captured and cruelly sacri-
d or buried alive. Thus perished three Roman legions.

he one bright spot in the disaster was the defence of Aliso by
ius Caedicius. The Germans made several attacks on his
1p, but he beat back every one, mainly by intelligent use of his
ners. When the Germans besieged his camp he broke out on a
k night and, though handicapped by many women and chil-
n, got his force through to Vetera, where he linked with two
ons under Asprenas. Arminius did not further molest the
nans; perhaps he knew that he had already secured the
ependence of his race.

The exact place in the Teutoburger Wald where the battle took place is
ossible to say because a very large area fits the description of the battle-
. However, I believe as did Sir Edward Creasy, that it is somewhere be-
n the modern towns of Bielefeld and Driburg. Some German historians
e the battlefield near Münster or Detmold.

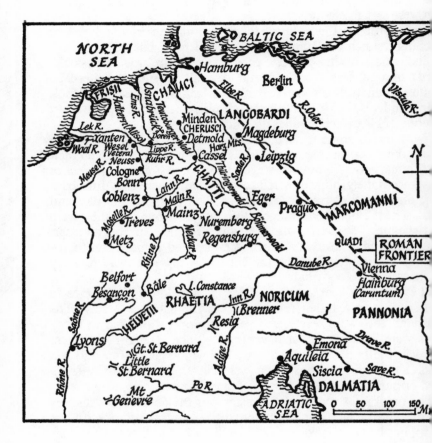

UTOBURGER WALD

In the early years of the Christian era the Romans militarily cupied Europe in much the same way that Hitler occupied it so ıny years later. And, in the same way, resistance movements rang up. Arminius led one such movement in the Cherusci be, which lived between the Harz Mountains and Teuto-rger Wald. It was here, in a classic guerrilla battle, that he ped out three Roman legions and other troops, under Varus. ıe debacle led within a few years to the Romans' final retreat to ə Rhine, which remained the limit of Latin imperialism.

The disaster shocked Rome and Augustus, who feared a G man invasion, though neither Arminius nor any other Germ leader contemplated invasion. Augustus sent the efficient Tiber to take over again the command in Germany. In A.D. 13 Germa cus, his successor, disembarking at the mouth of the E marched to the Weser, and camped somewhere near Minden. next day Arminius won a minor action against the Romans, the following day he was seriously wounded in a major ba in which the Germany infantry was mauled. The horsemen both sides fought a stand-off battle, but Germanicus claime complete victory. How complete it was may be gauged by the f that the Romans soon left the area and retreated to the left ba of the Rhine.

The Roman campaigns were mere superficial shows of a sup ority that no longer existed, and Augustus and his successor Tiberius was the first of them—abandoned all hope of perman conquest.

Nevertheless, Rome retaliated against Arminius in one of cruellest ways possible. Segestes surrendered to Germanicus a tricked his daughter into their hands as well. Pregnant, she v sent to Ravenna, where her son was born. At the age of four boy was led captive through the streets of Rome; in this despica way the Romans avenged themselves on Arminius, who ne again saw his wife and child. He waged a second successful v of independence, but was assassinated at the age of thirty-sev by some of his own kinsmen.

Tacitus called him "the liberator and incendiary of German and in this he was not far wrong. To reflect on what might ha been had history gone another way is an evocative pastin Arnold and Creasy praised Arminius more or less as the f founder of the British race. General Fuller points out m soberly that had Germany been Romanized for a further years—the Roman Empire endured for this period after Teu burger Wald—there would have been no Franco-German pr lem, no Charlemagne, no Louis XIV, no Napoleon, no Kai Wilhelm II, and no Hitler. So in more ways than one Arminiu victory was far-reaching.

His military legacy was equally momentous, but so far no F torian has gauged it. Other commanders before and after Ar nius have sought to take their opponent off-balance, but rar with such success. The utter destruction of the British Ar in its retreat from Kabul, Afghanistan, in 1842 is a mode

llel. Only one man got through the Afghan trap to reach
labad.

minius's technique of deception has been copied with fright-
g faithfulness by later German leaders such as Frederick and
cially Hitler. Hitler, too, pretended to be friendly while he
his trap; Hitler, too, swallowed up nations and their armies by
inian tactics and Arminian lightning blows. The word 'blitz-
;' was not coined until the Second World War, but Arminius
its principle 1930 years before. Like Arminius, but with far
excuse, Hitler was a wholesale butcher, and both practised
policy of separation-annihilation. Like Arminius, Hitler could
crowds and had an innate political sense. Both men man-
to keep their schemes secret from their enemies until the
ent for action arrived. Both had the utmost contempt for
enemies. The parallel does not end there, for, like Arminius,
r suffered at the hands of his own people.

nly two real differences existed between them: Hitler's
es were trained and had first-rate equipment; those of Armi-
were not trained and had no military stores. And Arminius's
ve for his actions was independence; Hitler's was domination.
elleius Paterculus, the most reliable ancient historian of
e's German campaigns, said that Arminius made use of
s's negligence as an opportunity for treachery, "sagaciously
g that no one could be more quickly overpowered than the
who feared nothing, and that the most common beginning of
ter was a sense of security." Could Hitler have read Velleius
rminius and applied his theory to his earlier conquests? If
d the chain of command came full circle.

CHAPTER SEVEN

Command from 378 (Adrianople)
to 732 (Tours)

OST military historians have 'skipped' the long period between the Roman wars and medieval times for the good
son that the sources for our knowledge of this period are less
iable and more fragmentary than those of earlier or later
ies. However, much martial activity occurred during the first
ousand years A.D. and as some of it has a direct bearing on the
quence of leadership a summary of it must be attempted. For
e purposes of this study the first important battle after that of
e Teutoburger Wald was the battle of Adrianople in A.D. 378.
was as salutary in its way and in its time as the firing of the
t musket or the dropping of the first atomic bomb. Fought be-
een the Romans and the Goths, it showed that the old tactics of
alanx and legion were finished, that bravery was the funda-
ntal aspect of shock warfare, and that cavalry was even more
the ascendant.

Infantry never had much to fear from cavalry provided it kept
order, but with the great increase in the use of missiles order
s practically impossible. The acute problem was how to com-
e defence against cavalry with missile power. Many men
rked at this problem, but, as we shall see, another 1300 years
uld pass before even a partial solution was found.

The Goths of this era used a laager, or wagon-fort—they them-
ves called it a wagon-city—as an integral part of any tactical
eme. They would form their wagons into a circle and use it

either as a mobile or as a stationary fortress from which the
fast, impetuous cavalry would make fierce raids. If pushed ba
by a superior force they would retreat into the safety of the
laager, which was practically unassailable. The Huns used t
same method. In the fifteenth century John Zisca, the Huss
leader, copied it, and in the nineteenth century the Boers used
most efficiently against the British and Zulus. Many wagon trai
crossing the American prairies during the nineteenth centu
formed a laager when threatened with Indian attack, but, havi
no cavalry which could emerge to fight off or harass the enem
these American wagon-forts were often overwhelmed.

In the year 378 the Goths and other nomadic bands were
militant and martial that they challenged the power of Rome
the East, where Valens, then co-emperor with his nephew Gratia
commanded. The Roman soldiers of this period—at least those
the East—were pathetically inferior to the men of earlier time
those under Valens were downright effeminate and soft, althou
Sebastianus, a competent general appointed by Valens as co
mander-in-chief, tried to salvage something from the wreck. F
appointment came too late.

Had matters been left to Sebastianus there would have been
battle of Adrianople, but Valens was ill-advised by others a
attacked the army led by Fridigern, the Goth general. Fridige
cunningly played for time so that his cavalry, then absent, cou
come up to support his well-placed laager. This cavalry dro
the Roman horse from the field, and the unsupported infantry w
fiercely attacked. Blinded by swirling dust, suffering intense
from thirst on a scorching August day, the Romans huddled i
potently together as arrows hissed into their ranks. Fridigern nc
unleashed his infantry from the laager, and in a bloody strug
the main Roman force was stamped into the dust. Valens hi
self was mortally wounded later in the day. With him died nea
every officer in the army and about 40,000 men.

Adrianople might almost have been a general signal for wa
The Goths and Vandals and other barbarian hordes attacked t
Roman Empire; in the next forty years Rome suffered as new
before or since, and the Vandals swept over Gaul to occu
Paris.

In 410 came the final indignity: Alaric the Goth, having twi
before besieged Rome, took it and sacked it. The great captai
of the past and their efficient soldiery would have turned in the
graves to see all that they had built up crumble to ruin. If ev

e was an object-lesson to prove that the price of liberty con-
of eternal vigilance and a powerful deterrent this was it.

he Huns also caused much devastation in the next century.
y were led in their most victorious days by Rua and then by
nephew Attila, who has often been stupidly held up as a great
ier but was in fact nothing more than a robber and gangster.
conquests were not due to any military skill or even to superi-
y of numbers, but merely to the extreme mobility of his bands
orse-archers and their Hun ability to exist under arduous con-
ns. The Hun hordes swept through an area like a hurricane,
rly destroying it and its people.

arly in 451 Attila, with a huge army of Huns, Ostrogoths,
ids, and a dozen other tribes, swept westward from the Rhine,
iging with unsurpassed fury an enormous area and sacking
burning such towns as Rheims, Metz, Arras, Mainz, Stras-
rg, Cologne, Trier. They besieged Orleans, which was saved
he arrival of the combined Roman-Gothic army under the
nan general Aëtius and King Theodoric I of the Visigoths.
y forced Attila to retreat, and late in June, at the battle of
lons, near Troyes, defeated him.

heodoric was killed but Attila escaped, or very possibly was
wed to escape. But one thing that all victors should learn is
an enemy leader must be made harmless—for good and all
pecially if he is the ever-restless, strife-causing type. The
s who fought against Napoleon learned this lesson in the end,
later the Kaiser was similarly rendered impotent. These were
tical decisions and not made by generals.

a 452 Attila invaded Italy, wiped out some cities, damaged
rs, massacred whole populations, and carried off others as
es. Fortunately for humanity Attila died of his excesses the
owing year.

hâlons has been represented as a victory which saved the
t from extinction by the Asiatics. This is too great a claim.
n had the Romans and Goths been beaten at Châlons Attila's
ire would have fallen to pieces on his death, for it was a per-
l empire without any national, religious, intellectual, moral,
olitical basis.

ess than a century later Rome was again in the middle of
e, this time under Justinian the Great, who through two com-
nt generals, Belisarius and Narses, again established Roman
emacy. The main battles of twenty years of almost constant
fare were Tricameron, 533, and Taginae, 552, at which battle,

on an Apennine plain, the eunuch tactician Narses defeated t
Goths by the first experiment in the use of bow and pike.

Narses had an infantry, phalanx-like front, with inward-faci
flanks of archers. With the Goths facing him in force, Narses ga
strict orders that no man could sit down to eat, go to sleep,
move his cuirass, or unbridle his horse. Similar commands, lea
ing to instant readiness, have won many battles, big and small.

Narses allowed the Goths to take the initiative, for his tact
depended on their doing so. They charged the pikemen, could r
break through, and were raked from the flanks by the Rom
archers, while a free-striking force of 1000 cavalry attacked t
enemy rear. After some hours, when the Goths were worn dow
the Romans advanced and routed them. Narses' flanks-forwa
formation was to be copied many times, sometimes with mod
cations, but it was such an obvious trap that no general worth l
job would be deluded into attacking straight against the centre.

By 534 the Mediterranean was again a Roman lake, with t
exception of a few isolated parts of the coast, but Italy was ruin
by her twenty years of war and unable to withstand the assau
and invasions of other races, notably the Lombards. Rome
conquered North Africa from the Vandals, but was unable
keep the Moors in check as the Vandals had done, and Afri
reverted once more to barbarism, and the area fell easily to t
Saracens in the following century. Justinian was no doubt pleas
with his victory at Taginae, but it was the greatest Pyrrhic victc
in history, for it was the climax by which Rome became a bac
number in world affairs.

By the year 630 the Romans and the Persians had exhaust
each other and had been further wasted by other wars over t
previous century. In that year, by no mere coincidence, begar
struggle which was to last a thousand years. This was the year
which Islam as a power began to rise. By 652 the Moslems h
taken Syria, Persia, Egypt, Iraq, Mesopotamia, Ecbatana, t
Persian Gulf, and Khorasan, annihilating Roman and Persi
and Byzantine armies in the process. In following years the Ara
many times tried to capture Constantinople,[1] and in the yea
717–718 they laid siege to it. The man who defended it, a p
fessional soldier called Leo the Isaurian—although he car
from North-east Sicily, not Isauria—created a new empire whi
was to become Europe's buffer against Asia for seven centuries.

[1] Named after the Emperor Constantine, who inaugurated the city on M
11th, 330, and took up residence there. It was often called New Rome.

eo's defence of Constantinople was a classic of its type, and
any ways was a precursor to the Battle of Britain. Constan-
ple was an almost impregnable fortress, with strong walls well
pped and manned largely by steady Anatolian troops. It was
practicable to storm the city—at least until the advent of gun-
der—so the Saracens attempted to storm it by sea—bringing
quadron of large ships, each with 100 armed men aboard,
nst the sea-wall.[2] After the assault failed the Saracens realized
blockade was the only feasible way of reducing the fortress.

eo's survival had therefore to depend on his fleet's being able
reak the blockade, just as Britain's survival depended in the
nd World War. But Leo's fleet was numerically much inferior
e Moslems'.

e defended his harbour by a great boom chain hanging be-
n two towers, and on one occasion, seizing an opportunity,
ad the chain lowered and made a lightning raid on an enemy
, destroying twenty with 'Greek fire'[3] and capturing others.

e was even more successful when he left the protection of his
m, caught the Moslem fleet unprepared—he had a good
onage system—and rammed or burnt many vessels in a one-
d battle. Exploiting his success, Leo ferried a commando
e across to the Asiatic shore and inflicted a sharp defeat on a
lem army.

his was one of the first examples of combined operations. It
also one of the first instances of a general instantly following
victory with another. Apparently, few commanders before
had even considered such a thing. When they won a battle
slaughtered their enemy until their blood-lust was satisfied
then rested on their laurels. Leo's idea of exploitation had a
ound effect on many leaders who studied his battles. His
ve months' defence of Constantinople was a military achieve-
t of the first order and a significant historical act. Had Britain
n to Hitler in 1940 the results would have been vast enough
efy conjecture. Had the Byzantines lost Constantinople in 718
Moslems would have surged through Europe and probably

ive hundred years later the Venetian Doge Dandolo captured Constan-
le by a similar assault against the sea-wall.
Greek fire was probably made from naphtha, sulphur, and quicklime, and
d spontaneously when wetted. Similar compositions had been in use for
ries, and many commanders tried to improve on their predecessors' efforts
e fire as a weapon. It was early used as an offensive weapon at sea, and
also be used in defence of a fortress, but its use by mobile troops was
ed until the Great War.

have stamped out of existence the crystallizing kingdom and e
pire of the Franks.

Militarily the Byzantines were centuries ahead of the West. T
Byzantine Empire was originally the East Roman Empire, so
its developments were built on foundations laid by the Roma:
in fact, nothing in Byzantium is more truly the heir of Rome th
her military policy. The first half of the seventh century is 1
distinctive period in which the historian would be inclined
place the rise of a 'Byzantine Empire', but the Byzantine Arr
had been well established for years. It had excellent military te
books more than eight centuries before the Western world,
not surprisingly the army itself was one of the most advanced
the world.

The Byzantine emperors divided their realm into army c
tricts, each protected by fortresses, linked by good roads.
Byzantine general rarely sought battle. When threatened
simply retired to a fortress, well provisioned against a sie
Eventually the besiegers had to raise the siege to find food, a
while they were doing this the Byzantines would emerge a
destroy them.

The Byzantine Army had two clear divisions—fighting troo
and administrative soldiers. In this too they were centur
ahead of their time. The administrative section included a sup
column, field engineers, a baggage column, and even an aml
lance corps—probably the first of its type. The fighting troo
were in three separate commands—infantry, cavalry, and ar
lery. Never before and only rarely since have troops been
well equipped and organized. Detailed movements had be
evolved to counter every possible form of attack, and all offic
were expected to study these movements.

Alone in Byzantine, in the Europe of the Middle Ages, 1
business of war was treated with scientific deliberation, each g
eration facing new problems and solving them by sustained stuc
Not numbers, but reasoned skill carried a battle, which was
mere *mêlée* but the disciplined co-operation of many uni
Byzantine generals could never afford to indulge in quixotic ch
alry, for too much depended on the preservation of their sm
forces. They used every possible subtlety—feigned flight, nis
attacks, ambushes, false messages designed to fall into ener
hands. The Byzantines believed that a general who relied on for
when he could achieve his object or objective by enterprise wa:
fool. The characteristics of the Byzantine soldier—as his lead

er ceased to tell him—were training, bravery, discipline, and
le in his profession.

3yzantine engineers studied in detail all the natural difficulties
ch might be encountered during a campaign. In the West an
iy might march for days to find a ford across a river. The
:antines built sectional boats, which were numbered and then
:ied by mules. When a stream was reached the sections were
ckly put together and caulked.

can find no direct evidence which might prove that later
erals of other nations, except those of the Ottoman Empire,
owed the many examples of efficiency set by the Byzantine
lers—the Byzantine military textbooks were not translated
several centuries—but I think it possible that von Moltke, the
at Prussian strategist responsible for the victories of 1866 and
0, profited from them. It is possible, too, that Isabella of Spain,
of the first great army quartermasters, knew of Byzantine
hods.[4]

\t Constantinople in 718 the Byzantines had stopped a mass
ss-country invasion of Europe, but, reaching the western end of
Mediterranean by sea, the Moslems and Moors had already
ndered Aquitaine and Burgundy, Narbonne, occupied Car-
sonne and Nîmes, and had even reached the Vosges. Despite a
eat at Toulouse, the Moslems were practically undisputed in
r progress through Southern France because the one man who
ht have stopped them, Charles (or Karl) Martel, son of Pepin
was enjoying a war on the Danube to secure his north-east
itier before he set out to bind the whole of Gaul into an
pire. Gaul at this time was a mere conglomeration of im-
manent barbaric kingdoms. The great bulk of the people con-
ed of Romanized Celts, the Germans sprinkled among them
usually dominant over them. The Teutonic Franks, too, had
ronounced superiority over the other conquerors of the great
on.

he local leader in the most dangerous position at the time of
Moslem incursion was Duke Eudo of Aquitaine, with the
slems menacing him in Spain and the Franks on his north-
. Duke Eudo wanted at least one secure frontier, so he made
illiance with a Berber chief, Othman ben abi Neza, who ruled

Unfortunately for the Byzantines, their empire was rotten with moral and
tual decay, and it was this inner weakness which largely led to their defeat
he Turks at the battle of Manzikert in 1071 and to the end of the magnifi-
Byzantine Army.

an area on the northern side of the Pyrenees. In this Eudo
merely doing what many leaders have done, so that he c₍
concentrate his forces against one enemy, not two. He mar
Othman's daughter and strengthened the alliance. The Mo₍
governor of Spain, Abd-ar-Rahman, was incensed at Othm
"traitorous step" and chased him into the mountains, w
Othman either jumped from a precipice or was pushed from it.

Abd-ar-Rahman turned his attention now to Aquitaine.
main intention in invading the region was plunder, but he
wanted revenge for the killing of some Moslem detachments n
of the Pyrenees. The possible conquest of France was incide
but no doubt considered by Abd-ar-Rahman, who was a ₍
petent and experienced general. He seems to have been hi
popular with his troops, probably because he allowed them
limited plunder, which is a dangerous way to buy popularity.

In the summer of 732 Abd-ar-Rahman crossed into Fr₍
near Irun, at the Bay of Biscay end of the Pyrenees, and m₍
into Gascony. How many men he had is conjectural. Arab wr
say he had 80,000, while Christian historians of the era
"many hundreds of thousands". Moslem armies were al
large, but never so large as this, and I think the figure was p
ably under 100,000, mostly mounted, with a strong detachr
of skilled Berber cavalry.

Some monks who recorded the Saracen invasion say that
Moslems brought their wives and children with them as we
their belongings, as if planning to settle in France. This may
count for the "many hundreds of thousands". It was natura₎
the figure to be exaggerated because the Saracens terrified
people of France. Time and again flourishes of horsemen w
swoop upon a settlement or farming community to plunder, r
and burn.

The size of the army would have appeared larger, too, bec₍
of the great number of mules, some to carry supplies but m₍
to carry plunder. Behind the army proper, mingled with the ca
followers, came a horde of petty but vicious criminals who
pended for their living on what the troops left them or thre
them.

Abd-ar-Rahman had nothing to fear from his rear; neverthe
further to terrorize Aquitaine, he detached a force to strike
east to Arles, near Marseilles, while he took the army due nortl

Abd-ar-Rahman's earlier successes had been largely due t₍
care in protecting his rear, which he did more by threat of a₍

an by action itself. It is impossible to assess how much these ctics influenced later generals since it is only common sense to fend the rear of a column in enemy country, but some generals ve suffered disastrously from not using such common sense.

Duke Eudo threw whatever forces he could scrape together into rdeaux, but they were overwhelmed and the prosperous city s stormed, looted, and burnt. As always, the helpless civilian pulace was cruelly maltreated, but in that era they looked on ch suffering as inevitable. No matter to what race soldiers be-nged they looted, raped, and burnt.

Abd-ar-Rahman crossed the Dordogne river and passed rough the fertile countryside, ever plundering—massacring ople as the whim took him, which was often. There was no cape for the people in the path of his army, for the cavalry nged far and wide, prodding peasants out of their hiding-places that they could be slaughtered.

Charles, successful in the east, was now south of Paris. He ossed the Loire and caused almost as much havoc in the region Berri as the Saracen general was causing farther south. Eudo, uke of Aquitaine, and Charles were deadly enemies, but Eudo s forced to swallow his pride and appeal to Charles for help. nd Charles readily agreed to give it on condition that Eudo sub-it to Frankish control.

Meanwhile Abd-ar-Rahman had invested Poitiers, about sixty les south of Tours, and was moving on to Tours to sack the bey, which he had heard contained great treasures. Like his en, Abd-ar-Rahman had an insatiable appetite for spoil.

Moslem tactics—if tactics they can be called—were very waste-, for they were nothing more than furious, ill-conceived charges. agically, this link in the chain of command seemed to be picked and used again during the Great War. It is doubtful if many lied generals of the Great War had read of Abd-ar-Rahman, t they must have read of the Saracens, and historical literature, uch of it legendary, has painted the Saracens as invincible horse-en. *Ipso facto*—perhaps a certain type of modern military mind asoned—the Saracen *tactics* must be sound and invincible. But e Saracens won most of their battles because they were lightning st while their enemies were laboriously slow; they were efficient hemers, but they knew little of tactics.

Their main weapons were the lance and sword, with which they re adept. The Moslems had very few archers. They relied on eir speed for defence and seldom wore armour.

Charles's army was formed almost entirely of infantry; even nobles used horses only on the march and rarely in battle. only professionals were the men of Charles's own private forc this applied to any Frankish general—while the rest of the ar was made up by militia levies, ill trained and ill equipped. one force which kept a Frankish army together was food, an the general could not see it was provided he could say goodby his army. The professionals mostly had armour—which again coming into fashion—and all the men carried a shi Their weapons were swords, javelins, daggers, a battle-axe, an throwing axe; a skilled axeman could split a skull at fifty ya There seems to have been no systematic organization into unit the various types of arms.

Charles's great quality was that he always understood enemy because he made a point of studying him. Any g general has always done the same. Charles's letter to Eudo il trates this quality:

> Follow my advice and do not interrupt their march precipitate your attack. They are like a torrent, which i dangerous to stem in its career. The thirst of riches and consciousness of success redouble their valour, and valour i more avail than arms or numbers. Be patient till they h loaded themselves with their encumbrances of wealth. . . . T will divide their counsels and assure your victory.

An Arab writer said that Abd-ar-Rahman attacked Tours w great ferocity, "almost before the eyes of the army that came save it; and the fury and cruelty of the Moslems towards the habitants of the city were like the fury and cruelty of rag tigers." He ascribed the subsequent downfall of the Moslems their excesses.

If Charles was aware of what was happening in Tours—and probably was—he must have needed great will to hold himsel check and not to attempt to drive the Moslems from the city. T would have been militarily rash. Nevertheless his approach force the Moslems to withdraw from the city, and they were hampered by their loot that they were no longer mobile. The armies now confronted each other for seven days. General Fu believes that in this time Charles was waiting for reinforceme to arrive while Abd-ar-Rahman was sending his plunder to rear. It is sound conjecture, particularly as it concerns Char but Abd-ar-Rahman would have found it impossible to ind

oldiers to trust their plunder to anybody else. The human
ls who followed the army would have taken it and spirited
ay to Spain. Neither could Abd-ar-Rahman order the plunder
abandoned, for his men would not have obeyed him.

obably the armies had a few fringe combats near Tours,
which Abd-ar-Rahman fell back towards Poitiers and some-
e near this town decided to accept battle—perhaps from
, perhaps to cover the withdrawal of his loot, most probably
use he did not want to be caught with the river Dordogne at
ack without room to manoeuvre.

arles did indeed understand his enemy. Once brought to
e the Moslems must attack; they had no option, because they
no defensive ability. Charles therefore arranged his army in
anx and waited for the inevitable wild cavalry charge, which
not long in coming. The Moslems charged many times—this
ideal cavalry country—but Martel's army stood "like a belt
e frozen together", as one ancient chronicler put it. As even-
approached Duke Eudo and his Aquitainians turned one of
enemy's flanks and attacked Abd-ar-Rahman's camp, thus
ng the Moslems to fall back; their loot was in the camp, and
were fearful for its safety. There is some doubt whether
ar-Rahman was killed on the first day or the second, but the
er seems most likely. According to one record he was
red to death while trying to rally his retiring troops, while a
heroic chronicler claims that he was killed as he charged
the midst of the phalanx.

obably fighting occurred on the second day, but some authori-
ay that during the night the Moslems abandoned their camp
much of their loot and fled south. In either case the Franks
won a decisive victory. Pursuit was out of the question, for
les had no cavalry, and being shrewd, he would not have
ed Eudo to feel perfectly safe from further Saracen aggres-
for so long as Aquitaine needed Frank protection the Franks
l control Lorraine. As it happened, the Saracens made no
er serious attacks beyond the Pyrenees.

isualties at Tours are beyond computation. They range
as high as 360,000 Moslems killed to as few as 1500 Franks
l. The Moslems certainly lost more than the Franks, and
losses would have been increased by attacks on their camp-
wers in their retreat to the Pyrenees. The one really sour note
harles's victory is that he took Abd-ar-Rahman's loot for him-
but this was an act in accord with his era.

Charles's feat supplemented—indeed, complemented that
Leo. Between them they had saved France. In later years Cha
forced the Moslems to withdraw from the Rhône valley. He
no doubt ironically grateful to Abd-ar-Rahman, for his defea
the Saracen gave him a tremendous reputation and enabled
to build his empire and to found an imperialistic dynasty, to
inherited in 768 by his grandson, Charles the Great—Cha
magne.

The contributions to the military leadership left by Cha
Martel—known as "the hammer"—are those of the wise
of studying an enemy before fighting him, of holding back
the right moment, even at the expense of suffering on the par
friendly people, of the superiority of sober valour over impet
courage, of method over dash. It is not without significance
Charles was Duke of the Austrasian Franks, the bravest and r
thoroughly Germanic part of the nation. The military qual
he showed at Tours are more Germanic than French, whic
perhaps why he was the subject of frequent lectures to off
cadets of the Prussian and German Armies from the tim
Scharnhorst onward. His place in military leadership is n
prominent than it appears to be.

---◇•◇---

CHAPTER EIGHT

Charlemagne; Genghiz Khan
and Sabutai; Edward III, Crécy

◥ HARLEMAGNE'S work as a military commander stands as an
◡ island of sanity in a sea of stupidity, for the Middle Ages
ɔvide few examples of genuine art in war.

Charlemagne was one of the first generals to organize an
ny highly. He wanted an army of quality, not quantity, and
ɩen he called upon his nobles to supply men he ordered that
ːh horseman must come equipped with shield, lance, sword,
d bow, and that foot-soldiers must carry sword, spear, and
w.

He wanted his army mobile, but this was impossible if it had to
y for its subsistence on what it could forage, so he organized
ʋpply-train as well as a siege-train. Because he ruled such a vast
ːa he established what were really forts at strategic points in
domains. Oddly enough, though this seems obvious military
ategy, it had been neglected for many centuries.

It was about this time, too, that warfare was given a great boost
the growing attitude that it was noble to fight in defence of
ɛdom and liberty—though no two definitions about freedom
d liberty coincided. The Church recognized that war could,
leed, be righteous.

In the year 990, for the first time, rules and regulations for war-
ːe were laid down in the *Pax Dei* ("Peace of God"). This code
ned at protecting women, clerics, peasants, church buildings,
ttle, and agricultural implements from the soldiery. Men guilty

of breaking the code faced excommunication, but the threat w
not as successful as its exponents hoped.

Between 850 and 900 the Scandinavians—the Vikings—l
their mark on martial development. During this half-century th
raided the whole of Western Europe, forcing their victims to e
ploy professional soldiers and to build strongholds. This mea
that military power passed into the hands of the nobility. In t
end many nobles had armies which were stronger than tho
owned by monarchs, thus giving rise to further warfare.

Continental countries relied on cavalry to beat the Viking
but in England King Alfred tried something different. He built
fleet and beat the Vikings on their own element. On land
relied on infantry and took no steps to raise cavalry.

Infantry was well developed in England by King Harold's da
At the Battle of Hastings, 1066, his men were armed with spea
javelin, two-edged sword, and the unwieldy Danish axe, b
bows were not popular at this time in Britain. The hostile No
mans carried lance, sword, and mace, and a short Norman bo
or the crossbow.

Harold's formation at Hastings was probably that of the shiel
wall, the best possible one against the Norman infantry a
cavalry. For a long time during the battle this formation, t
stolidity of the English, and the fierceness of their fighting block
the Normans. Had Harold maintained his position he may n
have lost the battle, but William lured his enemy from the
positions by means of a feint retreat—an old stratagem from t
Orient, as we have seen.

Finally he ordered his archers to fire at a high angle so that t
English would have to raise their shields. Harold himself was I
in the eye, and when he fell the English disintegrated.[1]

William the Conqueror's invasion of England in 1066 was
masterpiece of clever strategy and tactics, and probably he was tl
inspiration and model by which Norman arms were so remarkab
successful for the next century.

Some weapons, like the crossbow, were becoming more 'scie
tific'—so much so that in 1139 the Second Lateran Council o
lawed the crossbow, describing it as "a weapon fateful to Go
and unfit for Christians". The Council held, in fact, that lo
distance or missile warfare was unchristian.

The crossbow did not require the same muscular strength

[1] The death of the commander-in-chief in battle still meant the defeat of I
whole army, so great was his control and his power so great a symbol.

ate as the longbow, but it was much more complicated and
spanned (loaded) by various systems of leverage. Some types
: wound up. In action the archer sheltered behind a high
den shield known as a pavise, which rested on the ground
ported by a prop.

he Lateran edict did not keep the crossbow out of war, but it
have the effect of further ennobling warfare, thus giving it
antic qualities which appealed to chivalrous men of birth.

uring this period Earl "Strongbow" and his 200 or so
sh knights gave a splendid example of commando tactics, by
quering the greater part of Ireland and repulsing a powerful
se invasion. Strongbow's small but efficient hard-hitting
e were masters of every commando tactic and trick, and they
eved as much as Otto Skorzeny and his hand-picked Nazis
orth-west Europe in 1944–45.

rince Edward, later Edward I (1272–1307), left some strategic
ons for later commanders. His solution to subdue the Welsh—
rdy, fierce race—was to build castles at strategic points, the
cy of Charlemagne. He connected them by roads, and by
ing the enemy on the move he wore them down. The British
these tactics 600 years later in various parts of the Indian
ontinent.

the East Genghiz Khan made his impressive contribution to
tary history; by clever use of three armies in combination he
e up the powerful Kin Empire. In 1241 Genghiz Khan's
ing general, Sabutai, took two armies into Europe in as
stating and dynamic a military sweep as any in history. He
: his main army into three widely separated columns and
ced as many holes in Hungary to the Danube—cleverly keep-
the flank columns well ahead of the central column, the main
ing force. His second army all this time was guarding his
hern flank, decisively beating Bohemian, German, and Polish
ies. Near Gran the Hungarians had assembled on the far bank
e Danube and were in far too strong a position to be attacked.
utai staged a careful and convincing 'retirement', which de-
d the Hungarians and lured them after the Mongols. In an
on as clever as it was violent Sabutai wiped out the Hun-
an army, to become undisputed master of Europe's central
ns. What might have happened had the Mongols stayed on
conquered soil—nobody could have thrown them out—pro-
s fascinating conjecture. Strangely, they left a year later.

is difficult to resist the conclusion that von Moltke was

directly influenced by the Mongol strategy and tactics in his ca
paigns of 1866 and 1870. The point will be amplified later in
book.

Great military changes took place in the thirteenth and fo
teenth centuries. It was during the thirteenth that body armo
reached twin peaks of effectiveness and absurdity. A knight w
such a weight of armour that he suffered torment in a hot s
Many a knight needed two footmen to hoist him into the sado
and if he were struck from his horse during combat he was u
less; he might even be unable to rise to avoid being trampled
horses or clubbed to death by infantry.

By adding flaps, hinges, and over-pieces knights tried to co
up every possible chink through which an adversary might pr
them with dart, arrow, sword, or lance. Under his armour
knight wore a thick quilted garment, while over it and the ad
tional plates he wore his surcoat with belts. With his shield a
weapons he could well be carrying a load twice his own weight.

Saracen armour was much more practical. It was of ring-
chain-mail, strong, light, and flexible, and much more comfo
able. The Saracens played havoc with the Christian knights
crusaders—many of whom were burnt to death inside th
armour by Greek fire.

When they returned home the knights of the West brou
something with them from the East—memories of the magnifice
castles of the East—in Palestine, for instance. This led to a rash
castle-building in Central and Western Europe, and before lo
every district was dominated by a castle, to which peasants in
area looked for protection.

By a process of military evolution there came into being c
militias, then specialist mercenary soldiers. who were very w
paid. Late in the thirteenth century, too, France and England a
later Italy began to pay all soldiers, even the short-service or
Soldiering was becoming a regular profession in Europe.

Some mercenary bands, selling their services to the high
bidder, were superb soldiers. Others were mere opportun
and became brigands when there was no war.

During the first half of the fourteenth century France was ho
lessly in the grip of chivalry. Battles were fought by 'men
quality' on horseback. A knight thought it below his dignity
attack infantry, who were usually massacred after a victory. T
French were more concerned with taking prisoner oppos
knights and holding them for ransom than with killing the

the battle of Courtrai in 1302 the French nobility imagined
f to be the best fighting force in the world, but it was little
e than a gallant but undisciplined mob. The French knight
sidered himself far superior to any common soldier, especially
e soldier happened to be on foot. He regarded the appearance
he field of battle of spearmen, crossbowmen, or others as an
lt. He had no more regard for his own common soldiers than
ad for the enemy.

was unfortunate for France that this was the period of
vard III, one of the first 'modern' generals, and whose tactics
leeply offended the French. Edward's battle of Crécy has a
nite place in the British chain of command, for with this
ory came England's foundation as a military nation. That this
ild be is somewhat paradoxical, for Edward III had got him-
into a most dangerous situation at Crécy, and his victory was
largely to the French being even more rash and so allowing
nselves to become the vanquished in one of the most decisive
les in history.

t the time of Crécy the English Army was raised by ordering
landowners to provide men-at-arms, spearmen, or archers
ording to a set scheme approved by the English Parliament in
5.

he men-at-arms wore armour and carried the lance, sword,
ger, and a shield. Most of them were trained from early youth,
naps as boys of no more than ten or eleven. The cavalry
e called pauncenars, from the German *Panzer*, meaning a
: of mail. These lance-armed warriors were not so well
pped with defensive armour, but they did wear a sleeveless
: of chainmail known as the habergeon. The lighter cavalry
e an iron helmet, a thickly padded doublet, iron gloves, and a
rd.

he infantry consisted of Welsh spearmen who wore no armour.
ry man was given—at the King's expense—a tunic and a
tle made of the same material and of the same colour. This
y battle-dress was first issued in 1337.

he archers were the backbone of any English military force
he period. Some were mounted, but they used their horses
ely to hurry from one place to another. The archers wore
' iron caps for protection, but sometimes they had large shields
ited at the bottom, which could be driven into the earth.

English archers were extremely skilful. Their bows were
illy of yew and were 6 feet 4 inches long, the arrows being of

several lengths but generally described as cloth-yard shafts. T
arrows were fitted with a pointed barb of iron and fledged w
goose or peacock feathers. They could pierce oak to a depth
two or more inches.

A good archer could fire six aimed shots a minute with an eff
tive range up to 240 yards and an extreme one of 340 yar
Volley firing was devastating and demoralizing even to we
trained troops—as other British troops were to show at Mons
1914.

One advantage of the longbow over the crossbow—which w
used by French Genoese mercenaries—was that it was held p
pendicularly to the ground, and not horizontally like the cro
bow, so that the bowmen could stand closer together and co
centrate their fire.

Another formidable English weapon was the bill—evolv
from an agricultural implement—a staff weapon with a hoo
spike, and blade. A foot-soldier could drag a horseman from
saddle with the hook, then kill him with the spike or blade. T
blade could be used, axe-like, for wide and vicious swinging. T
pole-axe was also in use. Only a brave man would tackle a sold
wielding this long-staffed fiercesome weapon.

Edward disembarked his army at La Hogue between July 1
and 17th, 1346, reached Caen on July 26th, and here order
that all the men so far wounded and all the booty taken shou
be put aboard the ships. But the crews had mutinied and had
turned to England, forcing Edward to make drastic changes in
plans. Without communications he could not stay at Caen, but
he headed south he would clash with the superior army of
Duke of Normandy. Therefore he marched east, following
Seine towards Paris, which he approached on August 13th, le
ing a trail of devastation in his wake.

Peasants and farmers who were unfortunate enough to live
the line of an invading army's march rarely had warning of
approach. Suddenly soldiers would appear, rough, crude m
who took everything that was eatable or portable and fired a
thing that was not. They often assaulted women and would
any man who interfered. If they felt high-spirited they wo
fire the fields of grain, trample their horses through the vegeta
patches, or hack down fruit-trees until they tired. A 'friend
army was only a little less cruel than a foreign one.

Edward's men plundered and burnt town after town, and ev
abbeys were destroyed, though on one occasion when this ha

ed Edward hanged twenty of his officers for permitting the out-
e.

eaving the Paris area, Edward now pushed north and by
gust 21st had reached Airaines, south of the Somme river.
lip of France was now at Amiens with an army growing larger
the day. Edward had great difficulty in finding a ford across
Somme, but a big reward brought forward a French traitor
 led the English to a crossing-place ten miles below Abbe-
e. Despite fierce opposition from a French force of 2000 the
ay got across on the 24th, an hour before the French army
ae up—only to be stopped from fording the river by the rising
.

At Crécy Edward decided to fight. His reasons for selecting
 site have been much discussed. Edward has been praised for
icipating that Philip would advance by the Abbeville–Hesdin
d, but such anticipation required no great intellect. Edward
w that Philip could chase him by two roads only, and one of
se roads was practically barred to the French because of the
y thick wood for miles around.

imilarly he has been praised for realizing that the French
uld attack frontally; there was no other way they *could* attack,
 their blind instinct of chivalry demanded a frontal attack.
e French military mind of this period could not have con-
ved the idea of a flank attack. The position that Edward chose
ed his tactics and his strength, but many other such positions
sted in the area. He fought at Crécy because he was tired of
ning before the French, because—as Froissart says—he had
ched the area which was the inheritance of his grandmother,
 pride insisted that he defend it. More than that, Edward
s enclosed in a triangle—with the sea, the Somme, and the
nch army for its sides.

he country around Crécy is of rolling downs falling to two
ll streams, the Maye and Authie. The English lay on the slop-
banks of the Maye above the little town of Crécy.

dward gave a supper for his senior officers—a fine meal, for
e was to be had for the taking, and the country was rich in
ae and farm produce. The carts and carriages that followed the
glish Army were loaded with plenty of provisions—all looted.
ward then prayed at the altar of his oratory, a portable chapel.
was midnight before he retired to sleep.

hilip stayed at Abbeville, and that night he too gave a supper
all his dukes, barons, and other nobles. After supper he asked

that there should be no quarrelling among them, for his no
were very touchy about their pride and honour.

At daybreak on August 26th Edward and his son, the Princ
Wales—the young Black Prince—as well as many others, h
Mass and were confessed and given communion. This
Edward commanded every man to proceed to the field of ba
He ordered a park to be made by the woodside behind the a
and in this were put all the carts, carriages, and horses; the I
had decided that all would fight on foot. The one entry to the
was guarded by picked men.

Edward placed two of his three divisions in the forward s
of the rise east of the Crécy–Wadicourt road and the third in
rear. The Prince of Wales, aged seventeen, nominally c
manded the right-front division—consisting of about 800 r
at-arms, 2000 archers, and 1000 Welshmen—but the actual c
manders were Warwick the Earl Marshal and the Earls of Ox
and Harcourt. Northampton and the Earl of Arundel comman
the left division of 700 men-at-arms and 1200 archers, w
Edward himself commanded the 700 men-at-arms and 2
archers of the rear division. Edward's headquarters were a
windmill from which he could see the entire field of battle.

His dispositions finished, Edward mounted a pony, and, wi
white rod in one hand and flanked by his marshals, he r
slowly along the ranks encouraging his men. They had their r
day meal, then again formed battle-order, but sensibly were
to sit and rest in ranks, with their helmets and bows in from
them.

Philip now had his army assembled at Abbeville—8000 r
at-arms supported by 4000 foot and adorned by an extraor
arily illustrious collection of royalty and nobility. No fewer t
three kings fought with him—the half-blind King John
Bohemia, John's son Charles, King of the Romans, and I
James III of Majorca. Also were present many dukes and r
of the chivalry of France.

Early on August 26th Philip set out on the Abbeville–He
road with four knights forward as a reconnaissance patrol. T
knights discovered the English positions, and on their return
gested to Philip that the army should halt for the night, so
the whole army would be ordered for an attack on the follov
morning.

Philip gave orders to this effect, but now occurred one of
lamentable incidents which have so often marred French a

e leading French troops halted, but the nobles leading the fol-
wing men refused to halt until they too were at the front. The
nt men, turning and seeing the rear men still pushing forward,
umed their march. The King and his generals tried in vain to
p the army, which pressed forward in confused order until
y saw the English army drawn up. The sight was so unnerving
at the leading ranks turned about, alarming the men follow-
g. A short but violent storm now occurred, after which bright
n appeared again, shining in the face of the French. Many
glish archers lay on their bowstrings to keep them dry during
is storm.

The Count of Flanders and the Count of Alençon had by now
arshalled the Genoese into better order and marched them for-
rd into the Vallée des Clercs. The Genoese were ordered to
out so as to frighten the English, and they tried this three times,
t, as Froissart records, "the English never moved".

They left the first aggressive move to the Genoese, who opened
e with their crossbows; their bolts fell short. The English
chers then took one deliberate step forward and commenced
lley-fire. The effect was instantaneously devastating; many
enoese were hit, and others cut their bowstrings or threw their
ws away and ran. Philip ordered that the deserters be killed at
ice to save his army from mass panic.

The French knights needed no urging to fight; they trampled
wn the Genoese and hacked at them with their swords in their
gerness to get into battle, though English arrows were now fal-
ig among them. As shafts bit into man and horse, nailing hel-
et and armour to skull and flesh, chaos creased the French front
nks, and many knights were thrown by their rearing mounts. A
sciplined division, having been repulsed, would have cleared
s front so that the second division had a clear run to the assault,
it this did not happen at Crécy, and the second French division
llided with the wreckage of the first. On the Prince of Wales's
ont the situation was dangerous for a time because a portion of
e French force dashed against it, though more from the horses'
ight than by military design. Edward sent the Bishop of
urham—the ecclesiastics of this period were enthusiastic fight-
ig men—and 30 knights to reinforce his son's division. To a
essenger who had come from the Earl of Warwick, Edward
sked, "Is my son dead or hurt or felled to the earth?"

"No, sire," was the reply, "but he is hard-pressed and needs
our aid."

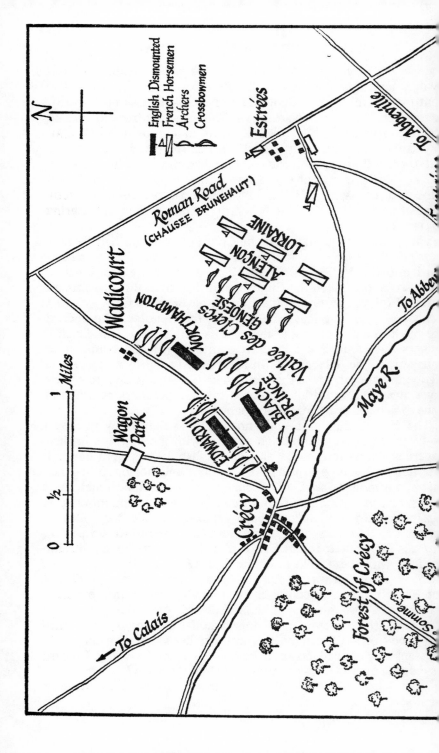

king into account the battle methods of his time, Edward
had chosen his ground well and had made competent dis-
tions for its defence. Considering the enemy weight of num-
, Edward knew he had to fight a defensive battle. However,
position would have been hopeless had the French leaders
any genuine tactical insight. They could easily have used the
of the day (August 26th) to bring up all the French force.
could have placed a third of it in front of the English and
ed the rest on columns of march on the right. At daybreak
morning these 40,000 men would have moved northward
Wadicourt, presenting the English with an impossible choice:
ght with an overwhelming force rolling up their line from
flank or to retreat rapidly. Such a plan was beyond the
ination of medieval generals. They could think only of
tal attack and if they had superior numbers, then all the
weight with which to push! At Crécy the archers with
longbows showed how futile such methods were against
tactics allied to steady discipline. Not even waiting for much
eir army to come up, the French charged to destruction.

Froissart quotes the King's reply: "Well, return to him an them that sent you and say to them that they send no mor me ... as long as my son is alive; and also say to them that suffer him this day to win his spurs; for if God be pleased, I that this journey be his, and the honour thereof."

While this was happening Northampton, probably u Edward's orders, was wheeling his division so as to attack flank of the French who were charging the English right divis The French were bloodily repulsed and fell back into the rank their third division, led by Philip himself. Fifteen times French assaulted and every time without any preconceived p No Japanese *banzai* charge was more fanatic than that of French chivalry; for them "Death before dishonour" were mere words.

The Welsh troops worsened the enemy's confusion, for w ever the French men-at-arms fell back the Welshmen rushed ward and slaughtered many fallen nobles—to the bitter fur Edward and his chief lieutenants; they could not get ransom a dead man.

Philip himself, wounded, and now with fewer than 70 lance guard him, rode frantically about the field, trying to mount one more desperate charge against the English lines. In the the Count of Hainault made the King see reason and induced to withdraw.

The French were routed, but pursuit was out of the quest for dusk had now fallen and Edward had no effective cava But he was a competent enough commander to keep his under arms, and next morning, when the French reinforcem came up, not knowing that their army had been defeated, English scattered them with heavy loss. After that, in a clea mist, the English troops were allowed to break ranks and ga in the loot, which meant stripping the dead of everything had. Even bloody clothing was useful to the poorer soldiery.

Not until the dead were examined by the three heralds sen to the field by Edward, and the few prisoners questioned, wa known that the King of Bohemia, the Duke of Lorraine, counts, and 1542 knights and squires had been killed. At 10,000 common soldiers were dead on the field, a scene of centrated butchery if ever there was one. According to report English casualties were fewer than 75 and included onl knights, but such a slight loss cannot be believed.

Among the French prisoners were the Bishop of Noyen,

chdeacon of Paris, and the Counts of Aumale, Montbéliard,
d Rosenberg.

Ordinary soldiers were buried on the spot, some being found in
shes and in hedges as well as in the open, but Edward sent
e bodies of French nobles to Montreuil to be buried in holy
ound. He also declared a truce for three days so that the
asants around Crécy could search for and bury any bodies
ey found.

Crécy will always hold its pre-eminent place in military
story. It was to the English what Marathon was to the Greeks
Anzac to the Australians. English troops had beaten the Scots
d the Welsh, but these campaigns had passed unnoticed in Con-
ental Europe. The English had fought under Henry III and
dward I in France, but their actions had been mediocre and
eir achievements few. Now, after Crécy and its sequel—the
ge and capture of Calais—English troops had such a remark-
le reputation that, by the principle of martial momentum, they
d to hold and enhance that reputation.

At that time no foreign general could understand how the
nglish had achieved their victory, and this made it all the more
pressive. A great part of the victory was due to the training the
wmen had received on their village green since their boyhood.
early 500 years later Sir John Moore, founder of the magnificent
ght Division which fought in Spain and Portugal, acknowledged
t he had made use of the pre-Crécy principle of rigorous
ining. Apart from this the victory was due to Edward's having
on a system of dismounted combat, using archers and men-
arms in combination.

The dictum by which the English and British were to win
ndreds of battles—it could well be expressed as 'shoulder to
oulder and keep the troops steady'—was so well founded at
écy that in the centuries to come it was rarely shaken.[2] And as
s steadiness and discipline were the weapons which won so
ny fights it might well be claimed that the link in leadership
ged at Crécy is one of the strongest.

[2] It might also be said that during the Boer War and the First World War
vish adherence to this dictum killed many British soldiers.

CHAPTER NINE

The Age of Innovation

The Janissaries; du Guesclin's 'Phantom' Army; Mahomet, Master Gunner; The Magnificent Defence of Constantinople; Isabella, Master Quartermaster; Gustavus, "Father of Modern War"

FEW years before Crécy—in 1338—the Turks, with the Ottoman Empire just rising, introduced a remarkable type of ier and called him Yeni Tscheri, meaning new army or new ier. The words became corrupted into European as 'Janis-.'.

he Janissaries were the invention of Ala ed-Din, who could that a feudal militia of Turkish horsemen, still educated in tradition of pastoral society, could not hope to conquer and an empire for the descendants of Othman, the first Turkish an. Turks could not be disciplined to the extremity required, new army was formed of sons of Christian, non-Turkish ects of Othmanli.

he conception was not new, but was a copy of the Mamelukes ded by Saladin and perfected by Es-Salih Ayyub. The plan to give the Christian boys the best practical education pos-, but they would have no parents or country and would swear giance only to the House of Othman. Gradually the Janis-es were educated as Moslems, but this was almost coincidental.

he experiment was an outstanding success, for the Janissaries, iired as children, aged between seven and twelve, and edu-d or re-educated to an artificial pattern, became the most com-nt and most feared body of men in the world, as soldiers administrators. Trained to think militarily and to act with ision, they achieved a degree of cold, inhuman efficiency

never equalled. They were as invincible as any military for
tion in history and they had a more far-flung prestige than Ron
legionaries, Swiss mercenaries, Cromwell's Ironsides, Engl
grenadiers, Napoleonic cavalry, Prussian guards, the Anzacs,
Hitler's S.S. Hitler definitely modelled the Hitler Youth Mo
ment on the Janissary system and demanded from his S.S.
same sort of personal renunciation imposed on the Janissaries.

But the Janissaries were little known in Europe in 1364 whe
stubborn, sometimes crude but always brilliant Frenchman,
Constable du Guesclin, began to make his mark on military
tory as one of the first systematic guerrilla-commando lead
The disaster of Crécy brought du Guesclin into prominence, a
before long he did his country the great service of applying
coup de grâce to the chivalry Edward III had so seriou
wounded. He also reduced the great English possessions in Fra
to a thin strip between Bordeaux and Bayonne. And he did
this without fighting a battle.

It takes a really great soldier to gain so much without a bat
yet du Guesclin has been decried by some of his own countryn
because, in effect, he suffered too few casualties. But oth
learned from him—among them the unique Turenne, Sa
Marlborough, Napoleon, Sherman, several German generals;
that anybody matched du Guesclin in his own field.

His strategy was simply to avoid battle with the main Engl
force while all the time he harassed and hampered enemy mo
ments and nibbled pieces from the territory they held. His pol
was 'No attack without surprise', and in accordance with
principle he swooped on one garrison after another, especi
those that he had heard were restless or mutinous or where
could induce local civilians to unbar the gates or let down scal
ropes by night.

He ambushed convoys and reinforcements, waylaid dispa
riders and enemy officers with weak escorts. Every action v
carried out with commando-like speed and violence. If sor
thing went wrong or a garrison was able to rally in time to ma
a fight of it du Guesclin called off the assault. Why get a bloc
nose when he could strike somewhere else and take the place w
out suffering even a bruise? Yet there was nothing negative ab
du Guesclin's methods, and the proof of their efficacy is that
achieved his remarkable successes within five years.

A new link in warfare was slowly being forged at this tim
artillery. The first use of gunpowder to launch objects with

ight of penetration may well have been in the Far East. Both
tars and Arabs made early use of hollow tubes of wood or
aboo, tightly bound with hide, hemp, or wire. They were
led from the muzzle with alternate charges of powder and an
ndiary ball, often of tallow. When the tube was ignited at the
zzle the fire worked around each ball and touched off the
der to discharge the ball ahead. The Mongols had machines
ch hurled melted fat and tallow-loaded projectiles.

oger Bacon certainly knew of gunpowder in 1252, and the
man monk Berthold Schwartz, who lived in Freiberg until
ut 1384, made countless drawings of cannons, but he did not
nt the cannon; nobody knows who made the first cannon and
n. In the fourteenth century both cavalry and infantry had
d cannons—little more than large tubes on the end of a pole.
soldier fired his cannon by igniting powder at the touchhole
a lighted length of rope or stick carried for the purpose.

n Arabic document mentions cannon in 1304; other documents
Ghent refer to cannon in 1313 and 1314, and Oxford has a
ure of a *pot de fer*—a dart-throwing vase—in use in 1324. In
8 there was a cannon at Cambrai, France, which fired masses
arts. In 1339, at the attack on Quesnoy, there were several
lar cannon. And from that time onward history refers to them
uently. In 1340 Augsburg, Germany, had a gunpowder mill.

he original cannon was small and fired darts or small lead
s, weighing 3 lb. at most. A great variety of early cannons
ted, some of them gigantic ones.

1 1368 in France there was the Master of the King's Cannons,
in 1383 the Bishop of Norwich used "the Great Gun of
terbury" in the siege of Ypres. In 1391 the Italian city of
ogna had a large supply of iron shot.

ulverins, a type of cannon, are heard of at this time. The Great
verin fired projectiles weighing 15 lb., the Bastard Culverin
., and the Middle Culverin 2 lb. By the end of the fourteenth
ury bombards were in existence, and could throw a ball of
e weighing as much as 200 lb. But they were of little practical
They were easily crushed by their own action, and they could
knock down a strong wall.

rtillery radically altered the face of war, but the many stories
have been told of the terror inspired by the early cannons are
fantasy.

hile artillery was struggling into life the French chivalry re-
itated itself, despite du Guesclin's exemplary work for his

country. Its revival was a tragedy for France; with a four to c advantage at Agincourt in 1415 the French indulged in a ridi lous frontal attack and were beaten bloody, to give Henry V England a famous victory that he could not have won had Guesclin been alive and in command.

The siege of Orléans followed as a consequence of the Engl invasion of France in 1415, but I do not propose to deal witl here. In 1851 Creasy said that "It may be asserted without aggeration that the future career of every nation was involved the result of the struggle by which Joan of Arc rescued 1 country from becoming a second Ireland under the yoke of triumphant English." This might well be true, but, beyond be the first siege in which any important use was made of artille the siege and battle of Orléans have nothing to commend th in the martial sense. The hysterical emotionalism which 1 always surrounded the Maid has somehow led some historian: who should be immune to emotionalism—to conclude t Orléans was a great battle. Without decrying Joan persona there is something peculiarly shameful and unmilitary in spectacle of an army being led by a teenage girl, and it is pleas to reflect that the innovation was not imitated.

In 1430 a year after Orleans, Sultan Mahomet II was bc Cruel and ruthless, but a student and an intellectual, Mahor became sultan in 1451, and avidly studied the lives and campai, of Alexander, Julius Caesar, and many other rulers and gener; It is significant how so many of the really great generals of hist have not been too proud to admit their debt to the past. Mahom who was one of the most outstanding men in Oriental histo certainly admitted his debt.

He lived and breathed war—as a dedicated general mus demanded the strictest discipline, and punished severely slightest insubordination. He had the great quality of never be discouraged by defeat, and he knew that to remain efficient army must remain active; he kept his troops continually on move.

In any study of military development he stands out as the fi great gunner; Napoleon, himself a master gunner, learnt fr Mahomet. When Mahomet set out to capture Constantinople had probably 13 great bombards and 14 batteries, each with f guns, of smaller calibre. His largest bombard, cast in Adrianop fired a stone shot of 1456 lb., and required 60 oxen and 200 n to get it into position. As it took two hours to load its effectiven

limited. On April 12th, 1453, Mahomet opened the first great
anized bombardment in history, thus establishing a sinister
enduring link. The Turks concentrated their shot on particu-
sections of the walls, and the artillery fire went on day and
ht, to the distress of the defenders and inhabitants of the city,
ch was defended by a maximum 8000 troops to Mahomet's
,000.

Nevertheless, the defenders beat back some large-scale assaults
inflicted thousands of casualties on Mahomet's troops, largely
ng to the defensive genius of the brilliant Genoese soldier
n Giustiniani, who was ably supported by the veteran German
itary engineer Johann Grant. On May 18th Mahomet made
irther attempt at storming the walls under cover of a *helepolis*
city-taker'—a huge wooden tower. The *helepolis* was dragged
to the walls, and from it heavy fire was poured into the de-
:es, but Giustiniani blew up the tower. Mahomet next resorted
nining, copying the methods introduced by Philip of Macedon
!40 B.C.[1]; that is, his miners dug tunnels and chambers under
walls, propping up the roofs as they proceeded. Then they
ild set fire to the props in the hope that the walls above would
apse into the cavity. But the defenders, directed by Grant,
nter-mined. Grant blew up the Turkish miners, smoked them
, suffocated them by stinkpots, or drowned them. At times
h sides met underground and fought bloodily with knife, spear,
axe.

'rustrated, at the point of despair, on May 29th Mahomet
iched his greatest assault—a combined one by army and
t. The main attack was made by three echelons of infantry,
Bashibazouks, the Anatolians, and the Janissaries, in that
er, the worst being first and the best last. The defenders, now
iced to fewer than 4000 fighting men, fought so hard that
homet had to make five separate assaults, but in the end he
mphed and the great fortress city fell. The attackers lost many
re men than the defenders, but this did not perturb Mahomet,
he was an exponent of the theory that the end was worth the
ins; his enduring influence in this respect was great, and
iy generals copied him, time and again battering at powerful
:nsive positions in the expectation that successive attacks
ild wear down the defenders. This Mahomet mentality often
its successes, but many of them were Pyrrhic. The Mahomet
itality was nothing more than an obsession for conquest

[1] When he laid siege to Perinthus (Eregli) and Byzantium.

regardless of cost, and it was much more of a negative appr(
to war than the sly tactics of du Guesclin. Extremely insidiou
corrupted even intelligent military leaders, and never more
than during the war of 1914–18, when generals hurled masse
men against fortress-like positions much more formidable t
Constantinople ever was. Mahomet had some virtues as a gene
but his vices and not his virtues survived in the chain of lea
ship. The siege and the taking of Constantinople was so po
cally, religiously, and culturally catastrophic and its effect
profound that for centuries it was regarded as a magnificent r
tary feat. The view prevails even today. But the praise bel(
to the defenders, not to the attackers. Mahomet made his firs
connaissance in force on September 6th 1452; despite his
numerical superiority he did not take the city until May 29th
following year. The clever, spirited defence of Constantin(
should be celebrated, not its capture. But evil influences
strong, especially when cloaked in success, and the Mahc
mentality has not yet been eradicated.

While Turkey was emerging as the great power of the Eas
Western Europe Spain was becoming powerful, with Qu
Isabella proving herself a great general and an even gre
quartermaster-general. Isabella, who with her husband Ferdin
assumed joint rule of Aragon and Castile in 1479, has a defi
place in the chain of command, and in my view is the only wo
in history who can be justly called a great captain. While of le
stature than Hannibal, Scipio, Gustavus, Frederick, and Napol
she nevertheless had unique qualities. And she was no n
copyist, but an innovator and initiator.

To conquer Granada—the first step in a series of campa
which were to establish the Spanish Empire—Isabella develo
artillery, engineers, and infantry. Her work with infantry f
shadowed a change as great in its way as the use of gunpow
She commenced her wars with the customary feudal levi(
groups of men provided by the nobles as part of the duty t
owed to the Crown. But Isabella soon realized, as man
general had done before her, that the levies lacked discipline
that their sense of independence made them unreliable. So
developed her police force into an army, an early form of natic
army of professionals, and finally she hired Swiss mercenai
then the finest infantry in Europe. Intelligent, trustworthy, and
the mercenary, however, owed his allegiance to his comma
rather than to the ruler who paid the commander. This cha

er from levies to professionals was a primary factor in the in-
oduction of modern war.[2]

Isabella's artillery was also formidable. Her bombards threw
on and marble balls and occasionally fire-balls which not only
t the defences on fire but terrified the defenders. Pioneers were
cruited in thousands to build roads for passage of the bom-
rds. Isabella's supply problems were immense, but she was
ual to them. Her supply train consisted of no fewer than 80,000
ck-mules; in all history there is no record of any greater num-
r of animals used in warfare. Isabella herself controlled dis-
bution of rations, managed the billeting of soldiers, and
anned the routes to be followed by her convoys.

She also introduced a field hospital—the first recorded instance
one—and a regiment of field messengers. These early signallers
oved invaluable in Isabella's campaigns. It should be said that
rdinand was commander-in-chief of the army and that he was
icient and capable, but he could never have achieved his suc-
sses without the magnificent staff work of his wife.[3]

With the surrender of Granada in January 1492 Spain, with
e exception of Navarre, was united into one great Christian
ngdom. The military consequences were as great as the politi-
l ones, for the war had brought forth the finest army in Europe,
d foreign observers were greatly impressed by it and its organi-
tion, and most European armies adopted Spanish infantry
ethods.

The outstanding inheritor of Isabella's innovations and of
anish military inventions was Gustavus Adolphus of Sweden
511–32), one of the chief figures of the Thirty Years War.
multaneously with the development of the chain of command

[2] During the feudal era rank and command, as we understand it, did not
st, but the employment of mercenary troops gradually evolved a system.
e monarch employed the army commanders and the colonels; the colonels
ected the captains who raised the companies; the captains chose their lieu-
ants, and the men were often permitted to select the non-commissioned
icers. This ancient device was substantially the system which applied to
lunteer regiments during the American Civil War. The growth of mercenary
ganizations made more severe methods of discipline imperative, and in the
teenth century Ferdinand in Spain, Francis I and Henry II in France, and
arles V in Germany made codes of laws for their respective armies. Punish-
nts were Draconic, and rewards were allotted for courage and outstanding
vice, but unless a general was able and deeply respected by his men no laws
ld keep up a discipline such as is taken for granted today.

[3] Her philosophy of life is best shown by her own admission that she knew
ly four fine sights in the world: a soldier in the field, a priest at the altar, a
utiful woman in bed, a thief on the gibbet.

there was a chain of inventions, and between 1450 and 1596 m: took place in Spain or were developed there. The main o were:[4]

1450 Matchlock or arquebus, the first infantry firearm.

1463 Bronze explosive shell.

1470 Explosive bombs; wheeled gun-carriage (first recor use).

1483 Pistol.

1487 Incendiary shell.

1520 Rifling (the grooving in a barrel, which gave grea accuracy, velocity, and range).

1521 Wheel-lock and Spanish musket.

1543 Wheel-lock pistol.

1560 Paper cartridges.

1573 Fragmentation shell (roughly similar to the la shrapnel).

1575 Hot-shot.

1588 Common shell.

1590 Fixed cartridges.

1590 Fixed cartridges (powder and ball in one).

1592 Rifled pistols.

1596 Percussion fuse.

Gustavus, who was only 16 when he became king, profoun admired Isabella, and her influence on him is as noticeable Gustavus's influence on later leaders. He enlisted all Swed males between fifteen and sixty who had no settled dwell of the rest all between eighteen and thirty were allowed to d: lots, and only the tenth was taken for the army. Those v worked in vital industries—such as mining or munitions—v exempted, as were food producing peasants who had no sons.

Sweden was the first country in Europe that built up for ! self a regular and at the same time national military organizat: As early as the sixteenth century the Vasa kings had laid foundation of a national regular army, and Gustavus perfected He also introduced a novel method under which each sold was supposed to own and be supported and equipped by a cer portion of land, rising in size and importance according to r; and grade. When war thinned his ranks Gustavus was compe:

---

[4] Some of the dates given are approximate only, as records are both inc plete and contradictory. The word 'lock' refers to the ignition system in arms.

list mercenaries, and regiments came to his army from all
of Germany, the Netherlands, and Britain, but the Swedes
the kernel of the force.

s artillery and engineers were vastly superior to anything his
ies had to show; they had nothing to compare with his regi-
al pieces, light iron four-pounders. He took with him to
pe a large force of miners and engineers, both of which
lla had used in strength.

t Gustavus Adolphus was too progressive a general to make
nistake of fighting his campaigns of 1630–32 with the old
ish system of weight, by now universal. He wanted mobility.
battles of the Middle Ages had been won by cavalry; for a
time no infantry could withstand the shock of large men on
horses. Then the English archers had found weak places in
il-clad line, and Swiss pikemen discovered that horses would
harge against a three-deep hedgehog of three-foot spikes on
ighteen-foot shaft. The Spaniards adopted the Swiss pike
cs and supported their pikemen with musketeers on the
s. As a result cavalry lost its proper place and horsemen
iorated into skirmishers and foragers.

ustavus gave war a new look by altering the equipment and
cs of his cavalry. He used only cuirassiers and dragoons. The
trouble with horse before Gustavus's day was its slowness
arging. Squadrons would ride up to the enemy, and each rank
d successively fire and then wheel away to reload. The heavy
lry lacked dash and never undertook the true rôle of horse,
he Swedish cuirassiers were taught to ride at a gallop, to fire
pistols at speed, and then push home with the sword. The
oons carried musket, sword, and axe and were really
nted infantry.

great infantry reformer, too, Gustavus reduced the length
weight of the musket and replaced the fork firing-rest then in
ersal use with a thin iron spike—the 'Swedish feather'—
h could be used as a palisade stake against cavalry.

le distinction between riflemen, who fired guns, and grena-
, who threw hand-grenades, dates back to Gustavus; the word
adier' was coined at the defence of Ratisbon by the Swedes
632, when the soldiers who took the risk of handling and
ng hand-grenades were given extra pay.

marches Gustavus dispensed with a rearguard when march-
orward and with a vanguard when marching from the enemy
d his men were rapid marchers. In battle he had a keen eye

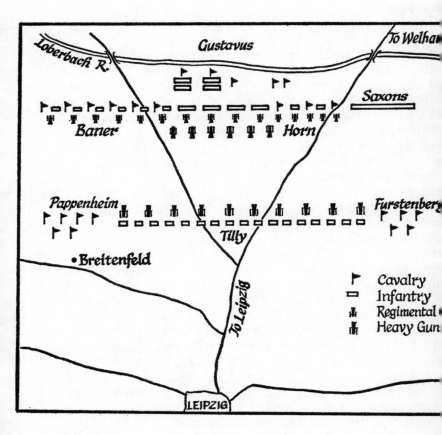

BREITENFELD

It is likely that had General Tilly faced any troops in Europe other than those of Sweden he would have won Breitenfeld. At the crucial point of the battle the Swedish left was exposed when their Saxon allies fled, and Tilly, a competent tactician, ordered an oblique move to the right, then a left wheel to threaten Gustavus's flank, and if possible to roll up the Swedish line. But the Swedes, much more individually intelligent than their enemies, could move twice as fast, so Tilly had no effective advantage. Gustavus simply told Horn to wheel to face Tilly's threat and sent reserves to lengthen Horn's line. Gustavus now acted decisively. He ordered Bäner to mount a cavalry attack on Tilly's left flank, while Gustavus himself led four regiments in a charge on the enemy's guns, which he captured and turned on to Tilly's troops. By this time the Swedish guns, firing three rounds to the Imperialists' one, had played havoc in the enemy squares. The Swedish reserve artillery, brought in at the psychological moment, completed the enemy's confusion.

for ground and the ability to make his three arms work togeth
The discipline of the Swedes was remarkable, religious duti
were strictly observed, and crime was very rare. There were re;
mental schools for soldiers' children, many of whom, as well
their mothers, travelled with the troops. Prostitutes, the bane
German armies, never accompanied Gustavus's armies. As
army was better in organization than any other in Europe, so
was superior in *esprit de corps*, largely because of Gustavu
personal example and because of the 'God is with us' conv
tion he imparted to his troops.

Again influenced by Isabella, Gustavus introduced field hos]
tals and regimental medical chests, and is sometimes credit
with being the originator of uniforms. In the modern sense t]
may be true, but Roman military dress had been uniform ma
centuries before.

The troops were fed from depots—one of the most importa
of Gustavus's improvements. He established these depots in su
able localities, and saw that his staff of commissaries kept the
full with supplies from Sweden or from contributions made
the countries crossed.

His moral and intellectual courage equalled his physic
courage; his march into Germany was only a trifle less audacio
than that of Hannibal into Italy; his attack-crossing at the Le
river—where he used smoke to cover the crossing[5]—was no le
dashing than that of Caesar at Zela. Alexander, Hannibal, a
Caesar—Gustavus had studied all three, and he possessed the
finer qualities. Like all three, he put his brain and soul into
work. In dealing with his half-hearted allies Gustavus showed t]
patience of Hannibal and the persuasiveness of Caesar.

The wars in the Netherlands in the second half of the sixteen
century had greatly developed engineering. Outworks grew
extent and importance, and inner works were built to enable t]
besieged to hold the fortress even after the loss of the walls. As
engineer Gustavus had learned all that the Netherlands had
teach and had improved on it. He adopted the system of fie
fortification brought to perfection in the Netherlands, but alter
it in many ways.

The Gustavian method showed its brilliance at the famo
battle of Breitenfeld, fought near Leipzig, Germany, on Septer
ber 17th 1631. Here Gustavus proved that mobility was superi

[5] In 1700 Charles XII of Swden used exactly the same ruse when he cros
the Düna in his war against Poland and Russia.

eight. His formations were much more elastic than those of
army of the Catholic League, commanded by Count Tilly.
cavalry was posted strategically at several points, his main
lery was a little left of centre, and the light guns were in front
heir respective regiments. Gustavus also had an artillery
rve—the first known instance of such a thing. He ranged his
ntry in small oblongs, and the largest unit had only 200 men.
h sub-unit, in which the musketeers were covered by the pike-
, was a small, mobile, hard-hitting human fortress. Actually
battle was not fought as Gustavus had intended, but this only
erlines the effectiveness of the new tactics of mobility, for be-
their advent it was virtually impossible to change the course
battle once the two sides were committed to the fight.

ustavus's tactics gave him more spectacular successes before
death in action towards the end of his climactic victory at
zen the following year. The American historian Colonel
ge, writing in 1890, said that from Alexander to Caesar the
f war rose to a great height; that from Caesar to Gustavus it
into oblivion, and that Gustavus re-created it. This is far too
eping a statement, but it does serve to indicate Gustavus's
ortance as "the father of modern war", as he is so often
lled. It also hints at the Swede's vital place in the chain of
mand, for with Gustavus began the third main period of war.[6]
e left valuable lessons for succeeding great captains. They
ided the benefits of methodical planning; careful accumula-
of supplies; energy in marches and manoeuvres; rapidity of
the value of taking and holding strong-points; the need for a
base and efficient communications; the value of sober morale;
immense security that is won by discipline; the fact that the
ulated risk was not synonymous with foolhardiness.

t a time when wars and battles were more frequent than they
now, when war was an accepted part of the way of life and
hed every man's life, the methods of great leaders were
ied more assiduously than they are now, and Gustavus be-
e the prime model for every ambitious soldier in Europe.
ustavus was not only the founder of modern Continental
tary organization, but also the founder of modern tactical
s. One man he profoundly impressed was Oliver Cromwell.

he first from remote antiquity down to the decay of Rome; the second
g the Middle Ages.

CHAPTER TEN

◆◆◆

Cromwell; The Ironsides;
The Battle of Naseby

s a man and as a ruler Cromwell was in most respects the equal
of Gustavus, so it is no slight to him to say that his military
was only a reflection of that of the Swede. In any case, every-
y else in Europe was imitating Gustavus—or trying to. It
much for Cromwell that he was such a worthy follower of
tavus.

1 1642, ten years after the death of Gustavus, the Civil War in
land broke out. Charles was at Nottingham with a scratch
y of 10,000 men, with Prince Rupert—"Rupert of the
ne"—in command of the Royalist cavalry. The Parliamen-
army had twice the Royalist strength, but was equally ill
ned. Little occurred for two years, except that in 1642 Crom-
began to discipline his Ironsides. He began his New Model
ipline with a 60-man troop, of which he was captain, but
e was nothing new in it. It was merely an imitation of Gusta-
methods. Cromwell was deep enough to understand what he
all other Englishmen had watched—the magnificent campaigns of 1630, 1631, and 1632 in Germany—and he was
enough to apply the lessons they brought out. Cromwell
ned himself as he trained his pious yeomen, rising from troop
tain to captain-general.

t Edgehill, on October 23rd, 1642, the Royalists had 12,000
, the Parliament 15,000. Tempestuous Rupert, on the Royal
t, charged and routed Essex's left, and then turned to plunder
ineton. The Royal left had equal success, and the day seemed

lost for the Parliamentarians, when thirteen troops of th
cavalry came up, among them Cromwell's, and rode down t
Royalist infantry. Rupert returned just in time to save the Ki
from capture and to cover the retreat.

But Cromwell knew that it was a near thing. The Parliam
tary army was made up, as he said to Hampden, of "old decay
serving-men, and tapsters and such kind of fellows". He want
"men of spirit, of a spirit that is likely to go as far as gentlem
will go". Later he raised these men, "men such as had the fe
of God before them and made some conscience of what th
did". As he saw it, leadership was useless without disciplir
followership.

People who ascribe the New Model Army entirely to Cro
well's own invention do his intelligence an injustice. Under
standards were serving many Englishmen and Scots who h
fought with the Swedes, and with the Thirty Years War drawi
to a close it is inconceivable that Cromwell should not ha
known what Gustavus had begun twenty years earlier. Cro
well learned the intricacies of drill from John Dalbier, a Dut
veteran, who had seen much service on the Continent, but
made his own rules of discipline, and so well conducted were
men that civilians did not run and hide from them as they usua
did when soldiers approached. Following Gustavus, he created
England the beginnings of a regular army.

In May 1643, near Grantham, he won his first independe
fight. Outnumbered two to one, his cavalry rode down the Ca
liers without a check. In July he met the Royalists near Gai
borough, and in close-quarter fighting with sword and pistol dro
them off and chased them, then astutely covered a retreat wh
not strong enough to face a larger body of Royalist infantry.
August he became second-in-command to the Earl of Manchest
and in October he again defeated a large force of cavalry ne
Winceby. A newsletter journalist recorded in May 1643: "As t
Colonel Cromwell, he hath two thousand brave men, well dis
plined; and no man swears but pays his twelvepence; if he
drunk he is set in the stocks or worse."

A letter Cromwell wrote to a friend on September 11th, 164
reveals the key to his system of discipline: "I have a lovely co
pany; you would respect them, did you know them. They are
Anabaptists, they are honest, sober Christians; *they expect to
used as men!*"[1]

[1] The author's italics.

n July 1644, at Marston Moor, Cromwell commanded the liamentary left wing with 4000 men. Seizing an opportunity, outflanked the Royalist right and utterly routed it. It was no -for-leather charge of the kind Rupert made, but a steady hodical trot with an occasional pause to fire and load. Its centrated, remorseless energy was even more frightening than ild sabre charge. "God made them as stubble to our swords", mwell said of the Royalists.

upert had made a successful charge too, but it had been so etuous that his squadrons were unsettled and ill ordered; mwell's were in perfect order. He struck at the Royalists be- : they could re-form, and they fled. This battle earned Crom- l and his yeomen the sobriquet of "Ironsides".

ut the Army was still far from popular with the public. Early 1645 the Committee of Both Kingdoms—the Parliamentary erning body—wrote to a colonel in the West of England to sure him for "the very great complaints of the intolerable :iage of the troops". They were guilty of all kinds of indisci- e and violence—robbery, arson, spoiling, drunkenness, sive behaviour, and all kinds of debaucheries.

he common people of England suffered almost as much as the abitants of any country racked by war—and from both sides. : heavy exactions of the Scots in Cumberland and Westmorland month after month reduced the inhabitants to despair. In thumberland and Durham the charges on the farmers were so vy that the landlord had little or nothing. On each side at this e the soldiers lived mostly by plunder. They carried off cattle cut down crops, sequestered rents, and assessed fines. They t up a multitude of small forts and garrisons as a shelter to ng bands who despoiled the country, parts of which were rife a squalor and brutality.

he New Model Army was to change much of this—at least on Parliamentary side. The New Model Ordinance was accepted he House of Lords in February 1645, and significantly was of er strength numerically than before, for worthless men were ded out. The Army consisted of 14,400 infantry, 6600 cavalry, 1000 dragoons. The whole body was given thorough drill and :ipline at Royal Windsor, and the effect was apparent the nent the Parliamentarians met the enemy, although a Cavalier :ribed them as "a collection of raw, inexperienced, pressed liers". It has often been assumed that because the New Model ny came to achieve so much its members must have been

volunteers. In fact, Parliament had to compel men to enlist, f
seemed England did not have 20,000 men of militant conscie
willing for the cause to leave shop and farm, wife and home
submit themselves to iron discipline and face all the perils of
active service.[2]

The artillery, up till now neglected, was reorganized, and
Army was given a powerful train, eventually brought up to
guns, some of 6-inch or 7-inch calibre, plus some 12-inch bo
throwing mortars. At this time, too, the red coat, earlier ado
by Cromwell for some troops, became general, to remain so
1914.

The Parliamentary soldiers were paid regularly, a clear inc
tion of Gustavian influence, for Gustavus had paid his men r
larly, an astounding thing for those times. The New Army sol
earned about as much as they would have done as ploughme
carters. They carried knapsacks but no water-bottles, and
man had a portion of a tent. Their staple rations were bread
cheese, considered adequate, honest food. Oddly enough, this
army had no field hospitals, and wounded men had to rel
what help their comrades could give them or on their own he
get them to some sympathetic housewife near the battlefield.

The establishment included a Judge Advocate General a
Provost Marshal General, under whom was a squad of mou
police. Up to sixty lashes could be inflicted, but flogging
rarely necessary in this army of Bible soldiers. Cromwell's
cessors were not so moderate; in later centuries lashes were
flicted in hundreds and even thousands of strokes.

The average substantive wealth in the Army was not high,
Royalists were fond of taunting the Parliamentarians with
poverty, vowing that the whole pack of them could not must
thousand pounds a year in land among them. Yet in the
Army, commanded by Sir Thomas Fairfax, thirty of the th
seven senior officers were of good family. Pride, a drayman, F
son, a cobbler, and Okey, a ship-chandler, were among
minority who rose from the ranks.

Throughout the war both sides showed remarkable lack o
formation about each other's movements, and many cava
were frankly contemptuous of the Roundheads' New army

[2] The Wars of the Roses, 1455–87, has resulted in such a deep-rooted d
for the professional soldier that for 150 years England was left withou
army—at a time when military organization on the Continent was becom
science.

re confident of winning the next battle. They amused them-
ves by carving a wooden image of a man which they called the
d of the Roundheads, and carried it in scorn and derision. Some
them even made the mistake of being contemptuous of Crom-
ll and Fairfax, though they made a powerful team, especially
en compared with the Royalists' leaders, Lord Astley, aged
ty-six and too old for effective command, and Prince Rupert,
enty-five and too irresponsible. All four were soon to play their
rt in the battle of Naseby.

Of all the battles which occurred on English soil only Hastings
more famous than Naseby, an interesting battle on many
unts. The Parliamentary Army had abandoned the siege of
xford, while Charles was stationed at Daventry, thirty-five miles
rthward, irresolute and hesitant because of the conflicting
vice Prince Rupert and Sir John Digby were giving him.

On June 5th, 1645, General Fairfax left Oxford and moved his
rliamentary Army north-east to Newport Pagnell. On June 8th
irfax and his aides decided to attack the Royalist Army, and
e following day the Parliament gave Fairfax *carte blanche* in
e conduct of the campaign—as a wise step. On the 10th Crom-
ll was posted to Fairfax as second-in-command.

On June 12th Fairfax drove in Royalist pickets, eight miles east
Daventry, causing the King to retreat hurriedly to Market
arborough, eighteen miles north-east. Fairfax, a student of war-
re for a long time, knew that an enemy retrograde movement
ould be pushed hard, so the next day he pursued Charles so
rcefully that his forward troops captured some Cavalier patrols
they made merry in an inn; according to some sources the
avaliers were playing a game of quoits. It was typical of them
t to have sentries on guard.

When the King heard of this development he called a battle
uncil. Further retreat, with the Roundheads pressing close,
ould be dangerous, so the Royalists decided to form a defensive
sition on high ground two miles south of Naseby and covering
e road from Naseby. Choice of the ground showed sound tacti-
l appreciation. The view was good, but, perhaps because of
orning mist, Rupert sent his chief of scouts to reconnoitre and
report on enemy dispositions. This officer returned to say that
had been about three miles forward but had not seen any
emy, a report that Rupert thought absurd—which it was.
upert took a patrol and rode forward to investigate for himself.

Fairfax had broken camp at 3 A.M. and with Cromwell had

ridden forward to seek a position covering Naseby. They cros
East Farndon ridge and descended into the valley, which
boggy and protected by a stream. Cromwell saw that
Royalists, who were strong in cavalry, would not either init
action or be drawn into it on such ground, so he suggested t
the Parliamentarians occupy the ridge. In this he was merely
lowing an age-old maxim to 'take the high ground'.

Rupert arrived at this time near Clipston, from which he s
the Parliamentary force riding back up the hill and reasoned t
Fairfax would occupy the ridge. He saw that to the right
better country and a gentle slope up which his cavalry might
vance in a flanking movement. He reached a point on the S
bertoft-Clipston road about a mile south of Sibbertoft.

But in turn Fairfax saw this flanking move and countered it
side-slipping to his left. By nine that morning both armies w
marching west on parallel lines about two miles apart. A sh
march of about a mile brought the armies to an open shall
valley between two slopes—Dust Hill Ridge and Red Hill Ri
—and here they both formed line about half a mile apart.[3]

The senior Parliamentary leader on the spot, Skippon, pos
the army forward of a ledge on the southern slope, Red I
Ridge, but Fairfax when he arrived withdrew the men behind
ledge, the better to make his dispositions in secrecy. Wellingto
act in keeping so many infantry lying down just below the cr
at Waterloo is strikingly similar.

Rupert had sent for the entire Royalist Army, and it form
up on Dust Hill Ridge, now with no hope of being able to tu
the Parliamentary flank. Still, Rupert was satisfied enough wit
frontal attack, for the terrain was good cavalry ground. Rup
took the right wing cavalry, Sir Marmaduke Langdale the l
cavalry, and Lord Astley commanded the infantry in the centre.

Together they formed a mile-long front, too great a distar
for 7500 men in 1645, for it gave the Royalists a reserve of o
800 under the King himself, who had a commanding view fr
Dust Hill Farm.

The Parliamentarians had the same frontage and much
same formation, except for one important difference. Cromw
commanding the cavalry on the right flank, had his horsen
slightly behind the infantry line so as to keep to higher grou
Commissary-General Ireton led the left-flank cavalry, whose l
edge was not quite flush with twin rows of strong hedges. Behi

[3] These ridges are now joined by the Naseby-Sibbertoft road.

e hedges Cromwell posted 1000 dragoons under Colonel
y—a remarkable decision, for the dragoons were not only far
ard of the Parliamentary line but well in advance of it as
on an exposed flank. They were supposed to enfilade
ert's horse when they charged, but were in such a dangerous
ion that they could easily be themselves enfiladed or attacked
the rear.

e Royalists should have stayed on the defensive; the weaker
usually does. But Rupert was not the type to play safe—
vhole knowledge of tactics seemed to be summed up in one
l, 'Attack!'—and without reference to Astley he induced the
to order an attack.

now, with so much obvious military activity in the area,
y of the villagers and farmers had fled, but just as many
ans stood at a safe distance from the scene, agog with ex-
tion. They included the human vultures who followed any
in the field, ready to race on to the field after the battle to
er plunder.

the Royalist infantry line moved Fairfax advanced his
try just forward of the ledge, where the men waited silently
e Royalists pressed across the field. The moment combat was
d Rupert led his cavalrymen in a charge. Keeping inside the
es he swept up the slope and smashed into the flank of Ire-
line. Rupert dashed on for another mile until he encountered
Roundheads' baggage-depot, where his Cavaliers wasted time
fruitless effort to capture it. Had Rupert been as well read as
as courageous he would have ignored the enemy's baggage,
cially as he had had a similar experience at the battle of
hill. For a full vital hour Rupert and his cavalry were away
the battle. Strangely enough, English and British cavalry
e this same mistake many times in many countries.

e Royalist infantry were at first very successful, and forced
Roundheads back over the crest. With Skippon wounded,
ax pushed in his reserves to bolster the breaking line, and,
g an example and fighting in the front himself, he succeeded
lding the Royalists. Ireton also showed sound leadership.
of his cavalry force had crumbled and disappeared under
mpetus of Rupert's charge, but as the Cavaliers were now
ere to be seen Ireton wheeled the remaining part of his
and attacked the Royalist infantry on the flank.

t these were fine, steady troops, and they stopped the cavalry
k and captured the wounded Ireton. At this point Okey, also

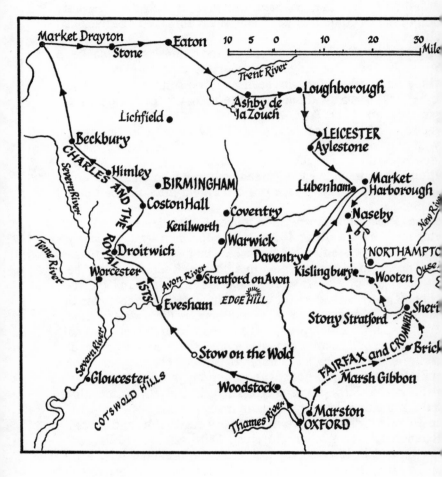

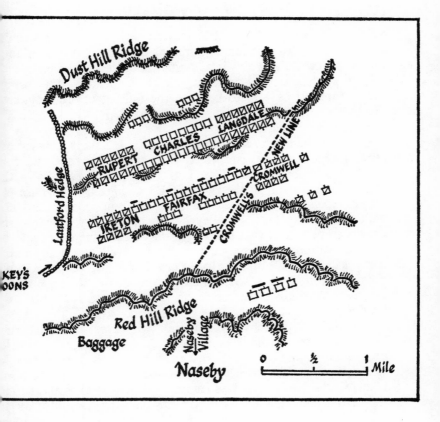

NASEBY

Naseby had four main phases:

1. After the initial manoeuvring the Royalists opened the battle moving into the attack to climb the Roundheads' ridge. hen Ireton was wounded his wing lost cohesion, and Prince upert and his cavalry caused great damage to the left of the oundhead line.

2. In the centre the infantry battle became hopelessly confused, t the Royalists had the advantage.

3. Cromwell on the right took his 3600 horsemen downhill to et Langdale's regiments, decisively defeated them, and turned lf his force against the exposed left flank of the Royalist fantry.

4. Because of a misunderstanding among the Royalists their ntre was left isolated and at the complete mercy of the Round- ads, horse and foot.

relieved of pressure from Rupert, and waking up to his opp(
tunity, led his dragoons in a charge against the Royalist infant
The whole centre was now in a confused, massed struggle.

This was the critical moment. Whichever leader could bring
strong force of cavalry to bear on the milling centre would w
the battle, or, as the historian Professor S. R. Gardiner put
"would have England at his feet".

Langdale had been leading his Royalist left flank cavalry ov
fairly difficult country sprinkled with rabbit warrens and fur
brush at the bottom of Red Hill Ridge, and eventually th
reached the bottom of the rise which was here steeper than els
where. Cromwell had been watching their approach, and no
with fine timing, with Whalley he led his cavalry downhill in
charge so relentless that the Royalists—outnumbered two to o
—were scattered and pursued. But Cromwell was too much
control to allow all his cavalry to charge off into the blue in wi
pursuit. He ordered three regiments to pursue the fleeing Royalis
but kept the bulk of his force on the field, and remained at
head.

He wheeled this cavalry, and in two waves sent them in
attack the exposed flank of Astley's Royalist infantry. Attack
on the three sides, these men were forced back into the valle
where, fighting desperately, they hoped for rescue by the Kin;
reserve. Charles himself was leading the reserve towards the m(
dangerous spot, the left flank, despite the intervention of at le;
one of his officers, when somebody shouted, "March to t
right!" This unauthorized command was passed down the ranl
and the whole force turned about and retreated rapidly.

Charles managed to pull them up within a quarter of a mile—
commendable display of control. It was still possible to make
charge—the battle raged only 600 yards away—but Charles he
back while the Roundheads surrounded his infantry. Rupert, to
had now returned from his ridiculous rampage, his horses t
blown and his men too out-of-hand for a further effective charg
So the Royalist cavalry watched helplessly while their infant
fought gallantly but hopelessly. Eventually, out of ammuniti
and facing annihilation, the survivors surrendered.

Fairfax re-ordered his infantry and prepared to continue t
advance, and Charles, conceding total defeat, retired to Leicest
with Cromwell in close and continuous pursuit.

The Royalists lost the battle because their cavalry left the
infantry unsupported, a sharp lesson in the need for strict bati

pline. The Parliamentarians won the battle because their
lry supported their infantry and because of Cromwell's tacti-
ppreciation. A nineteenth-century German military historian,
nig, believes that there was "scarcely a battle in history where
lry was better handled than at Naseby".[4]

might be said that Rupert was personally responsible for the
at of his own side. One of the most colourful soldiers in
ry, he was also one of the most irresponsible. I think it pos-
that his deplorable example at Naseby might have led in-
tly to British generals being given restricted commands and
ctives so that no one leader could endanger the safety of all.

the cold and wind the battlefield of Naseby was a grim scene
night. Lady Herbert searched over it, with a retainer, for the
of her husband. They met stragglers laden with loot, and
and there lay a wounded man pleading for help they had no
ns of giving. Practically everybody fit and still active had
ed on, leaving the still heaps of dead and the ghastly writh-
and gaspings of the still dying. Mangled limbs were scattered
t, mixed with the carcasses of horses and the wreckage of
carriages and supply carts. Small arms littered the field, and
nents of clothing and feathers fluttered in the wind. The
lers of the dead had practically finished their work, but a few
women still moved among the dead, some of them trying to
a body not too far gone to try to patch up. Others were
ering spoil.

ady Herbert went up to one of the women and asked if she
d tell where the King's Guards had fought. "Aye, gossip,"
woman said. "Be'st thou come a-riffling, too? But i'faith
'rt of the latest. The swashing gallants were as fine as pea-
s, but we've stripped their bravery, I trow. Yonder stood the
's tent, and yonder about do most of them lie; but thou'lt
ce find a landing for thy cattle now."

ady Herbert found the fragments of the Royal tent, where
dead lay wedged in heaps, indicating long and desperate
ing, with combatants often fallen clasped together.

romwell went from victory to victory, though his successes
marred by the so-called massacres of Drogheda and Wex-
. "I forbade them to spare any that were in arms in the

{ajor H. G. Eady, a capable analytical historian, considers Gustavus and
well "the greatest cavalrymen of history" (*Historical Illustrations to Field
e Regulations*, Operations, 1929). I do not subscribe to this interesting
oint, but Cromwell was certainly the best cavalry commander Britain
ver had.

town,"[5] Cromwell explained of Drogheda, but no doubt ma
non-combatants perished as well. Cromwell was God-drunk, a
his conduct was the essence of narrow Puritanism, but it was
way of war in that era.

Cromwell's campaign of 1651, at the end of the Second C
War, was a supreme example of a general's artistry. On the
protected rear of an enemy facing hunger and desertion he d
berately left just one door open for his enemy, and they ente
it, to be trapped at Worcester by four separate converging for
and destroyed on September 3rd. Three thousand enemy w
killed, 10,000 taken; Cromwell lost 200 men.

This was his final personal battle, but he initiated the Du
War of 1652–54, which ended to England's advantage, and
Spanish War of 1655–59, which, though theoretically a victory
England, ruined her trade to the benefit of the Dutch and cau
a serious economic depression. But Cromwell, who had died
September 3rd, 1658, did not see this disaster.

Few British people appreciate the fact that Cromwell is one
the few great commanders of history who were never beaten;
other notable exceptions are Scipio and Alexander the Great.
is significant that neither Cromwell nor Scipio ever made a dir
approach, and their faithful adherence to this principle had mi
to do with their success. Judged by the success of his nine-ye
military career, Cromwell emerges as a greater soldier than
measured by the rules of the art of war. His tactics were bet
than his strategy, and, judged by opposition—a paramount asp
in assessing a soldier's greatness—he does not stand high. I
losses in storming strong places, except at Clonmel, were alwa
small and testify rather to poor defence than to brilliant atta
Colonel Dodge, one of many foreign historians and generals w
have studied Cromwell's campaigns, has likened him to Geo
Washington as being "eminent in arms". This is a fair asse
ment; he was not a great captain, and he does not quite reach
stature of Turenne, Marlborough, and Eugène, but he certai
holds a secure link in the chain of command.

He proved that the morale of the commander himself and
morale of the troops themselves were vitally important a
equally so. At Dunbar in 1650 he appeared to be in an alm
hopeless position, but his resolution was astonishing. He was s
rounded by the Scots and outnumbered nearly two to one,

[5] At the taking of Magdeburg by Tilly in 1631, 40,000 people were massac
in one day.

munications with the sea were interrupted by weather, and his
ps were practically starving, yet he indomitably maintained
position until the enemy was led to make a mistake. Crom-
at once took advantage of this, and almost annihilated the
ttish force by battle and pursuit.

is influence in the British military sphere is especially notable,
much of the enduring character of the British Army is even
based on the New Model Army—the organization of regi-
ts, a fixed establishment for artillery and transport and many
inistrative details, the origin of British military discipline,
uding the great tradition that an army marching through a
ntry must take nothing without payment.

CHAPTER ELEVEN

Turenne; Marlborough;
Eugène; Charles XII

'HE many wars between the end of the Thirty Years War
(1618–48) and the beginning of the War of the Spanish Suc-
sion in 1702 were indecisive, largely because the development
fortifications had outstripped that of weapons, hence the de-
sive was dominant. Also, an army was still not formed of
-contained formations but moved and fought as an entity;
cramped manoeuvre and movement, with the consequence
t during the wars of the Fronde (1648–55), then the Devolu-
t and Dutch Wars, until the War of the Grand Alliance
39–97), only one campaign was decisive—that of Turenne
ing the winter of 1674–75, when France was fighting for her
against a coalition of enemies.

Vhat the later generals of history owe to Turenne is immense
incalculable. He has the distinction of having commanded in
:e campaigns than any other general in history, and he is also
sual in being one of the few great commanders who improved
1 age—most others deteriorated alarmingly,[1] as other historians
» have noted.

{is last campaign—he was killed soon after, aged sixty-three—
» his finest, if only because he showed that even in seventeenth-

_ refer, of course, to those leaders who actively commanded for a reasonably
period and into their fifties and sixties. Alexander the Great died at the age
urty-three. Epaminondas was of the Turenne mould. Almost fifty when he
n his military career, he might welll have improved still further with age,
ie was killed in action twelve years later.

century warfare a decision could be reached by use of inte
and enterprise.

France was in a desperate position, and her allies had all
over to the hostile coalition. Turenne was forced back across
Rhine as the Elector of Brandenburg moved to unite wit
large army under Bournville at Enzheim in October 1674,
was then forced to retire to Dettweiler. The Germans meanw
occupied Alsace and took up winter quarters in the many to
between Strasbourg and Belfort.

Turenne had always believed in du Guesclin's policy of
attack without surprise'. But he improved on this principle,
he realized that 'surprise' did not necessarily mean 'surf
attack'. His first surprise in 1674 was to decide on a midwi
campaign, a remarkable decision in that era when there wa
almost unwritten law that gentlemen did not wage war in wi
Turenne lulled his enemy into a false sense of security by pla
his fortresses in an obvious state of defence, while he led
entire field army secretly into Lorraine.

Then, with the Vosges to hide his movements, he marched
men quickly south. After a while he split his army into more
twenty smaller units to confuse and distract enemy spies. T
groups were ordered to press on through rough country de:
the weather—they encountered several snowstorms—and
rendezvous near Belfort. Many a lesser commander would I
spent at least a day here consolidating and resting his
Turenne knew that the slightest delay could be fatal. He laun
his army into Southern Alsace—to the utter astonishment of
enemy, who thought he was far away to the north. At Colm:
mid-Alsace the Elector of Brandenburg had enough tim
organize a defensive position, and as he had as many me
Turenne he probably felt fairly confident.

But the psychological advantage was with Turenne; his
were winning, the enemy's troops were shaken. Cleverly he n
a tactical indirect approach to Turkheim, where the dec
battle was fought. The enemy army melted away completel
a dispatch to Paris Turenne could say truthfully that not
enemy soldier except prisoners remained in Alsace.

After a comfortable winter Turenne took the field to meet
Austrian general Montecucculi, who had been called to do
others had failed to do. Turenne nearly out-schemed him,
and clearly would have defeated him on the Sasbach river, w
Turenne was killed by a cannon-ball.

I believe that Wellington was consciously influenced by
Turenne in that he always chose a position which would provide
concealment and free movement for his reserves, as shown by
his position at Talavera, 1809, and especially at Waterloo,
1815.

Turenne was a sympton of France's development as an aggressive nation. Louis XIV saw himself as an heroic figure and pas-
sionately wanted to make France supreme in Europe. His
ambitions were applauded and helped by his brilliant ministers
Louvois and Colbert, who between them moulded France into a
first-class military nation. Louvois took over the army, centra-
lised its administration, and established an *esprit de corps*. His
reforming and innovating hand was everywhere. He improved
army equipment and sanctioned much that was new, including
the flint-lock musket. Realizing that certain arms of the service
were smarting under a sense of injustice and inferiority, he raised
their professional status. The infantryman became a man to be
admired and the engineer, formerly rarely heard of, a hero.
Louvois also improved the artillery and established military
magazines at strategic points. While he did all this his col-
league Colbert, was building the French Navy into a formidable
force.

Both ministers were helped by the military engineering genius,
Sébastien Vauban. In his long life of military service Vauban
built 33 forts, repaired or improved 300 fortresses and ports, conducted 53 sieges, and was present at 140 actions. He became a
marshal in 1703, only a year before Blenheim, and when he died
in 1707 he left to the French Army a legacy that endured for the
next 200 years. Napoleon, a century later, could be grateful for
what Vauban did for France.[2]

Louis, with such men as Colbert, Louvois, and Vauban to aid
him, made rapid progress, and by 1678 had added large slices of
Europe to France. By 1688 France and Britain had begun their
long and bitter duel for colonial territories. France at this time
had the strongest army in the world. It is interesting to note that
at his accession in 1643 Louis found only one regiment of
dragoons in the French Army. By 1690 France had 43 such
regiments.

Despite Louis's strength the German princes rallied against
him, and to help them William III of England formed the Grand

Unfortunately, he also sowed the seeds of the Maginot Line mentality,
which helped to defeat France in 1940.

Alliance—England, the United Provinces, and the Holy Ro**
Empire—to meet France. The end of this war was the Treat
Ryswick in 1697, but it in no way reduced France's ar**
strength.

After much political manoeuvring and one crisis after ano**
Louis's ambitions again got the better of him, and in 1701 he
vaded the Spanish Netherlands and Milan and seized some D**
forts. He also barred British merchants from the Ameri**
trade and later stopped English goods from entering Fra**
The Grand Alliance was revived by England, Austria, and **
United Provinces, and England prepared for war. It was at **
point that William III died of injuries following a fall fror**
horse and was succeeded by Queen Anne. Louis believed, **
some justification, that William's death would cause the colla**
of the Grand Alliance. Nevertheless in May 1702 war was **
clared—and into the spotlight stepped John Churchill, l**
Duke of Marlborough.

Few generals have faced such a complex task. His soldiers w**
were Dutch, German, and English and they were separated **
language, time, and space; one of his allies, Austria, **
threatened by enemies on three sides. As Allies, France had S**
and later Bavaria. Marlborough had to stop the French swa**
ing the United Provinces and to stop both the French and **
Spaniards from swallowing Austria.

In view of his success in stopping them it is important to rem**
ber that Marlborough, in his impressionable early twenties, **
seen much service under Turenne, a fact that is not gener**
appreciated.

Communications remained primitive, armies were still of m**
erate size, and cavalry remained the decisive arm. Because of **
last factor, strategy was largely dictated by the availability **
forage—always a tremendous problem.

Because transport was slow and unreliable, generals tended**
establish stocks of ammunition in secure places and to fight eit**
at these places or within ready reach of them. This, in turn, le**
the acceptance that defence was more important than attack **
was certainly easier; less effort was required and the run-of-**
mill generals never exerted themselves more than absolu**
necessary.

But Marlborough was no run-of-the-mill general. He br**
away from this type of warfare and returned to the offen**
strategy of Gustavus and the attack tactics so successfully p**

by Cromwell in England and by the Great Condé of France,
in 1643, during the Thirty Years War, had finally smashed
Spanish military system at the battle of Rocroi. Marlborough
also impressed by Turenne's ability to manoeuvre, he was
ued with Cromwellian respect for system, and he knew per-
lly or had closely studied his opponents.

most of his battles his platoon or 'divisions' (a division was
it a company strong) first fired on the enemy at a range of
y to fifty paces. Under cover of the smoke made by the dis-
ges his men then bayonet-charged. Repeated infantry attacks
down the enemy and softened them for a shock attack by
lry. Marlborough issued his cavalry with only three rounds
mmunition, to be used strictly for defence. This was how he
:d his horsemen to use the sword.

s system was helped by two great changes which had taken
: since 1631—the universal adoption of the flint-lock musket
the replacement of the pike by the bayonet. The British
ally adopted the flint-lock in 1690. This weapon became
lar in history and legend as "Brown Bess". The bayonet,
nificant though it seemed at the time, was to revolution-
actics. Some writers claim, extravagantly, that it marked
end of medieval war and the beginning of modern

fantry had become more diverse. Between 1650 and 1700
kinds existed—pikemen, musketeers, fusiliers, and grena-
. But by 1703, only a year before Blenheim, the four had been
ced to one main type, armed with flint-lock and socket
net. Officers still used a sword.

le lesser number of weapons simplified both tactics and for-
on. Firing lines were in four and three ranks, replacing the
column and six ranks. Battalions were now subdivided into
ler, more readily controlled groups—such as platoons and
ons, Gustavus-style.

fter campaigning indecisively in the Lowlands for two
ns Marlborough had more far-reaching plans for 1704. He
ided to strike right through from Holland to the Danube,
nquer Bavaria, and relieve Vienna, capital of the tottering
 Roman Empire, from the threat of capture by the Franco-
rian armies of Louis XIV. For those days he was stretching
nes of communication remarkably.

the spring he set off along the Rhine. This march was mag-
ntly organized—organization was one of Marlborough's

great gifts[3]—and the troops found meals, shoes, bridges, and
pitals waiting wherever they were needed.

The night's stop was always known in advance, and all the
had to do on arrival was pitch their tents, boil their kettles,
lie down to rest. Captain Robert Parker, who took part in
march, wrote: "Surely never was such a march carried on
more order and regularity, and with less fatigue both to man
horse." But there had been such a march—that of Clau
Nero's to the Metaurus.

The climax of this great march, which set a standard for o
generals to emulate, was the battle of Blenheim, Engla
greatest victory since Agincourt. The campaign showed
superiority of concentration and decisive battle over det:
operations and sieges, in which the French had been indulg
Marlborough and Eugène had concentrated forces in an
portant territory, and the result of the victory was outstand
although Marlborough's most admired manoeuvre was the for
of the great French defensive Ne Plus Ultra lines in 1711.

Allied tactics at Blenheim were certainly not perfect, but
battle was a logical successor to Breitenfeld, and an object-le
in warfare. The main lesson, probably, was that trenches, hea
garrisoned fortresses, and miscellaneous defensive tactics c
not prevail against aggressive spirit and opportunist skill.
subsequent art of war owed a debt to Marlborough and Eu
for their conception of the value of fighting over mere manoe
ing. They opened the way for Frederick the Great and Napoleo

But before Frederick's birth in 1712 another soldier who wa
leave his mark on Frederick and the military chain had rise
his zenith and was within five years of death—Charles XI
Sweden, whom General Fuller calls "the most extraordi
soldier in the history of war". Charles's place in military his
is unique, for it was his martial character rather than his ab
as a general which his successors strove to copy. His men ha

[3] With Eugène he was responsible for probably the most interesting exa
in history of the organization necessary to move and protect a convoy.
the successful action at Oudenarde in 1708 the Allies decided to besiege
and Marlborough collected at Brussels the mass of material needed. The s
train was 15 miles long, and comprised 80 cannon with 20 horses apiec
mortars with 16 horses apiece, and 3000 ammunition wagons with 4 h
apiece. By remarkable planning and attention to detail Marlborough
Eugène moved their stores 75 miles through enemy country, from Brusse
Lille, crossing the Dendres and Scheldt rivers in the process, without mi
Their achievement astonished Europe. "Posterity will have difficult
believing it", the contemporary historian Feuquières wrote.

th in his leadership which had not previously been surpassed
l which remained unequalled, despite the intense loyalty given
Alexander, Marlborough, Frederick, Wolfe, Napoleon, Moore,
l, Graham, Buller, Lee, and Montgomery, among senior
nmanders.

He was young, and his effective military career was relatively
rt and spiked with disasters, but he is mentioned remarkably
quently in the writings of the great captains and in military
tories and treatises. This is partly explicable by Charles's ex-
ordinarily fervent love for war and its hardships; he was prob-
y more interested in fighting than in victory. Nothing per-
bed him, and he delighted in dangers and hazards. He was
/ays optimistic, always honest, and though a disciplinarian he
s invariably fair. His personal courage was as outstanding as
 energy, and he had the tactical eye of a born soldier. When he
·k the field to prevent Peter the Great of Russia and Frederick
gustus of Poland from stealing his Baltic provinces Charles
s only eighteen years of age. After much arduous campaign-
, with his soldiers at times suffering indescribable hardships,
arles met the Russians in the great battle of Poltava late in
ıe 1709, and, despite the great bravery of his troops, he was
·isively beaten and became a refugee in Turkey. His defeat
s due to his blunder in moving deep into enemy country—and
ssian country at that—in defiance of communications and
ıply and in refusing to accept the good counsel of his senior
.cers.

Whatever Charles did was somehow invested with glory, as at
nder, in Turkey, on February 1st, 1713, when with no more
n 40 men he defended an unfortified house against 12,000
rks and 12 guns, and not until 200 Turks had been killed—10
Charles alone—was he overpowered and taken prisoner.

Throughout November 1715, with quite incredible heroism,
 defended Stralsund—on the Baltic coast of what is now East
rmany—against a coalition of Hanover, Russia, Prussia,
·ony, and Denmark. With Stralsund reduced to rubble,
arles escaped on December 23rd and raised another army.
. December 12th, 1718, while besieging the Norwegian fortress
Fredriksten, he was shot dead in a trench.

Charles was a soldier-leader who would not accept defeat.
ıunded, captured, emphatically beaten, he frustrated his
:mies by refusing to lie down; he won battles but lost wars. All
rope talked about him; generals were inspired by him, military

writers practically deified him. He impressed even Marlborou[g]
who was sent to Leipzig in 1706 to interview him. He brought
military leadership a 'one-sword-against-the-world' attitu[
which certainly infected Frederick and Napoleon and many
their senior officers as well—such as Seydlitz and Ziethen a[
Soult and Murat. Many other successful generals have been l[
consciously influenced by Charles, but owe to him something
what Marshal of the Royal Air Force Sir John Salmond, co[
mander in the field of the RAF in 1918, called "the virus qual[
in the blood" and which Salmond had himself.

Charles does not qualify as a great captain—Dodge says
would have done so had he possessed a "balance wheel"—but
was a great soldier and as personally brave, probably, as Sir Ro[
Gillespie (1766–1814), who is often regarded as "the brav[
soldier".

CHAPTER TWELVE

———————◆•◆———————

Frederick and his System;
the Battles of Rossbach
and Leuthen

HEN Frederick succeeded to the Prussian throne in 1740
everybody expected a placid and tractable king, for as a
ce he had devoted himself to poetry, literature, art, gardening,
philosophy. But overnight Frederick gave up many of his
ceful interests and became a warrior intent on creating a
hty Prussia. General Fuller, a discerning historian, believes
, "except for Alexander the Great and possible Charles XII,
lerick was the most offensively minded of all the Great
tains." That he was so is partly due to his study of great
lers of the past and to a conscious effort to mould himself in
r image and his tactics on theirs, with due improvements of
wn.[1]

particular the battle of Cannae fascinated him, for this was a
le of annihilation, and such battles were to become Frederick's
and, through him, the aim of every German general ever
r.

rederick wanted the most efficient army in the world, but his

Ancient military leaders have always fascinated the Germans. Field-Marshal
der Goltz Pasha wrote: "We would know what Alexander the Great was
even if the humblest of his infantrymen were to rise from the grave and
ar before us. Everything that Alexander was would be found in the
, the gestures, the glances, the laughter, the anger of that infantryman."

methods were vastly different from the crude ones of his fath
He gave his soldiers tremendous *esprit de corps* and accommoda
them with private citizens and not in barracks, so as to "ke
them human".

Nevertheless, night marches were avoided, and men detailed
forage or bathe had to be accompanied by officers so that th
could not run away. Even pursuits of the enemy were stric
controlled "lest in the confusion our own men escape". Oth
armies could afford a percentage of deserters; Frederick's sup
of men was limited. His recruiting sergeants plied their trade
vigorously as had those of his father. Captured soldiers we
nearly always forced to become Prussians and to be prepared
shoot down their fellow-countrymen—though there was noth
new in this system. Some young foreigners were given office
commissions, but as soon as they had crossed the border in
Prussia they were reduced to the ranks.

Before long an English traveller, John Moore, noted that "
Prussian Army is the best disciplined and the readiest for serv
at a minute's warning of any now in the world or perhaps th
ever was in it".

Frederick sought his officers far and wide and for their spe
ality and paid them highly, the amount varying according to
officer's abilities and qualifications; many officers received dou
that of their British counterparts. The pay of the common sold
was 1s. 4d. a week, out of which he had to spend threepence
washing and in materials for cleaning his arms.

The training of the Prussian Army was highly advanced, w
war situations produced authentically and carried out with
vigorous realism that was much ahead of its time.

History has given too little importance to Frederick's cava
and artillery. When Frederick became King the cavalry was cc
posed of large men mounted on powerful horses and carefu
trained to fire both on foot and on horseback. The force was
the heaviest type and incapable of rapid movement. In fact,
cavalry of all European states had degenerated into unwiel
masses of horsemen who, unable to move at speed, charged a
slow trot and fought only with pistol and carbine.

Frederick, quick to see the error of this system, followed
example of Charles XII and introduced reforms which made
cavalry one of the most efficient bodies of horsemen that e
existed. Frederick paid close attention to the training of the in
vidual cavalry soldier in horsemanship and swordsmanship.

is first change was to prohibit the use of firearms mounted
to rely upon the galloping charge, sword in hand. He taught
horsemen, who were hand-picked, to disregard enemy fire
to charge home. He lightened their equipment and armament
trained them to move rapidly and in good order over every
l of ground. Even so, cavalry serving as flank guards, scouts,
n outpost duty carried firearms and used them efficiently.

Guibert, a French observer, said: "It is only in Prussia that
le horsemen and their officers have that confidence, that bold-
ss in managing their horses, that they seem to be part of them
id recall the idea of the centaurs. It is only there that 10,000
orsemen can be seen making general charges for many hun-
reds of yards and halt in perfect order and at once commence
second movement in another direction."

he great Marshal Saxe,[2] the real victor of the battle of Fon-
y in 1745, had already laid down that cavalry should be
ible of charging at speed for 2000 yards in good order. The
lry of most countries could not reach this standard, but
lerick wanted an even higher standard. Frederick's older
rals opposed his innovations, but he was capably supported
helped by Seydlitz and Ziethen. Von Seydlitz was one of the
t brilliant cavalry officers in history, and in his day he had
reputation of being the best cavalry officer in Europe. He
Ziethen, another dashing cavalry leader, were probably the
officers on whom Frederick most heavily relied.

ut of twenty-two great battles fought by Frederick his cavalry
at least fifteen. At no time in ancient or modern history have
e brilliant deeds been performed by cavalry than were
eved by Frederick's horsemen in his later wars.[3]
rohibiting cavalry from firing was to expose them at times to
lly fire from artillery and infantry without a chance to
liate. To remedy this defect Frederick developed horse artil-
, which, by its rapidity, could follow all the movements of the

axe was a great soldier. He had written, quite seriously, in his *Mes
ries:* "I am not in favour of giving battle, especially at the outset of a
I am even convinced that a clever general can wage war his whole life
iut being compelled to give battle." This was du Guesclin's theory.
he brilliant Australian and New Zealand Light Horse were mounted
itry more than true cavalry. Mounted infantry did not normally fight on
eback but used their horses merely as a way of reaching a scene of action,
e they fought on foot. Cavalrymen, of course, fought while mounted. The
nventional Australian Light Horse regiments fought some actions as
lry, the most outstanding being their charge at Beersheba, Palestine, in
ber 1917.

cavalry and camp and fight with it. By keeping the enemy's t
teries and infantry at a distance and by its fire it paved the v
for the cavalry charge.

For more than thirty years, until 1789, Prussia had the o
efficient horse artillery in Europe. Frederick had howitzers for
army, too—large, booming guns with which he lobbed sh
on the Austrian reserves sheltering behind hills.

While welding his army Frederick was thinking deeply ab
strategy and tactics. He concluded that he had only one ba
problem—how to take a superior enemy by surprise. It was tal
for granted that any enemy of Prussia would have superior nu
bers. He evolved this solution: concentrate the inferior stren
of my own forces at a particular point with the apparent int
tion of launching a main attack. This will throw the enemy
balance. Now—how am I to launch my main attack successful
By finding the answer Frederick achieved immortal fame, but
do so he went back to history, dragging out and dusting off
secrets of Epaminondas, Alexander and Scipio. Also, follow
Gustavus, by whom he was directly influenced, Frederick plan
wars of mobility and rapidity of fire.

The difficulty of Frederick's method, which was always ain
at launching an attack on his enemy's flank, was the skil
development of the column on the march to form the bat
order. The slanting battle formation demanded of the officers a
NCO's a high degree of efficiency in giving orders and of
men not only obedience but also an instinctive realization of
situation, the ability to feel what would happen the next mint
and to react with the spontaneity of a *corps de ballet*.

Frederick's drill was intended, as he explained himself, to ma
the soldier in battle feel conscious of his heart as the result of
harmony between the pace he took and his heart-beat. His mar
ing pace made him calm, and drill had trained him in what
ought to do.

The marching pace allowed officers and NCO's to form
their fighting units and to move them precisely to the inch as tl
needed them. With the muskets of those days it was impossible
take particular aim. The men merely fired straight in front
them. By directing, moving, and forming his men exactly as
required them the NCO or officer took aim for all. A man act
on his own initiative could throw the whole line into confusion.

The Germans did not invent the idea of marching in step. T
idea probably first occurred to the Greeks. The Prussians, in

enteen-thirties, developed the marching pace from march-in step.

Frederick's system of manoeuvres came to be called Prussian ll, which was simply the method by which Frederick taught his talions how to respond quickly and decisively to orders. Some ters have called Prussian drill brutal. It was certainly hard, it was not brutal. It was hard because Frederick, unlike many ers of his day, did not regard war merely as a rough game. He ;aged in a war or battle with the object of winning it quickly; civilian population suffered during long wars, and the longer ampaign went on the more soldiers tended to lose their will to t.

Basically Frederick's tactics were extremely simple. He saw t if his army was much more mobile than that of his enemy he l only to wait until the enemy had deployed into line of battle, n attack it violently on the flank. This was the Epaminondas tic.

For this flank attack he used only part of his force, for he be-ved—and he proved—that 30,000 men could defeat 70,000 in ble-quick time. The remainder of his army he held ready for emergency or to move in when the rout started.

Probably Frederick was the first great leader since the Byzan-e generals, at least seven centuries earlier, to state that many itary lessons could be learnt from books and to insist that his cers study their textbooks. In speaking of officers who relied on ctical experience alone he said caustically, "The Prussian nmissariat department has two mules which have served ough twenty campaigns—but they are mules still."

His textbook *Military Instructions* is a masterpiece of com-n sense, for few of his maxims were profound. Here are some hem:

The first object in the establishment of an army ought to be naking provision for the belly, that being the basis and founda-ion of all operations. [The origin of the famous expression "An army marches on its stomach".]

It is an invariable axiom of war to secure your own flanks nd rear and endeavour to turn those of your enemy.

The conquering wing of your cavalry must not allow the enemy's cavalry to rally, but pursue them in good order.

To shed the blood of soldiers, when there is no occasion for t, is to lead them inhumanly to slaughter. [A lesson not taken o heart by the generals of the Great War.]

Though our wounded are to be the first objects of our at
tion, we must not forget our duty to the enemy.

In war the skin of a fox is at times as necessary as that o
lion, for cunning may succeed when force fails. [An echo
Gideon.]

Those battles are the best into which we force the enemy,
it is an established maxim to oblige him to do that for whicl
has no sort of inclination, and, as your interest and his
diametrically opposite, it cannot be supposed that you are b
wishing for the same event.

Some of Frederick's maxims might appear cynical, but in
light of the standard of education and of the class distinction
his era they make good sense. This one, for instance:

All that can be done with the soldier is to give him espri
corps—a higher opinion of his own regiment than of all
other troops in the country—and since his officers someti
have to lead him into the greatest danger (and he cannot be
fluenced by a sense of honour) he must be more afraid of
own officers than of the dangers to which he is exposed.

Political intrigue soon absorbed Frederick's attention. Ma
Theresa's Chancellor, Prince von Kaunitz, had convinced Fra
that the old rivalry between Austria and France was point
now that Prussia was so aggressive. He proposed a bargain
France would help Austria to regain Silesia she could have
Austrian Netherlands. Wooing France carefully, Maria The
and Kaunitz pointed out that the French-Austrian coalition
70,000,000 could crush Prussia's 4,000,000. In January 1
Prussia and England made an alliance, but in May France
Austria signed the Treaty of Versailles, creating a defen
alliance in which they were supported by Russia, Sweden,
Saxony.

Faced with all these enemies, Frederick, in July, posted 11,
men to watch the Swedes, 26,000 to watch the Russians
37,000 to garrison Silesia. In August, with 70,000 men he
vaded Saxony without declaration of war. The chances of survi
let alone victory, seemed slight. England provided money, but
world-wide conflict with France prevented her from giving e
tive military support.

Frederick claimed to have irrefutable documentary informa
that Austria was only waiting until her preparations were c
plete to launch the whole forces of the coalition against him.
one chance was to strike first and to deal Austria a blow wl

uld cripple her offensive. At the end of August he marched his
ny into Dresden, Saxony, where he found other documents
ich he said, proved that he was to be attacked by no fewer than
first-class powers—Austria, France, Russia, Saxony, Sweden
l the German States. It was a rare compliment, and, in a way,
lelighted Frederick, for it meant that Prussia was now taken
iously. He blockaded Pirna, and in October he defeated the
istrians at Lobositz.

The campaign of 1757 opened at Prague, held by 133,000
istrians under Prince Charles. Frederick had 120,000 men at
s time, his army having been increased by the conquest of
xony. He took Prague, but at great cost; 18,000 Prussians fell,
:luding Field-Marshal Schwerin, "who alone was worth 10,000
n". Frederick then marched on Kolin, held in strength by
:ld-Marshal von Daun. Frederick devastated his own army by
owing battalion after battalion at the Austrian guns. He did
t realize that he had been defeated until an officer, replying to
: King's order for yet another charge, said, "Does your Majesty
:an to storm the batteries alone?"

Scenting victory, the Allies now moved to strangle Frederick
a circle of steel, using 400,000 men against him, and by the
d of May the ring was tightening. Frederick was undismayed,
d, though he suffered losses and Prussia was reeling under the
ws, he struck back, sending his cavalry to raid enemy camps
d regrouping his scattered troops. Berlin, his capital, was oc-
pied by the Austrian Count of Hadik, who accepted a ransom
300,000 thalers to depart.

The Russians devastated parts of Prussia, inflicting horrible
rbarities on the civilian population. By October Frederick's
sition was so critical that even he began to believe that the war
is lost, but throughout the war the world was amazed at
ederick's capacity to recover.

Training went on continually. Seydlitz exercised his cavalry at
ll speed over very broken ground, and men were often killed.
ederick once commented on the number of deaths. "If you
ike a fuss about a few broken necks, your Majesty," Seydlitz
id, "you will never have the bold horsemen you require for the
ld." It was a significant statement in view of later German
ining.

Prussian cavalry was taught to rally to the front instead of the
ar, in other words to rally after a charge while pursuing, which
evented a reckless, disorderly Rupert-of-the-Rhine pursuit and

enabled the commander to follow up victory with greater
tainty. The usual task of hussars was to harass a retreating a
in detached parties; Frederick's hussars charged in a large b
like heavy cavalry.

Seydlitz displayed decision and daring on November 5th, w
the French and Austrians at Rossbach foolishly offered t
flank to the Prussians. Virtually the whole of the Prussian cava
in beautiful formation and moving at "incredible speed", a
French officer described it, charged the enemy. Four times
Prussians cut their way through the French, under Soubise,
routed them.

Where the Allies were still in column the Prussian artil
destroyed them, and then the systematic Prussian muske
smashed into those Allied infantry who held their ground.
retreat became a rout. The French and their allies lost 3000 ki
and wounded, 5000 prisoners (including 8 generals and
officers), 67 cannon, many colours, and most of their bagg
Those who survived became a rabble on the run.

The Allied leaders showed no generalship at Rossbach. T
must have won had they held a line along the Saale river and
mained on the defensive, for Frederick had not the strength
attack a static line. Inept at manoeuvre and relying on superio
of numbers, they offered battle—which was exactly w
Frederick wanted them to do.

In those days battles were rarely fought in winter. Armies
tired to winter quarters, and no military activity more seri
than patrolling was carried on until the spring, but Frederick
studied Turenne, and on November 13th he marched fr
Leipzig on a winter campaign. Frederick himself captured N
markt, where he learned that Prince Charles and Field-Mars
Daun had advanced to Lissa. Their right rested on the village
Nippern and their left on that of Sagschütz.

Their army, impressively strong, consisted of about 70,000 r
(possibly as many as 80,000), including strong cavalry squadr
and supported by 210 guns. Their 5½-mile front had the ri
protected by bogs and the left covered by an abattis. The cer
was at Leuthen.

Against this strong force in its strong position Frederick
only 36,000 men, made up of 24,000 infantry and 12,000 cava
His artillery consisted of 167 guns, including 71 heavy pie
The battlefield was an open plain, over which Frederick
manoeuvred in times of peace.

n December 5th, at five o'clock on a cold morning, Frederick
his army towards Leuthen. A few miles off he assembled his
rals and briefed them for battle. "I should think that I had
: nothing if I left the Austrians in possession of Silesia", he
. "Let me tell you, then, that I shall attack the army of Prince
rles, nearly thrice as strong as our own, wherever I find it. I
t take this step, or all is lost. We must beat the enemy or all
sh before his batteries. So I think, so will I act. Now go and
:at to the regiments what I have said to you."

he last instruction is revealing, for it was rare in that era for
men in the ranks to be told what the commanding officer had
iind. Frederick believed, rightly, that if he took the men into
:onfidence they would fight better.

s usual his plan was uncomplicated. He would advance
ight up the Breslau (Wroclaw) road, feint at the Austrian
t, march across Charles's front, and attack his left to cut his
imunications. The vanguard moved off, with the men singing
ymn:

> Grant that I do whate'er I ought to do,
>   What for my station is by Thee decreed;
> And cheerfully and promptly do it too,
>   And when I do it, grant that it succeed!

An officer asked Frederick if he should silence the men. The
ig said, "No, with such men God will certainly give me victory
ay." All later German generals believed they had the Deity in
ir ranks, but this applies to most commanders of Christian
iies.

The inhabitants of the area had scented trouble days before,
h foragers, scouts, messengers, and cavalry patrols continually
movement along the country roads. Everybody knew a battle
s brewing, but exactly where? Into which villages would the
diers move for quarters? Which houses would they fortify?
iich fields would be mashed into mud by the thousands of
rses and the hundreds of wheels? For many miles around the
:a farmers had already had their horses, carts, and stores re-
isitioned—a euphemistic term for stolen—or lived in fear of
:ir being taken. Had the season been summer many families
uld have evacuated the arena and lived in the open until the
rricane had passed. But this was winter, so most of them stayed
ere they were until, as fighting broke out and engulfed their
mlets and homes, they were summarily evicted or they fled.

The villagers of Borne were the first to hear or see conflict,
here an Austrian force—a detachment of five regiments ur
General Nostitz—barred the road. Dawn was just breaking,
the horsemen could be dimly descried through a mist. Frede1
ordered a charge and the detachment was scattered and 800 ta
prisoner. Nostitz was mortally wounded.

When the mist cleared the whole Austrian army was visi
regiment upon regiment, rank after rank—a formidable and
pressive sight.

The taking of Borne gave Frederick a vantage-point, and
height screened from view the advancing Prussian columns.
this point Frederick sent his cavalry against the Austrian rig
where they made such a display that Count Lucchesi, comma
ing the Austrian right, called for support. In haste, Field-Mars
Daun sent the reserve cavalry and even part of his cavalry fr
the left wing.

While this was happening the four Prussian columns forn
into two, and at Borne they wheeled right under cover of h
ground and marched south, the whole movement being carr
out with the usual Prussian precision, with an advance-gu;
under General Wedell. Then came, on the right wing, Gene
Ziethen with 43 squadrons and Prince Maurice of Dessau wit
battalions. The left wing consisted of the major infantry fo
under General Retzow, flanked by 40 squadrons under Gene
Driesen. Each body of cavalry was supported by 10 squadrons
hussars, while in the rear was Prince Eugène of Württemb<
with another 25 squadrons.

The Prussians seemed to be retreating, and this pleased Prir
Charles and Field-Marshal Daun, who observed the movem<
from the mill at Frobelwitz. Daun said delightedly, "The Pr
sians are off! Don't disturb them."

But just after noon the columns wheeled again, formed line
battle and drove towards the Austrian left near the village
Sagschütz. General Nadasti, the Austrian commander on t
spot, saw the overwhelmingly superior force advancing towa1
him and ordered away rider after rider, asking Charles urgen
for help. Help could not come in time. At one o'clock Wed<
supported by infantry and artillery, stormed the defences
Sagschütz.

The Austrians had learned something of the spirit in whi
cavalry should be handled, for Nadasti dashed out with l
cavalry and charged Ziethen's leading squadrons. The Prussi

rsemen regrouped behind their six supporting infantry bat-
ions, then followed Ziethen in a counter-charge against
dasti, over difficult ground. The Prussians were skilled in
ing over such terrain while the Austrians were not; they were
oken and driven into Rathener Wood. In ninety minutes the
ire Austrian wing was scattered, with Prussian hussars pur-
ng the flying Austrians. Then the Prussians began to roll up
: enemy line like a carpet, with their heavy artillery enfilading
: Austrian positions farther along.

A fierce fight developed at Leuthen itself, where the Austrians
ight gallantly. Unfortunately for them, their generals had not
rnt the bitter lesson of the French at the battle of Blenheim—
.t a village should not be overcrowded with troops. Leuthen
s packed as tightly as Blenheim, with the troops in places
m 30 to 100 deep. Artillery case-shot played havoc in these
id lines. With requisitioned farm horses Frederick had brought
 many of the heavy guns from the fortress of Glogau. This
midable artillery, as much as the redoubtable infantry and
shing cavalry, won the battle.

The Prussian Guards assaulted the Austrian positions and
rried them. Possession of Leuthen did not help Frederick im-
diately, for the Austrians had formed another line at right
gles to their first and had brought up artillery in support.

Frederick's infantry was held off until he sent for his heaviest
is and established them on high ground called the Butterberg,
m where they drove the Austrians back. Frederick was master
 the battle throughout. He had riders bringing him information
istantly, and so was able to move infantry, guns, and cavalry
out the large battlefield as necessary. This was unusual for
: period; normally once an army was committed the com-
nder could do little to influence events but had to depend
 the initiative of his subordinate generals. Frederick gave
 trusted leaders plenty of rein, but he rarely allowed overall
itrol to pass from his hands. Adolf Hitler, who professed him-
f a student of Frederician methods, also kept control in his own
ids.

The battle raged with little respite until four o'clock and dusk
s approaching. Count Lucchesi, a brave cavalry leader, had
embled a large force of horse and saw his chance to use them
en Prussian infantry under General Retzow was held up.
cchesi made a flank attack, but he had not seen forty squadrons
der General Driesen hidden behind the village of Radaxdorf.

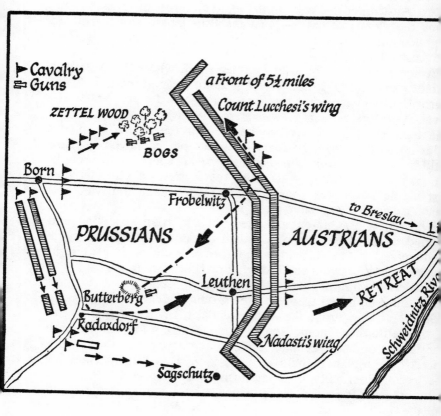

rederick's victory at Leuthen was a perfect example of the
ck of a long line from the flank, the attack rolling up the
nce from left to right. The Prussians, in two parallel columns,
ed through broken, hilly country and stretches of pine wood
ch screened their march from the Austrians, who stood ready
hours wondering what was happening. The attack was a
ical surprise, with assaults on the Austrian flank and even on
r rear. Marshal Daun found his long line crumpling up. All the
trian commanders had expected to hold a fortified line
nst a frontal attack, but the fortified line for all practical pur-
s had ceased to exist. They tried to form a new battle line
ace the Prussians, but it was never completed. The Austrians
ht fiercely in Leuthen, but their masses were vulnerable to
ssian artillery. Finally, Driesen, lying hidden in a hollow to
left rear, countered a charge of Austrian cavalry against his
advancing infantry; caught between the Prussian infantry and
lry, the Austrian cavalry was severely mauled.

Waiting for just such a moment as this, thirty of Driese
squadrons charged Lucchesi frontally while five drove agai
his flank and the other five galloped round the Austrian re
These enterprising tactics overwhelmed Lucchesi, who was kil
as his troopers broke and scattered. After losing so much of th
cavalry support the Austrian infantry was vulnerable. Dries
charged them in the rear, while General Wedell attacked th
flank near Leuthen.

The anecdote about Frederick which the Prussians like best
all tells how Frederick rode frantically about the battlefield af
hearing that von Wedell, his favourite, had been killed. Frederi
shouted his name continually: "Wedell! Wedell!"

While the King was shouting a corporal lying among a heap
dead and wounded with great effort said, "Your Majesty, we i
all Wedells here."

Frederick stopped, gazed at the dying man, and said, "Y
have taught me a good lesson and I thank you for it."

Hopeless confusion followed as darkness fell and the Austri
force disintegrated, many of the troops bolting towards Lis
Frederick, victorious but tired, also made for Lissa, riding throu
mobs of broken Austrians.

He rode into the grounds of a château and outside the buildi
met about a dozen Austrian officers. "Good evening, gentlemer
Frederick said courteously, "I dare say you did not expect i
here. Can one get a night's lodging along with you?"

The Prussians lost about 6000 men killed and wounded. T
Austrians lost 10,000, plus 21,000 prisoners, 116 guns, 51 colou
and 4000 wagons. But this was only an instalment. Prussi
troops took 2000 more prisoners on December 9th, and on t
19th Breslau surrendered 17,000 men and 81 guns to Frederick.

As a power Austria had lost her reputation, while Prus
emerged as the most dangerous military power in Euro
Frederick had retaken the whole of Silesia except for a sin
fortress, Schweidnitz.

Few victories have been so enthusiasticaly acclaimed
Leuthen. Frederick's system and success astonished those w
were accustomed to calculate effect by mere quantity. His tact
were to fascinate even Napoleon, who wrote:

> The battle of Leuthen is a masterpiece of movemen
> manoeuvres, and resolution. Alone it is sufficient to i
> mortalize Frederick and place him in the rank of the great
> generals. All his manoeuvres at this battle are in conform

ith the principles of war. He made no flank march in sight of
s enemy. . . . He carried out things I never dared to do. He
as above all great in the most critical moments. . . . It was not
e Prussian Army which for seven years defended Prussia
;ainst the three most powerful nations in Europe, but
·ederick the Great.

ut Frederick had trained that army. Frederick's biographer,
eral Tempelhoff, wrote:

Ancient history scarcely furnishes a single instance, and
odern times none that can be compared either in execution
· consequences with the battle of Leuthen. [This is not true.]
forms an epoch in military science and exhibits not only the
eory, but also the practice of a system of which the king was
e sole inventor.

he victory at Leuthen was largely due to the perfect co-
·ation of infantry, artillery, and cavalry, but the confidence of
ordinary soldier in Frederick as a general was the most de-
·e factor.

hinking over his victory, Frederick realized how important
lery was. He transferred all the 24-pounders he had captured
ustrian fortresses to his field army, and with these guns de-
:d the Russians at Zorndorf in 1758. Even when the fortunes
var changed Frederick remained true to his fundamental
ciple that the battle was won when the heavy artillery domi-
d the decisive heights and when the light artillery was made
nobile that it could be used on any part of the battle-
. Thus he became the real developer of field artillery. He
ced all the light guns to 3-pounders and attached them to the
lry. He gave the field artillery medium howitzers so that it
d cope not only with moving targets but also with fortified
tions. As a result of this reform he was so strong that he was
to support the natural deterioration of his infantry during his
; wars. He started with 1000 guns and finished with 10,000.
rederick consistently used his central position to concentrate
nst a part of the enemy's forces, and by employing tactics of
rect approach he won many victories, despite his numbers.
vever, at Hochkirch, 1758, and Künersdorf, 1759, superior
bers defeated him. At Hochkirch he opposed 37,000 men to
00 and at Künersdorf the Russians had 70,000 to Frederick's
00. But with only 30,000 he beat the Austrians at Liegnitz in
); they had 90,000.

In this he created a precedent. For the next two hundred ye Prussian and German troops were outnumbered almost eve where they fought—with a few important exceptions.

Memories of many battles fade; those of Rossbach and Leutl became brighter. Their importance can hardly be overemp sized, for they have dominated German history. They were rocks on which German pride and sense of superiority were buil

A German historian, writing in 1942 in the middle of Hitle war, claimed that Leuthen was "the model and ideal of all fut battles of annihilation".[4] He omitted to say that Frederick was spired by Cannae, but there is much truth in what he says, for the architects of Prussian and German might who follov Frederick acknowledged that they were building on the foun tions he had laid—especially the martial foundations.

Cavalry formations and tactics of most armies were based those evolved by Seydlitz and Ziethen, and many other arm copied parts of the Prussian military system, but the Prussia Germans, Bavarians, and Austrians, made most use Frederician examples.

The near-obsession for a great weight of artillery which fected German generals from the time of Frederick until the v of 1939–45 is directly attributable to Frederick's use of it. is Moltke's passion, a century later, for mobility. A successful m always has his imitators, and Frederick was *very* successful.

[4] When Hitler planned his last great assault, the Battle of the Bulge, he s to some of his generals, "History will repeat itself . . . the Ardennes will be Rossbach and Leuthen."

CHAPTER THIRTEEN

———— ◆·◆ ————

War in Three Continents

Clive, Wolfe, and Washington; Prussian Influence on the American Army; The 'New Era' at Valmy

the year that Frederick won Leuthen and Rossbach the ̲nglish clerk-turned-soldier Robert Clive won the battle of ̲ssey, which, though little more than a skirmish in extent, pro- ̲ed, in Fuller's view, a "world change in its way unparalleled ̲ce Alexander overthrew Darius at Arbela".

̲uller was echoing Malleson, who said, in *Lord Clive*, "There ̲er was a battle in which the consequences were so vast, so ̲nediate and so permanent. . . . The work of Clive was, all ̲ngs considered, as great as that of Alexander." Politically this ̲rue, as Clive himself realized at the time: "It is scarcely hyper- ̲e to say that tomorrow the whole Moghul empire is in our ̲ver."

̲live was a capable general. His conceptions were as brilliant ̲ those of Cromwell, his plans as masterly as those of Marl- ̲ough, his execution was as effective as that of his contem- ̲ary Frederick, and his courage and resolution were as in- ̲nitable as those of Charles XII, all of whom, as a student, he ̲w much about. Clive had not been trained as a soldier, which ̲haps explains why, at that time, he was so successful. His ̲d was stultified by military conventions, and he was free to ̲on inspiration which, I feel, was fired by his military reading.

̲Iis compatriot-contemporary James Wolfe was, in contrast, an ̲ent and highly educated soldier, aged only thirty-two when ̲en his momentous independent campaign. His background is ̲ortant, too, for his father had fought under Marlborough. ̲nes himself had fought with distinction at Dettingen, 1743,

Lauffeld, 1747, and during the Forty-five Rebellion was pre
at Falkirk and Culloden.

Wolfe had studied war and battle; he knew that discipline
a weapon. His orders to his battalion, the 20th Foot, which
commanded at Canterbury in 1755, made this obvious:

> The battalion is not to halloo or cry out upon any acc
> whatever . . . till they are ordered to charge with their bayo
> . . . There is no necessity for firing very fast; a cool, v
> levelled fire, with pieces carefully loaded is much more dest
> tive and formidable than the quickest fire in confusion.
> When the enemy's column is within about twenty yards,
> men must fire with good aim.

This type of preparation, together with the training of
officers—no British commander in the field ever had finer offi
than did Wolfe—made him victorious.

His General Orders issued between May 16th and Septem
12th, 1759—that is, during the Quebec expedition—show
Cromwellian effort he took to form his small army into as per
an instrument of war as possible in the time available. Ther
much of Cromwell in the phrasing of the orders and in their c
tent. The best qualities in the fighting man were "vigilance
caution". Plundering was strictly forbidden, as was swearing.
insisted on a high standard of discipline and behaviour and ca
cleanliness.

> No churches, houses or buildings of any kind are to
> burned or destroyed without orders . . . peasants who yet
> main in their habitations, their women and children are to
> treated with humanity; if any violence is offered to a woman,
> offender shall be punished with death.

But he hated Indians—"scalping is forbidden except when
enemy are Indians or Canads dressed like Indians".

Although he was capable of threatening soldiers with death
punishment he disliked flogging and on occasions used ridic
as a punishment, such as making a defaulter stand at the latri
with a woman's cap on his head.

Wolfe had intelligence enough to learn from others. His
conventional tactics clearly show that he had studied Gene
Braddock's disastrous defeat in ambush in 1755. He had app
ently also studied the elastic-square system devised by Brigadi
General Henry Bouquet, a noted English tactician.

However, this system, which, briefly, enabled a force to move
er rough, broken, and forested ground with ability to change
ection quickly and fight to front or rear or either flank, was
t Bouquet's invention; Eugène had experimented with it in
rmany.

After a battle of wits with his adversary Montcalm, Wolfe
ened a campaign of 'frightfulness', by bombarding Quebec,
tting off supplies, and laying waste to the country by burning
d wrecking. It is so easy to forget, when we complain of
ightfulness' by our enemies in our own age, that all nations,
cluding our own, have been guilty of it at some time or another.
priest and twenty men who formed the garrison at St Joachim
re scalped.

Wolfe's eventual attack, made with the help of the Royal
vy, was as complete in surprise as any in history. His troops
led the river heights to reach the Plains of Abraham, where
ey won their famous victory against the French.

Fortescue was to write in *The History of the British Army*;
With one deafening crash the most perfect volley ever fired on
ttlefield burst forth as if from a single monstrous weapon, from
d to end of the British line." The British reloaded, stepped
ward, and fired again, and did this for about eight minutes,
which time the battle had been decided and was practically
er, although it could be said that the mental and moral dis-
ration of the French had contributed as much to their defeat as
d British force of arms.

Wolfe's contribution to the leadership was important, for his
ining and his tactics reaffirmed the need for steadiness for
ich British troops were fast becoming noted. About half a cen-
y later Sir John Moore adopted Wolfe's system as the basis for
ining his remarkable Light Division. Also, Wolfe, with his
val colleagues, showed that amphibious and combined opera-
ns, intelligently and co-operatively handled, could produce
ectacular results.[1]

George Washington, though he proved himself a competent
neral and a great leader of men, brought nothing new to war,
t he and his Americans did show that tactics had to be adapted
the terrain and vegetation, a lesson the British were tardy to

Admiral of the Fleet Lord Keyes wrote in 1943, in his *Amphibious Warfare*
d Combined Operations: "The lessons of history are invaluable and the
ords of scores of amphibious operations ... are available from which to
n inspiration and guidance." Lord Keyes showed that much could be learned
m Wolfe's campaign.

absorb. Again, it was Sir John Moore who benefited most fro study of the American campaigns. The finest light infantry of day were the 500 riflemen who served under Colonel Da Morgan. Mostly Pennsylvanians of Scottish-Irish stock—for so reason they were called "Morgan's Virginians"—they marc extremely light, refused all wheeled transport, and in one per of three weeks covered 600 miles. Moore had these outstand light infantrymen in mind when he trained his own light infantr

The American War of Independence was a combat of irregu rather than of parade movements, and in this it broke away fr European tradition. Shooting to kill and deliberate trickery a deception were quite contrary to the rules of eighteenth-cent warfare, although they were commonplace facets of Indian w fare. The Americans pretended to surrender and then contin fighting; they swore allegiance one day and attacked the next; the disgust and exasperation of the Redcoats, they fired fr hiding-places and killed British soldiers even in the act of dri ing from rivers. Washington himself on one occasion order some of his troops who wore red coats to sew on to them buttons of an English regiment, pass through the lines, and k nap General Clinton. From this war forward all the so-cal rules of war—the moral rules—became absurd, although natic kept on making them.

Actually, despite the initial success of militiamen at Conco and Bunker Hill and the obvious supremacy of initiative ov pattern, of irregular warfare over the conventional, Washingt was sure, as early as September 1776, that the militia was adequate and possibly even harmful. He began a struggle wi Congress for a semi-regular army enlisted for the duration of t war. However, the American belief in the invincibility of milit men persisted for many years. Even generals who knew bett than this had to be careful how they expressed themselves. "T Americans possess as much natural bravery as any people earth," wrote General Nathanael Greene cautiously in 1776, b fore daring to add, "but habit must form a soldier."

If no general owes anything in particular to Washington, i directly Washington owes much to Frederick the Great. Indee the United States Army from 1778 was founded on Fredericia principles—a fact which American historians seem to ignor When Washington took his army to Valley Forge for the wint of 1777–78 he was joined by Baron von Steuben, who had serve on Frederick's personal staff during the Seven Years War. As H

a remarkably able and perceptive administrator Washington
inted him Inspector-General, and von Steuben went to work
a will to organize, discipline, and train all branches of the
ling army. Imbued with Prussian thoroughness, trained by
erick, fired by enthusiasm, von Steuben was largely respon-
for turning the Americans into a real army; European leader-
had crossed the Atlantic, and Frederick the Great helped to
the British from America.

euben, although commissioned at fourteen, passed through
y rank from private, mainly so that he could learn, and
to teach, the manual of exercise. He demonstrated at Valley
e the manual of exercise he wanted to introduce into the
rican Army, and he made the officers undergo the gymnastics
e Prussian cadet so that they could instruct their men. But
ben was far too intelligent to suppose that Prussian discipline
l be transplanted on to these soldiers, and he cut the Frederi-
maximum to a minimum.

wrote the first standard set of regulations for the American
y. The prime object of the captain was, he said, to "gain
ove of his men by treating them with every possible kindness
humanity". This was certainly not Prussian teaching of the
nteen-seventies, but it was nevertheless a typical Prussian
oach to get the most out of the men. Some parts of the
sian military doctrine Steuben forcibly impressed upon the
ricans. In the interests of economy of men the Prussian code
ade use of soldiers as officers' servants, a habit which had
lly developed in the American Army. Steuben wiped it out
had the soldier-servants returned to their military duties.

ddly enough, the Americans had an overweight of supply
nization. Steuben said that at Valley Forge he found more
termasters and commissaries than in all the armies of Europe
her.[2] Indirectly Steuben was helped by many foreigners who
served in Continental armies. Their influence cannot be cal-
ed, but it must have been significant, despite the proud
rican assertion that this was a national war.

either in America nor in Europe were the chief military
ns learned or heeded. In 1785, when the young Gneisenau
ned from America to Prussia, Frederick posted him to one
e worst battalions of infantry, commenting that the people
ning from America "think a great deal of themselves and of
knowledge of war, and they must learn war all over again

[2] History would repeat itself in the twentieth century!

in Europe." But Gneisenau, whose link in leadership is for
secure, had learned a lot in America, and later he had a ch
to apply it. The conservatism of European officers is psycl
gically understandable, but that of the Americans is puzz
They convinced themselves that the militia had really won
war, that Washington had been misguided in employing Steu
and that a standing army was unnecessary.

This is not to say that the American military system was I
sianistic; on the contrary, many of its details were in absolute
trast with all Continental and even with the British system.
Americans saw the army as an agency of civil power, to
organized and disciplined with that purpose in view, and no
an end in itself.

From the military, not the political, view-point a much r
important battle than any fought in America was the Cannoi
of Valmy in September 1792, which distinctly marked the be
ning of a new form of warfare. Goethe, who was present on
Prussian side, said to his comrades as he left the field, "F
today and at this spot there begins a new era and you can say
were present." He meant that Valmy was the symbol of the
ginning of unlimited war, of total war.

At Valmy the Prussian war machine was held up for the
time. Germany has always played down this unusual battle
did not accept it as a reverse, but Valmy was a Prussian dei
and no amount of German juggling with facts can disguise
reverse—though it was a defeat of Prussian leadership rather i
of Prussian troops. Yet the Prussians were commanded by
Duke of Brunswick, a nephew of Frederick the Great and
garded everywhere as the greatest soldier in Europe. His riva
the field was General Charles Dumouriez, a political
military adventurer lifted to high rank by the Revolution—b
capable commander nevertheless.

Brunswick's reputation was founded largely on his succes
campaign in Holland in 1787, regarded as an example of per
generalship. This was true enough, for the Dutch had acte
Brunswick expected them to behave, and, having the typ
methodical Prussian mind, he had been able to counter all t
moves. But Brunswick was handicapped by his mona
Frederick William, who thought of himself as another Frede
the Great—without the slightest justification. There was
unity between Brunswick and the King, except that Brunsv
usually dutifully deferred to his monarch.

The Prussian plan was to invade Lorraine with three armies, :h a total force made up of Prussians, Hessians, Austrians, and :nch emigrés, a total number of about 80,000. Brunswick had ne initial victories, including the taking of Verdun, after which planned to take Sedan and go into winter-quarters and so ablish himself for the following spring.

But the King, the leading emigrés, and several of Brunswick's n officers opposed the plan. They pointed out that the French-n confronting them were not a normal army but an "un-ciplined, revolutionary rabble" who could not possibly stand to the superior discipline of the Prussian Army. During the xt few days the Prussians moved slowly and Brunswick acted ptly and missed two chances to destroy large parts of the :nch Army. Dumouriez was acting with more skill and speed. 1ally the Prussian king countermanded an order of Bruns-:k's that might have saved the day and set in train the inevitable sco.

Incredibly the Prussians, without making a reconnaissance, :hout sending forward a single officer, and without any plan battle, moved towards the known French positions, where the :at French soldier Kellermann was one of the senior com-inders. Through no brilliance on the part of the Prussians the :nch were caught unprepared and forced on the defensive, but imouriez had no intention of abandoning the offensive al-;ether and ordered two audacious attacks on the Prussians— e on their rear and the other on their baggage-train.

For some reason the Prussians expected to find the French in :cipitate retreat, but about noon as the morning fog cleared they w them drawn up in line of battle. Kellermann, posted at a mmanding point near a windmill, raised his hat, adorned with :ricolour plume, on his sword and shouted, "*Vive la nation! ve la France!*" And the men, taking up the cry, replied, "*Vive tre général!*"

The French had 52,000 men in the vicinity that day, but only ,000 were present at Valmy. The Prussians had 34,000. At this int the 58 guns of the Prussian artillery, commanded by the re-wned General Tempelhoff, were in position, or hurriedly getting o position, to face Kellermann's 40 guns, under General Aboville, on Valmy Ridge. The distance between them was out 1350 yards.

French artillery was the best in Europe, largely because of the rk of Lieut.-General de Gribeauval, who had split artillery into

four distinct sections—field artillery, siege artillery, fortress art‖
lery, and coastal artillery, every detail being worked out wi‖
great skill for each arm of artillery. Gribeauval's system ‖
mained in force from 1765 until 1828 and was partly responsib‖
for French successes.

Goethe wrote: "Now commenced the cannonade of which
much has been spoken, but the violence of which at the time it‖
impossible to describe.... The whole battlefield trembled."‖
probably did, for each side fired more than 20,000 shot. B‖
1350 yards was a long range for cannon of 1792, and as t‖
ground was sodden clay much of the shot buried itself.

Brunswick ordered an attack on the Valmy position, but t‖
moment the Prussian infantry advanced Kellermann's artille‖
smashed their lines, and Brunswick stopped the advance before‖
had gone 200 paces.

At 2 P.M. a Prussian shell blew up three ammunition wago‖
behind Kellermann and both sides stopped firing. Two Fren‖
regiments broke, but Kellermann rallied them. The Prussia‖
again considered storming the ridge, but the French artillery ca‖
into play again. Brunswick was impressed by the steadiness of t‖
French infantry and noticed that the French cavalrymen stood ‖
their horses. He well knew that once a Prussian infantry atta‖
was under way the French cavalry would charge. He pondered t‖
problem, then called a council of war at which, for the first ti‖
in months, he acted as a real commander-in-chief and actua‖
made a decision. He called off the battle.

A Prussian general, Massenbach, wrote, "You will see h‖
these little cocks will raise themselves on their spurs. We ha‖
lost more than a battle. The 20th of September has changed t‖
course of history. It is the most important day of the century."

The French under Dumouriez and Kellermann had repuls‖
the most formidable army in Europe and had discredited the m‖
famous commander. Brunswick never admitted it publicly, ‖
the French generals and their men, throughout the campaign, h‖
been superior to him and to his slow-moving, slow-thinki‖
deliberate troops.

Less than a year after the cannonade the French National C‖
vention passed a law which was, in effect, a declaration of to‖
war.

> The young men shall fight ... the married men shall fo‖
> weapons and transport supplies; the women will make tents a‖
> clothes and will serve in the hospitals; the children will ma‖

d linen into lint. The old men will have themselves carried to the public squares and rouse the courage of the fighting en, to preach hatred against kings and the unity of the public. . . . The public buildings shall be turned into bar- cks, the public squares into munition factories. . . . All fire- rms of suitable calibre shall be turned over to the troops. . . he interior shall be policed with shotguns and cold steel. All ddle-horses shall be seized for the cavalry; all draft-horses t employed in cultivation will draw the artillery and supply- agons.

n August 29th, 1793, six days after the publication of this ificant document, one of Massenbach's "little cocks" found self with the opportunity to raise himself on his spurs. On day the French besieged Toulon, held by the British, and in mand of the artillery was Napoleon Bonaparte.

CHAPTER FOURTEEN

❖◆❖

Napoleon, Product of History

TWENTY-ONE of twenty-five military writers I regard as being
qualified to express an opinion on the subject nominate
[Nap]oleon as one of the really great captains. "One would have
[t]o back to Hannibal or even to Alexander to find his equal
[am]ong his precursors]", says Cyril Falls in *The Art of War*.
[Am]ong the world's great autocrats and conquerors Napoleon
[has] but two compeers—Alexander the Great and Augustus[1] ...
[As a] strategist he has never been excelled ... as a tactician he pos-
[sesse]d a wonderful eye."—Fuller in *Decisive Battles of the
[Wes]tern World*. The German Colonel-General Ludwig Beck,
[thou]gh not an Historian, saw him as "The most colossal military
[geni]us of all time."

[B]ut the other four bypass him. Wavell, for instance, says, in
[Sold]iers and Soldiering, "I cannot rate him as high as Marl-
[boro]ugh or certain others ... an indifferent tactician ... his hand-
[ling] of cavalry and infantry on the battlefield was often clumsy
[and] wasteful."

[I] admire Wavell as a general and as a man, but his estimation
[of N]apoleon shows his defects as an historical military analyst.
[H]owever, he admired Napoleon, for elsewhere he wrote:

When you *study* military history get at the flesh and blood of
[it], not the skeleton.... If you can discover how a young un-
[k]nown man inspired a ragged, mutinous, half-starved army
[a]nd made it fight, how he gave it the energy and momentum

[1]Augustus Caesar Octavian—first Roman Emperor.

to march and fight as it did, how he dominated and control
generals older and more experienced than himself, then y
will have learnt something.

I have myself criticized Napoleon indirectly,[2] but he must be
garded as having no betters and few equals.

Napoleon is the linch-pin in my study of the chain of comma
for among generals he was one of the keenest, most intellig
students of military history, making use of everything valua
and practicable that had happened in antiquity and in mod
times. And those who came after him benefited from everyth
that Napoleon modified, amended, or improved upon. He lear
too from the mistakes of his precursors, although not all of
successors learned from *his* mistakes.

Napoleon did not initiate the ideas of his own military age; th
initiation was the work of Marshal de Saxe, Guibert, Pierre
Bourcet, and others. Saxe, a military genius with wide
perience, summed up his philosophy of arms in his *Mes Rêver*
—somewhat misnamed, as it was really an outstanding analysis
war systems and war psychology. Few commanders have a
nowledged any debt to Saxe's book, and Napoleon even sp
disparagingly of it—which shows that he had at least read it. F
few men are big enough to admit that an idea which they h
proved successful might have been another man's brainchild, a
this applies as much to soldiers as to fashion-designers.

Saxe's book is important, for it clearly shows the interc
nection of old and new ideas and looks ahead to 'revolutiona
innovations. Knowing that the Greeks and Romans had inven
military music to make troops march in harmony and not mer
to lull them, Saxe wanted to apply music to induce men to for
the hardships of long marches.

He urged the use of light infantry in conjuction with the regu
infantry. The light soldiers would be placed about 200 paces
front of the regiments to disturb the enemy, harass him, and c
ceal the manoeuvres of the regiments. He proposed that ev
infantryman should carry a breech-loading fusil—although
had not then been invented—and he wanted the men to fire at
as a target presented itself because he felt that firing at comma
cramped the natural style of aiming and shooting. This
sheer heresy to orthodox officers.

[2] In fact Napoleon brought nothing new to war. What he did was to
prove on everything that had gone before...with much more skill than
predecessors." (*The Face of War*, Abelard Schuman.)

Saxe further urged physical-fitness training, in which jumping
and running would be prime activities. And, more heresy, he
wanted the soldier's hair cut short, for comfort, cleanliness, and
other efficiency. This was a sane idea, but other proposals were
less reasonable. He wanted marriages to last only five years so
that more soldiers could be produced; boys of any union would be
put into a military school. In this he was resurrecting the Janissary
principle and encouraging Nazi eugenic ideas of the future.

In his famous work *Essai Général de tactique* Guibert revealed a mind profound enough to analyse the military weak-
nesses of his time. He wrote:

> Suppose there were to spring up in Europe a vigorous people,
> possessed of genius, power and a favourable form of govern-
> ment; a people who combined with the virtues of austerity and
> a national soldiery a fixed plan of aggrandizement who never
> lost sight of this system; who, knowing how to wage war at
> small cost and subsist by its victories, could not be reduced by
> financial considerations to laying down its arms. We should
> see this people subjugate its neighbours and overthrow our
> feeble constitutions as the north wind bends the slender reeds.

This concept of a nation in arms—of a return to Spartanism, in
effect—which Guibert formulated in 1781, with a total disregard
of the rights of individuals, depended for its accomplishment on
speed and elasticity, and he evolved details to bring these
qualities about. Divisions should practise forced marches, passage of rivers, forming column from line and line from column,
with speed and simplicity. Infantry should fight three deep, as that
of Frederick had fought against armies which used a six-rank
formation.

An assault in column was absurd and ineffective, Guibert said,
as depth gave no weight to attack. Horses should not be galloped
for the entire distance of a charge; the first 200 yards of a 600-
yard charge should be covered at a slow trot, the second 200 at a
fast trot, and the climactic 200 at the gallop. He ranked cavalry
as a secondary arm, for exploitation of an infantry victory, for
shielding a retreat. All this Napoleon imbibed. And, we may suppose, Hitler, too, lapped up Guibert's philosophy of war even if
he was not specially interested in his tactics. "*We should see this
people subjugate its neighbours. . . .*"

Guibert was an even more ardent advocate than Saxe of gymnastics. Swimming, running, and climbing should take up much

of a soldier's training, while manual exercises and military ev
tions should be cut down. Guibert had a twofold purpose in
vocating gymnastics: they would show the soldier what sor
accidents and conditions might occur in war, and they we
make him more fit and supple and enable him to take a qui
step—120 paces a minute against the customary 70. Finally ir
duced into the French Army, this rapid pace ennabled
French to outmarch their enemies.

Guibert, too, demanded individual and independent fir
musketry practice against war targets, concentrating effective
against a given point. Noise in itself was not deadly, he poin
out, though many officers seemed to think it was. Half a mil
musket-balls might be fired in a battle and would make a fears
noise, but perhaps only 2000 men would be hit.

Guibert reminded his contemporaries that the Romans
others had lived on and at the expense of the country in wl
they were fighting and quoted Cato—"War must support w
Supplies or the need for supplies should not command
general, he said. When, because of the nature of the cour
supply-trains were necessary they should all be entirely militar
and should not be planned or controlled by other Governn
departments or by private contractors, as so many trains wer
those days.

Napoleon certainly learned from Guibert. By comparison
baggage-train of a French army in 1806 amounted to only
eighth or one-tenth of that dragged behind them by an equal b
of Prussian infantry.

Napoleon most probably studied the work of Pierre
Bourcet, a staff officer who served during the War of the Aust
Succession and the Seven Years War and later wrote a textb
about mountain warfare. Napoleon's own tactics in mountair
country seem to have been strongly based on de Bourcet's p
ciples, while some of his many maxims echo points made by
staff officer.

This is not to say that Napoleon was a mere military plagia
He campaigned and fought on new principles, but, as with all
other innovators, he made use of conditions which he him
had not brought about. Napoleon was partly the product of
times; for his early days as an officer were passed in the turn
of revolution, and he found this atmosphere refreshing. He o
much of his attitude to war to the Baron du Theil, comman
of the Artillery School at Auxonne, at which Napoleon serve

twenty-year-old gunnery officer. Commandant du Theil en-
uraged Napoleon to study the entire art of war, and among the
rks he studied was a work on artillery tactics by the com-
ndant's younger brother.

As Napoleon did not initiate the striking changes of his era, so
did not create the army which was to put them into practice.
e Revolution had forged this army, and the passions inflamed
the Revolution had inspired the men who filled its ranks. The
anges wrought by the Revolution are vividly illustrated by
'de-generalling' of the Army.

On the eve of the French Revolution the French Army was
ssly over-officered. It had no fewer than 1171 generals against
y 80 in the Prussian Army, which was slightly larger than the
ench. The Austrians had 350 in an army of roughly the same
e. By January 1st, 1791, the Revolution's radical cleansing had
luced the number of French generals to 34 among a total of
06 officers. The law of February 1780 had put an end to pur-
asing of commissions; everybody had to start at the bottom.

The Revolutionary armies put to death, generally by order,
atever chivalrous notions still remained alive. Carnot was
gely responsible for this, just as he was largely responsible for
apoleon's first major appointment. The spirit which permeated
wn from above infected the ordinary soldiers with martial ruth-
sness, with a truly professional zeal for use of arms, as distinct
m pseudo-professional zeal shown by the regular soldiers of
her armies. These French soldiers, like the irregulars of the
nerican armies of the War of Independence, shot to kill. To
ke war loss more permanent French decrees of September
92 and May 1793 banned the ransoming of prisoners—another
il in the coffin of gentlemanly war. All this was, in a way, a
row-back to barbarism—but it was disciplined, methodical bar-
rism based on a national political obsession. Under Napoleon
e whole system became Caesarian and militaristic.

Inheriting an already dashing army, Napoleon moulded it into
magnificent striking force. The infantry was good, but he
ttered it by improving its discipline. The artillery was good, but
ere was not enough of it, and it was roped to the infantry.
apoleon enlarged this arm and made it independent. The cavalry
s good, but tactics up till now had confined its movements and
ade it, too, closely dependent on the infantry. Napoleon en-
led it to reconnoitre, harass, and pursue.

Millions of words have been written in an attempt to explain the 'mystery' of Napoleon and the 'secrets' of his success. word 'genius' simply is not adequate, no matter whether we it a practical or a poetic definition. I see neither mystery secrets. Napoleon's actions and writings show clearly that he a passionate sensitiveness for war—as an adventure, as an i lectual exercise, as a vehicle for application of lessons from past, and as a means to an end. This passion gave him an int ambition to be the greatest soldier ever, which meant that had to study other great commanders to find out their 'secr to which he was acutely sensitive.

While conceding that Napoleon transformed war it would difficult to overestimate his debt to the historical literature arms. Napoleon was more than an avid reader of this literat he was a firm believer in the value of study of military hist When about to take over command of the French armies in I in 1796 he sent for a history of the 1745 campaign of Marsha Maillebois in the mountains in which he himself was to fight. parcel of books was lost, but Napoleon obtained others.[3]

Napoleon, when First Consul, prepared a pamphlet enti *Parallel between Caesar, Cromwell, Monk[4] and Bonaparte* flew it as a kite to see which way the wind was blowing. political significance of this act is immaterial to my analysis, here is further proof that he had studied these commanders.

Napoleon certainly studied the great soldiers of antiquit such as Alexander, Caesar, Hannibal, and Scipio and urged o ambitious commanders[5] to do the same, and though I can find documentary proof of it I think it extremely likely that he studied Miltiades, Arminius, and England's Edward III. He closely conversant with the tactics and methods of Condé, (tavus, Turenne, Vendôme, Eugène, and Marlborough. His ca cious, retentive, and probing mind was pondering stratagems possible plans long before the immediate need for them arose.

[3] The first parcel was found aboard a captured ship and was sent to Nelson
[4] General George Monk, Duke of Albemarle (1608–70). Napoleon's opinion of Monk is significant, for Monk used the power of the Army means of awing the English Parliament, and the plea of duty owing to Pa ment as a means of controlling his army.
[5] The Archduke Charles of Austria said, "A man does not become a g commander . . . without a passion for the study of war." Also: "Success is obtained by simultaneous efforts, energetic resolution and great swiftnes execution." Charles came very near to defeating Napoleon at the bl battle of Aspern-Essling in May 1809; Marshal Lannes was killed in battle. Liddell Hart calls Aspern-Essling "Napoleon's first serious defe but I feel that it was more of a drawn battle, despite the Austrians' nume superiority.

e himself said:

All great captains have done their great deeds by conform-
g to the rules and natural principles of their art, and by the
undness of their plans, and the proportioned connection
aintained between their means and the results they expect,
tween their efforts and the obstacles to be overcome. They
ve only succeeded by conforming to rules, whatever might
ve been the boldness of their designs and the extent of their
ccess. It is on this ground alone that they are our models and
is only imitating them that we can hope to rival them. . . . If I
ways appear ready to meet any emergency it is because I
ve long meditated on the possibilities. It is no sudden in-
iration that tells me what to do; it is study and meditation.

hort, there were times when Napoleon had long-dead com-
ders at his elbow.

r all of Napoleon's hundreds of maxims there is an actual
ct-lesson. Take, for instance, the maxim usually numbered 17:

In a war of marching and manoeuvring, to avoid battle
ainst superior forces, it is necessary to entrench every night
d to occupy always a good position of defence. The position
nich nature usually furnishes cannot shelter an army against
perior forces without the help of art.

apoleon could have pointed to the campaign of the Duke of
vick against the Portuguese in 1706—and probably he did.
Duke, with a French and Spanish army, covered almost all
pain. He commenced the campaign at Badajoz, and after
ng manoeuvred through the two Castiles, ended it in the king-
of Valencia and Murcia. Berwick's army made 85 camps
was not once surprised. The entire campaign was fought
out a general action, but it cost the enemy 10,000 men.
nd Maxim 26:

is acting against the truest principles to allow separate action
two divisions which have no communication with each other,
face of an army centralized and with easy internal com-
unication. [Not to be confused with the dictum of "March
parately, strike together", discussed elsewhere.]

he Austrians lost the battle of Hohenlinden in 1800 by neglect
iis principle. Their army, under Archduke John, was divided
four columns and marched into an immense forest in order

to join on the plain of Danzig, where they were supposed to prise and attack the French. But these divisions, which had intercommunication, were compelled to engage singly the Fre under Moreau, who had concentrated his forces. He caught Austrians in the forest, attacked them on flank and rear, devastated them, killing 7000, capturing 11,000, and ta cannons and all the baggage. The whole action was reminiscer the Teutoburger Wald.

Neglect or ignorance of this maxim was one major reasor the defeat of the German armies on the Russian front in 1! 44. Too many separate actions were fought against an enemy internal communications.

Napoleon was an attacking general—"I think, like Frede that one must always be the first to attack"—but he fully ap ciated the importance of trenches. They were, he said, "n injurious, always useful, often indispensable".[6] He had n precepts to guide him. In 52 B.C. at the siege of Alesia Auxois), it has been calculated, Caesar's troops dug out 2,000 cubic metres of earth from their trenchworks. The Roman Caesar's day owed as much to their entrenched camps as to legions, for their camps were practically unattackable. Napo must have known, too, that the Emperor Charles V used tren extensively in the wars of the sixteenth century and that by m of them he successfully opposed an army twice as large as his In Marlborough's campaigns both sides regularly dug themse in. Probably the most notable instance of trench warfare in eighteenth century was in 1761 when Frederick made his stan Bunzelwitz in Upper Silesia. With everything going wrong, not more than 50,000 men under his command, and menace 130,000 Austrians and Russians, Frederick from behind trenches held them off until shortage of supplies forced t to retire.

Some of Napoleon's maxims merely echo his precursors for instance, "Secure yourself all possible chances of suc when you decide to deliver an important engagement." years earlier Marshal Saxe had said, "War should be made s to leave nothing to chance."

The quickness of Napoleon's tactical eye, as extolled Fuller, is well shown in the taking of the Fort of Bard, w

[6] But as early as 1793 he had written, 'It is an axiom in strategy th who remains behind his entrenchments is beaten; experience and theory a one on this point."

pped the French Army on May 20th, 1800, after it had sur-
unted all the obstacles offered by the St Bernard Pass. Lannes
de desperate attempts to carry the fort by assault, but was re-
sed with heavy loss. Napoleon climbed a rocky precipice on
e of the mountains forming the pass controlled by the fort and
tantly saw the possibility of capturing the place. That night he
d a road covered with mattresses and manure, and in extreme
nce had his guns carried over it in ropes and straps, to a point
ere they could dominate the enemy fort. In single file cavalry
d infantry followed the path marked out by Napoleon and
ere no horse had ever climbed before. The fort was easily
en.

Frederick had said, "In war the skin of a fox is sometimes
necessary as that of a lion, for cunning may succeed when
ce fails." This principle was hardly profound or new—it was
least as old as Gideon—but Napoleon followed it many
es.

In desperate circumstances at Arcola in 1796 Napoleon sent a
all cavalry detachment with trumpeters behind the Austrian
es to sound the charge and generally make a commotion to
eive the Austrians into thinking that they were surrounded;
ruse worked and the usually steady Austrians fled in panic.

Had he studied the tactics of the ancient Gideon? Did he know
t Bahram of Persia had stampeded his opponent's cavalry
ring a night attack by tying bags full of rattling stones around
necks of his horses? Anyway, I feel reasonably sure that he
indeed know of the two almost bloodless victories—at Car-
nish and outside Constantinople—won by Belisarius with a
xture of bluff and daring which persuaded his opponents he was
ich stronger than he actually was.

Napoleon never advanced towards any 'natural position' held
an enemy, but sought for his own natural position—often
oss an enemy's rear. This policy greatly influenced Clausewitz.

It was commonplace for a commander to rouse the fervour of
troops by a stirring speech, especially before a battle, and
ny such speeches have come down to us.[7] But few commanders
ve had Napoleon's magnetic personality with which to infuse
ir words with fire. At the age of twenty-seven, when he took

Condé once inspired his troops before battle without saying a word.
ame with ardour and unattended, he rode the length of his lines, looking
the eyes of almost every man. It must have been one of the most im-
ssive pre-combat acts by a general.

over the Army of Italy on March 27th, 1796, Napoleon su
posedly made a famous proclamation:[8]

> Soldiers! You are famished and nearly naked. The Gover
> ment owes you much but it can do nothing for you. Yo
> patience, your courage have done you honour, but can give y
> no glory, no advantage. I will lead you into the most fert
> plains in the world. There you will find great towns, rich pr
> vinces. There you will find glory, honour and riches. Soldi
> of Italy, will you be wanting in courage?

Victories followed in rapid succession, among them Montenot
Mondovi, Millesimo, Dego, Lodi, Arcola, Rivoli, Mantua.

Napoleon carried martial public relations to a height not aga
reached for another century and a quarter. He made a point
remembering—or seeming to remember—old veterans who h
fought in earlier battles; he gave numerous 'pep' talks and issu
many proclamations; he displayed interest in the welfare and co
fort of his soldiers, and stories of his concern circulated co
tinuously among his troops.

But again, propaganda was not Napoleon's idea. As early
1792 General Massenbach, who had warned about the Revo
tion's "young cocks", complained of this "new French meth
of attack, not with sword and cannon, but with far more dangero
weapons, by which they tried to inspire the common soldier wi
Republican sentiments", Massenbach conveniently ignor
Frederick's own blatant propaganda campaigns among co
munities he had captured.[9]

Some French propaganda tactics were enterprising. Groups
unarmed French soldiers would appear at Prussian or Austri
outposts, talk in a friendly way about liberty and equality, a
leave packages of propaganda leaflets with their 'friends'. The
activities completely baffled the Prussians and Austrians, t
such passionate belief by common soldiers in political princip
was incomprehensible.

Mishaps for which Napoleon was personally responsible
attributed to dead men or others not in a position to defend the
selves.

[8] Supposedly, because I can find no reference to this speech in contempor:
accounts of the campaign. It appears that Napoleon first dictated it, fr
memory, while on St Helena. No doubt he made a proclamation, but the
Helena version could be a polished one.

[9] Propaganda had figured in the Civil War in England, when religious a
democratic ideas were brought into the service of Cromwell's army.

'hen he took Arcola—and he was in personal danger here—
nade sure that paintings showed him on the bridge, tricolour
and, although in fact he had been in muddy water at the foot
ie dyke. His own account of his being first across the bridge
so successfully implanted that it has been perpetuated by
tically every historian since the event.

he American historian Alfred Vagts appears to condemn
oleon for this deception, but I think it justifiable. The per-
lity and popular image of the commander was vital in those
;—more so than it is today. It would never have done for
oleon to be shown up to his waist in dirty water. He needed to
te a hero-image to inspire his army further, and this he did.
"first across the bridge" story was merely good tactics; the
lour in hand was the Gallic touch.

apoleon's stern manner, the certainty of his commands, and
rapidity of his movements terrified the older French officers
nuch as they terrified the enemy. In building a new military
em he had first to break down all the old rules and conventions.
promoted men from the ranks to be officers, he gave junior
ers more authority and initiative, he insisted on efficiency and
officers being on duty twenty-four hours a day during a
paign.

was from Frederick that Napoleon saw the necessity for
ility, and in 1804 he based his army on the divisional system.
; was not new—French generals had been experimenting with
sions for seventy years—but under Napoleon each division
ime a self-contained fighting unit, as it is today.

ι this year, 1804, the period of constant war started, and in the
' nine years Napoleon had 50,000 volunteers and 2,400,000
tees, in addition to seamen and *gardes d'honneur*. Up to 1806
ich losses, within the boundaries of 1793, amounted to
0,000 dead out of 29,000,000 inhabitants—the battle losses
: far less than those due to illness—a precedent for the prodi-
y with which French generals, bewitched by Napoleonic
nd, expended men in later wars. Decimation due to illness was
ywhere great in this period of mass armies.

owever, Napoleon was never deterred by losses, and con-
red them merely as commensurate with the magnitude of his
ories.

CHAPTER FIFTEEN

◆◆◆

Austerlitz, a Lesson in
the Art of War

˙APOLEON'S favourite fight—his own term—was Austerlitz,
1805. In later years he was fond of quoting Austerlitz as an
ιnple of fine reconnaissance and planning, of firm decision and
d action. It was, he said, a lesson in the art of war, a reason-
claim seeing that Austerlitz was the most sweeping and final
l his victories.

he approach march to Austerlitz really began at Boulogne,
τe Napoleon had made his headquarters at a small house
e he prepared to invade England.

was here that he heard that the French fleet, under Vil-
uve, had turned back to Ferrol. This was the final reason of
y why Napoleon could not proceed with his invasion of
land. The news arrived about four in the morning. Napoleon
for his secretary, Daru, who found him aflame with anger. He
d about the room, abusing Villeneuve for "ineptitude and
ardice". Then he ordered Daru to sit down and write.

aru sat down at a desk littered with papers and maps and
down a remarkable document—the advance against Austria,
h was to culminate in the triumph at Austerlitz—the second
test tactical victory in military history. (The first was Cannae,
B.C.) Without reference to notes or to maps Napoleon gave
u the complex details of the march and its halts, the various
es for separate corps, numbers and quantities, times and dates.
he end the entire campaign was on paper. Later Daru was to

marvel at the incredible way in which everything fell into pl
exactly as Napoleon said it would. This is why the prelimina
to Austerlitz are as interesting as the battle itself.

In an incredibly short time he gathered his scattered army
marched to meet his foe. Carnot initiated and Napoleon develo
the idea that divisions while operating separately should
operate towards a common goal. The ability to travel light
celerated the mobility of Napoleon's armies and enabled them
move freely in forested or mountainous country. Being unable
depend on supply-trains for food and equipment gave thrust
hungry and ill-clad troops in striking at the rear of an enemy w
had great supply-trains on which he depended.

Napoleonic armies marched rapidly, too. "The strength of
army, like the quantity of motion in mechanics", Napoleon s
"is estimated by the mass multiplied by the velocity. A s
march enhances the *moral* of the army and increases its power
victory." On one occasion a corps under Marshal Lan
covered 65 miles in 50 hours; Bernadotte marched his men
miles in 69 hours.

Napoleon also said:

> The first quality of a soldier is fortitude in enduring fati
> and hardship; bravery but the second. Poverty, hardship
> misery are the school of the good soldier. . . . Tents are
> healthy. It is better for the soldier to sleep out, for he sle
> with his feet to the fire, which soon dries the ground on wh
> he lies; some planks and a little straw protect him from
> wind. . . . Commanders should be ordered never to sleep i
> house. . . . Tents give an enemy information as to your num
> and position.

Poverty, misery, and hardship Napoleon's soldiers got. Ot
armies of those days had long supply and baggage colum
Napoleon's were much shorter because his soldiers had to live
the land—which meant that they robbed the peasants wh
farms they passed. Whenever it was known that an army
coming the farmers would hide everything they could and dr
their stock some distance away. But Napoleon's troops were
pert foragers, and they could sniff out hidden bags of apples
flour as easily as they could a pig. A large Napoleonic force p
ing through the country left a swathe of poverty in its wake a
seized everything eatable. Only once in a while was a farmer p
for what the Army took. In enemy countries it stole everythin
could carry, eatable or not. Tents were not provided, so the n

ot under whatever cover they could find—in a barn or a hay-
ck, under a cart. If no cover was available they simply slept in
 open, around a fire if the weather was cold. Often they slept
 ough heavy rain.

Battles followed in quick succession as Napoleon marched into
 heart of Europe ... Günzberg, Hallach, Albeck, Elchingen,
mmingen. Then, before the Austrians knew what was happen-
, 30,000 of them under Field-Marshal Mack were surrounded
 Ulm and had to lay down their arms.

These first defeats were followed up with typical Napoleonic
ce. Those corps which had escaped the disaster at Ulm were
sued and, one after the other, destroyed. The Tyrol was over-
 and its strong positions were occupied by Marshal Ney. From
y Napoleon heard of Masséna's successes against the re-
wned Archduke Charles, while at Dirnstein, Marshal Mortier
 defeated the Russian First Army under Kutusov.

n the midst of all these victories Napoleon heard of the French
eat at Trafalgar. "I cannot be everywhere," he said simply.
 could not alter the course of the war at sea, but he could make
ory on land. He marched on.

Napoleon had seven corps, under Bernadotte, Marmont,
vout, Soult, Lannes, Ney, and Augereau, with cavalry led by
rat and the Imperial Guard as a reserve. It was a magnificent
ce brilliantly led, well deserving its new title—the Grand Army.
The men who formed Napoleon's "brotherhood of marshals"
e an inspiring group: Murat, the dashing, brilliant cavalry
der who had led French horsemen on all the battlefields of
y and Egypt; Lannes, glorious at the battle of Montebello; the
eran Soult, hero of Altenkirchen and of Zürich, experienced
years of war in Germany; Bernadotte, a statesman as well as a
ed leader; Davout, stern and strict, his gallantry and deter-
ation unsurpassed; Ney, *le brave des braves*, who had risen
n simple hussar to general of division in eleven years;
gereau, veteran of the Pyrenees, the East, Italy, the Rhine,
 the Netherlands, another man who had risen from the ranks;
rmont, long a comrade of Napoleon and a brilliant artillery-
n. At the time of Austerlitz, however, Marmont was still not a
rshal; he received his baton in 1809. There was also Marshal
thier, Napoleon's brilliant Chief of Staff, a wonderful admini-
tive soldier and tactician, whose duty it was to transmit
poleon's orders. And we must not forget Masséna, the money-
ing smuggler and military genius.

In all Napoleon had twenty-six marshals, although at the
of Austerlitz there were only eighteen, and many were on
elsewhere. They were young, too, with an average age of a
thirty-nine. Napoleon himself was only thirty-six. Berthier, a
fifty-two, was an old man in comparison with the rest. The y
of Napoleon's marshals had a lot to do with the spirit with w
they conducted their campaigns and battles.

On November 13th, 1805, Napoleon entered Vienna, wit
resistance, for the enemy had gone. He then began to spread
his corps. But before any army could push northward ou
Vienna the Danube had to be crossed. Napoleon's only r
was across the Spitz bridge, which the Austrians held in stre
Also, the bridge was mined and would certainly be blown u
the first sign of attack.

Napoleon wanted the bridge intact, and he told Murat
Lannes so; these two swaggering Gascons promised to captu
singlehanded. How they achieved their boast makes one of
finest stories of the Napoleonic period.

They put on their most magnificent uniforms—ostrich feat
gold-embroidered tunics, blue trousers, red morocco boots.
their breasts were their shining decorations, on their belts
diamond-hilted swords. Then together, but without escort,
cantered calmly towards the bridge.

The Austrians could not help but be aware that the stran
were men of importance, and the word soon went round that
of Napoleon's famous marshals were approaching. They cro
the bridge and asked for the commander, who happened t
Prince Auersberg, a rather old and indecisive commander.

The Prince asked why they had come.

"Haven't you heard of the armistice?" Murat asked.

"It has just been signed, and by its terms the bridge has
handed over to us," Lannes said.

Prince Auersberg was surprised and suspicious, and an a
ment occurred. While Lannes and Murat kept the Austrian
mander busy another adventurous French commander, Oudi
was bringing up a party of his noted grenadiers. They were cr
ing towards the French end of the bridge, where they shie
sappers who uncoupled fuses from demolition charges.

But the charges remained at the Austrian end of the brid
and they were covered by guns. At this point Prince Auers
decided to retire from the bridgehead. Not all his men wer
gullible. A sergeant saw Oudinot's grenadiers, and, putting

d two together, he ordered his men to fire on the marshals.
nnes and Murat pretended to be amused. Murat, casually, said
Auersberg, "Is this your famous Austrian discipline, where
geants countermand the orders of generals?"

The Prince was stung by this and had the sergeant arrested.
t an Austrian gunner, who could also see that the whole thing
s a French trick, laid his gun on the marshals. Lannes
mptly sat on the barrel. Oudinot ordered his grenadiers on to
bridge, an act suspicious enough to arouse even Prince Auers-
rg's doubts. "Why are those men advancing?" he demanded.
"They are not advancing at all," one of the marshals said dis-
ningly, "but the weather is so cold that they are marking time
keep their feet warm."

Auersberg had no more time to wonder about the proceedings.
idinot ordered his men to double, and within minutes they
d secured the bridgehead. It was a brilliant and audacious feat,
oical of Napoleon's marshals.

Nevertheless, it was about this time that Murat, and Soult too,
gan to lose their nerve. Napoleon's position was certainly
ngerous, for his corps were spread out along hundreds of miles.
arshal Masséna was coming up from Italy, but he was a long
y off, and it was very doubtful if he could arrive before battle
sued. In fact, Masséna was finding Venetian territory too
ofitable in loot to want to reach the barren lands between him
d Napoleon.

Napoleon pushed on towards Brünn, which he reached on
ovember 19th. At this point he had 65,000 men, and much of
s army was still dispersed, for he had been forced to post some
oops to keep check on Hungary and Bohemia and to garrison
e captured Vienna. But only 40 miles away was a force of at
ist 83,000 Russians and Austrians, under the Emperor Alex-
der and the Emperor Francis II. Within three weeks these
rces would be doubled by armies moving towards them. In
dition, another 200,000 Prussians might also soon take the
ld. So rapid had French movements been that many soldiers
d fallen out of sheer exhaustion; one battalion of the Guard
d temporarily lost 400 men from this cause. A saying current
the Army was, "The Emperor makes more use of our legs than
r arms!"

But morale and the will to fight were so high that the stragglers
re doing their best to catch up before the battle they knew was
evitable. At Brünn, Napoleon gave his army a week to recover

its strength, recover its strays, and to repair its boots
weapons.

But Napoleon himself took no rest, and on November 21s`
reconnoitred the wide, high plateau of Pratzen. It must have b
a striking scene, and in its way this scouting expedition
even more important than the battle which was to follow.

First came watchful vedettes—the scouts whose duty it
to protect Napoleon and his party in front and on the flanks. T]
on a grey horse, came the short, sallow-faced Napoleon him;
dressed in a grey overcoat and wearing long riding-boots. On
head was a low, weather-stained cocked hat.

He was followed by a large group of officers, their senior r
proclaimed by the heavy lace on their plumed hats, unifor
and saddle-cloths. Behind these officers was a strong squad
of carefully picked cavalry in dark-green dolmans with fur
pelisses slung over their shoulders and huge fur caps surmoun
by tall red plumes.

Napoleon rode in silence over the plateau, his alert, intense e
missing nothing. He studied carefully the little village of Prat
and the steep slope down to the muddy stream below, the G
bach river.

None of his staff spoke to Napoleon, for they knew better t
to interrupt him in the midst of one of his famous reconnaissan
Finally he drew rein and turned to face his staff. "Gentleme
he said, "examine this ground carefully. It will be a field
battle upon which you will all have a part to play."

So discerning was Napoleon that he had seen at once that I
the battle must be fought. Every day after that he scouted
country, drew maps, and studied them closely all the time
sisting that his generals also examine the terrain. Before
battle of Austerlitz commenced Napoleon accurately predic
the exact order of events, and even forecast the time of day
each incident in the series that would make up the fight.

Napoleon had lived with the theory of Austerlitz long bet
he ever saw the place. It could be described as a 'pivot batt
Napoleon may well have used this term himself.

Basically it depended on the swinging of a line from some
pregnable hinge at one end, while the other end, either fa
back under pressure or voluntarily retired, would progressiv
weaken the enemy centre. Napoleon's idea was that when
situation had developed to the point where his own line was
danger of being outflanked he would attack the enemy with

:pected reserve. This extra weight, delivered at the critical
t and time, would decide the issue. Just where he had especi-
hoped for success the enemy would find himself hopelessly
ngled. Inevitably his strength would be further drawn to-
ls the threatened point, his centre would be still further
:ened and might even be pierced. Once broken into two
ons the enemy army would be lost beyond redemption.

was now certain that the united army of two mighty empires
close by, and that both the Russian and Austrian mon-
s were prepared to trust their fortunes to trial by battle. With
generals and their soldiery they were eager to retrieve their
ious misfortunes and disgraces at Napoleon's hands.

ley had already beaten back the French advanced guards at
:hau, and this gave them confidence. It is fairly safe to
ne that Napoleon had ordered his Guard to give ground in
r to lead the enemy on. This was a favourite ruse of his.
it fell back from Posoritz and Soult from near Austerlitz.
Russian Emperor, Alexander, convinced Francis of Austria
they should attack Napoleon before he could collect more
)s.

is was precisely why Napoleon needed a little more time.
adotte had not come up with his corps, and Davout's corps
1 only be present if action was postponed.

ipoleon halted the retreating French troops on his chosen
efield. The outlying corps of Bernadotte and Davout were
led. By discipline and training Davout raced his corps 70
s in 48 hours to take part in the attack on the right of the line.

unitions, food, and ambulances were placed at chosen points.
oleon then confidently announced that the battle would take
 on December 1st or 2nd. He had only to wait for the enemy
me to him.

ipoleon sent Savary to present his compliments to the
eror Alexander—and also to see as much as he could of the
iy preparations and morale. On his return Savary told
oleon that the Russian leader was surrounded by "a set of
g coxcombs" whose every look and gesture expressed over-
ing confidence in themselves and contempt for their op-
nts.

1 the reverses of the previous campaign against the French
 the result, the Russians said, of unpardonable cowardice
ng their allies, the Austrians. The first battle would show
'rench how well the Russians could fight.

Later the Tsar sent a young aide-de-camp to return the ⟨com⟩pliment carried by Savary. Napoleon then stage-managed a s⟨cene⟩ of desperate haste in the French lines, so that the young o⟨fficer⟩ could return to Alexander with the news that the French we⟨re⟩ near-panic. This added even further to the Russians' confiden⟨ce⟩ which was what Napoleon wanted. His one fear was that ⟨the⟩ Russians might decide against battle.

The Goldbach marked the front of the French army. ⟨This⟩ river rose across the Ormütz road, flowed through a steep-s⟨ided⟩ dell and then into Menitz Lake. At the top of its high left ⟨bank⟩ was the wide Pratzen plateau, which Napoleon did not occ⟨upy.⟩ It seemed to Napoleon's staff that he had erred in giving up ⟨this⟩ useful ground to his enemy.

"I have granted the plateau to the enemy deliberately," ⟨he⟩ told them. "By holding it I could here check the Russians, ⟨but⟩ then I should have only an ordinary victory. By giving it u⟨p to⟩ them and refusing my right, if they dare to descend from ⟨these⟩ heights to outflank me, they will be lost. I will devour them."

Napoleon rested his left on a rugged height which som⟨e of⟩ his veterans called "the Santon", after a similar height in E⟨gypt.⟩ On the crest was a little chapel whose roof had the appear⟨ance⟩ of a minaret—and the French veterans remembered min⟨arets⟩ from Egypt.

Napoleon strengthened this height with field-works, whic⟨h he⟩ armed and provisioned like a fortress. He specially chose ⟨its⟩ defenders and put the Santon under command of the able Ge⟨neral⟩ Claparède. "Fight till your last cartridge and, if necessary, ⟨die⟩ here to a man," he told Claparède.

He meant exactly what he said—and he never doubted ⟨that⟩ his troops would fight to the death. No troops specially sele⟨cted⟩ for such a task ever betrayed his trust.

His centre was on the right bank of the Goldbach. Here do⟨uble⟩ lines of troops under Soult and Murat, Duroc and Oudinot, ⟨lay⟩ concealed by the windings of the stream, by scattered clu⟨mps⟩ of wood, and by undulations of the ground.

His right was entrusted to Davout's corps, but only one div⟨ision⟩ of infantry and one of dragoons had been able to come into ⟨line⟩ in time. Posted at Menitz, they held the defiles passing M⟨enitz⟩ Lake and the two other lakes of Telnitz and Satschan. Napo⟨leon⟩ had need of a determined general here, and Davout was that m⟨an.⟩

In general, Napoleon's line of battle was an oblique one, ⟨with⟩ its right thrown back. Napoleon had deliberately given it ⟨this⟩

pearance of being defensive, even timid. He wanted the enemy
commit themselves to an attack on the right in an effort to cut
lines of communication and line of retreat to Vienna. If they
uld be led into this trap the difficulties of the ground would
eck them long enough for Napoleon to send help to Davout.

At the same time, with his left impregnable and his centre
dy to punch hard, Napoleon expected to be able to attack the
sso-Austrian flank and rear.

The Russians and Austrians were not stupid. They knew their
ntre would be weaker than elsewhere along the line, but they
lieved that they could cover the weakness by advancing on to
plateau and holding it. They fully believed—and this was
ir big mistake—that Napoleon intended to remain on the
fensive. He was only pretending to be on the defensive. The
lies believed that Napoleon was worried about his communica-
ns. In fact, he hardly gave them a thought, for he knew he
uld not be retreating.

The right of the Russo-Austrian army, under Princes Bagration
d Lichtenstein, rested on a hill near Posoritz. Their centre,
der Kollowrath, occupied the village of Pratzen and the large
teau, while their left, under Doctorof and Kienmayer, stretched
vards Satschan Lake and the marshes.

The village of Austerlitz was to the rear of the Russo-Austrian
sition. The Emperors of Russia and Austria slept here the night
fore the battle—and this was why Napoleon gave his victory
: name of the village. It was a vanity typical of the man.

Napoleon might have been pleased with his choice of battle-
ld, but the people who lived in the villages through which the
ht would rage were desperately unhappy. By now nearly all
d abandoned their homes and shops and farms, taking what-
r they could carry. They had little hope of finding their build-
;s intact after the armies had fought and moved away. Some
uld be destroyed during the battle; the soldiers would burn
ers in the frustration of defeat or the exuberance of victory, or
rhaps simply to keep themselves warm. They would take away
ything portable, useful, or valuable and probably smash any-
ng they could not carry. 'Glorious victories' were never
rious for the people who owned the battlefield.

Napoleon's actions so puzzled the enemy's headquarters that
y thought he might even be planning a retreat before action.
: withdrew the mass of his forces still farther, till they were
ng the Goldbach river. He no longer held the plateau at all,

which seemed extraordinary. It was such a natural defensi
position that the Austrians and Russians actually wondered
Napoleon was losing his nerve.

Then, at a distance of about a mile, the two armies waited
bivouac, with piled arms, eating and resting around their fires
the Allies covered by clouds of Cossacks, the French by a th
line of vedettes.

The weather was cold but clear, and Napoleon, established
an old hut, could see the entire field. From here he could mo
brigades, battalions, and squadrons about the field like so ma
chess-pieces. In the afternoon he saw through his telesco
Russian columns on Pratzen plateau moving from their centre
their left, concentrating opposite the front of the French positi
at Telnitz.

Their intentions were obvious even to a subaltern in his fi
action. They had convinced themselves that the French intend
to act on the defensive and that they would not attack in fror
Therefore, the Russians and Austrians reasoned, they had only
mass troops on the right, cut off the French from Vienna, a
then destroy them.

They forgot that by moving major forces to the left th
weakened their centre, and that on their right they were leavi
their own line of retreat unprotected.

Napoleon was so pleased that he trembled in anticipatic
"What a shameful manoeuvre!" he said. "They are runni
into the trap. They are giving themselves up! Before tomorr
evening that army will be mine."

Napoleon had more of a sense of humour than history giv
him credit for. He ordered Murat to take some cavalry towar
the enemy, to move about uncertainly and hesitantly, and th
to retire as if alarmed. The ruse was successful, and Napolec
when he heard of it, chuckled.

The Emperor now issued a proclamation to his troops, off
ing them certain glory in the coming battle, assuring them of l
personal leadership, and promising them cantonments and pea
after the victory.

Napoleon did more than give orders to his subordinate co
manders. He decided on a novel way of encouraging his men. I
gave orders that each battalion was to be paraded and that
commanding officer was to read out to the men the plan for be
ing the Russians and Austrians. He did not much care if t
enemy heard the plans. He assumed that if they did hear, th

would think the whole thing a trick. It certainly was a new
, for at that time and for many years to come private soldiers
 told nothing about the plans for battles in which they
;ht. Much later General Montgomery was to emulate
oleon in this way.

he men settled down to their evening meal—some biscuits
 stale bread and some pieces of half-cooked meat. Lucky
 had a few potatoes or the luxury of an apple. They drank
, tea,[1] or plain water. Then the veterans went to sleep—lying
hat bitterly cold weather with their feet to the fire. The
iger, newer soldiers lay down as ordered, but they did not
.

s always, Napoleon went quickly to sleep. Before midnight
as awakened to be told of a sharp enemy attack on the right.
ad been repulsed, but Napoleon mounted and rode out be-
n the two armies to check dispositions. He rode right into a
sack outpost and had one of the narrowest escapes of his life.

he Cossacks attacked him at once, and he would have been
d or captured only for the courage of his escort, who held
he Cossacks while the Emperor rode for safety. His horse be-
e bogged in the marshes, and Napoleon had to make his way
ot through his lines.

n extraordinary incident now took place. A soldier made a
h of straw to light Napoleon's way, and in the flame he
ared to the soldiers near by almost as a vision. As this night
 the anniversary of the coronation, they were prepared to
ve that his appearance among them was a supernatural
n.

ldom has an army shown such spectacular devotion to its
ral as the French did to Napoleon that night. Napoleon, at
 annoyed and then a little embarrassed, was really deeply
d of the men's spontaneous affection. "This is the happiest
t of my life," he told his staff.

xploiting the moment, he moved from camp-fire to camp-fire,
ring the men, thanking them for their loyalty, assuring them
ictory, explaining that medical aid would come to them as
kly as possible if they were wounded.

Promise us," shouted a veteran grenadier, "that you will
 yourself out of the fire."

I will do so," Napoleon answered; "I shall be with the
rve until you need me."

[1] A popular drink in French armies of the period.

The thousands of enemy who saw the blaze of light along
French front were first of all startled and then pleased a
heartened, for they thought that the French were burning th
shelters as a preliminary to retreat.

For the men in the ranks the coming battle might have be
an exciting prospect, but it was also a grim one. That night,
the field of Austerlitz, the battle-hardened men were under
illusion about their chances of survival.

The battle would be fought at close quarters. Muskets had
accurate range of less than 100 yards, and there was no point
firing at a greater range. Many times infantry advanced to wit
20 yards before firing, and as reloading took about a minute ev
shot had to count.

Napoleon relied heavily on individual initiative, though
troops were capable of a shoulder-to-shoulder British-style mo
ment when necessary. Soldiers stood steady in their ranks, p
haps for hours, while enemy cannon-balls tore through the ran
This was a stern test of discipline, both imposed and personal.
the restricted front of battle, from a few hundred yards to, rar
three or five miles, bodies would lie in heaps about the troops s
standing.

There was a good reason for these rigid tactics, for if infan
were caught out of formation the hovering cavalry would pour
and cut them to ribbons. The only real infantry defence agai
cavalry was steadiness. As men fell, so the survivors closed tl
ranks, always presenting that shoulder-to-shoulder wall of res
ance, for after the cannon fire and the musket volleys there wo
be bayonet fighting.

Often a soldier's sufferings began only when he was carried
when he staggered into the barn, house, or tent being used a
hospital. Here surgeons wielded saw and knife and probe w
more enthusiasm than skill, amid a foul mess of blood, rags, a
dirt.

Less than 50 per cent of wounded could expect to surv
gangrene, loss of blood, or tetanus. Operations were perform
without anaesthetic, hence surgical shock was severe and of
fatal. The wonder of it is that any wounded man surviv
Vinegar was the only antiseptic, disinfectant, and dressing
wounds. Typhus, caused by lice, killed many soldiers who l
survived wounds, while dysentery and ague were common.

Soon after dawn on December 2nd Napoleon had a mea
breakfast, buckled on his sword, and said cheerfully to his st

ow, gentlemen, let us commence a great day." His marshals
ered for detailed instructions. First of all, however, Napoleon
ined his basic plan. Briefly, it amounted to this:

e would wait and check the enemy's attacks on his flanks,
e he made a violent attack on the Allied centre to cut their
es in two. Then he would turn an overwhelming force on
extended left and crush them into pockets among the lakes.

he Allies had a numerical superiority of 22,000, and probably
 thought they had other advantages. But, in fact, Napoleon
two overriding advantages: the Allied lines was completely
sed to view, while Napoleon's was hidden; the French line
more compact and uninterrupted.

 thick, cold mist the Allied attack began about eight o'clock.
oleon listened to the thunder of artillery and the rattle of
ketry and permitted the enemy to become fully committed.
as one of his maxims never to frighten off the enemy before
 could engage their troops to the point of no recall. Just be-
 the fighting began the mist broke over the field and the sun
e brilliantly through. Napoleon took the "Sun of Austerlitz"
 he afterwards called it—as an omen of success.

s the guns opened Soult mounted to ride off to his command
ing in the ravine, where they were quite out of sight.
ult," Napoleon said, "how long will it take your men to reach
ummit of the plateau?"

Twenty minutes, sire," Soult said.

bout this time, in the centre of the line, the two enemy
erors—Alexander and Francis—were climbing the eastern
 of the plateau, which was deserted and apparently open for
 occupation.

Ah! Then we can give them another quarter of an hour,"
 Napoleon, looking at his watch. For another fifteen minutes
French right held while the French centre stood silent, wait-
Then Napoleon waved his arm. . . .

o the blaring music of regimental bands, divisions led by
damme and St Hilaire, spearheading the corps of Soult and
nadotte, went up the Pratzen height at the double and
cked the Russians, right, centre, and left.

he Russians, still busy in their general movement to the left,
 taken completely by surprise. They managed to scramble
 some sort of formation, but French bayonet charges broke
y line they formed, and as early as nine o'clock Napoleon
manded the plateau.

Meanwhile Prince Lichenstein had paraded 82 squadr
of cavalry, and Bagration supported them with many infan
divisions and a strong artillery force opposite the Santon. H
Lannes and Murat fought an independent battle to Napolec
pre-arranged plan.

Facing the Allied might, Lannes had General Caffarel
division on his right and Suchet's division on his left. They w
supported by the guns of the Santon. Two massive columns
cavalry—comprising the divisions of Kellermann (son of
victor of Valmy), Nansouty, Walther, and d'Hautpoul—w
on Caffarelli's right, while some light cavalry was pushed forw
to observe.

Murat gave the Allies no chance to take the initiative. To o
the fight he sent in Kellermann with his light cavalry, and i
brilliant general charged and put to flight the enemy vangua
Uhlans under the Grand Duke Constantine attacked Kellerma
who retired his weaker force through Caffarelli's infantry, wh
musket fire stopped the Uhlans. Kellermann reformed a
charged again. Then the battle really boiled. Murat led seve
charges, taking with him Kellermann, Walther, and Sébasti
all of whom were wounded, the first two seriously.

The French 5th Chasseurs broke a Russian battalion a
captured its standard, a tremendous and encouraging feat
battle in those days. To capture a standard was virtually
destroy a unit. Caffarelli's infantry forced an Austrian battal
to surrender. Seeing this, a regiment of Russian drago
dashed to the rescue. Mistaking them in the smoke for Fre
troops, Murat ordered other French infantry to cease firing.

The Russians were able to break through the French ranks a
to surround Murat himself. Splendid horseman and swordsm
Murat fought his way out of the trap to safety. At this point
Allies went on the offensive, but Murat and Lannes were
really worried. Murat ordered Nansouty to attack with his cui
siers—big men on big horses and armed with long, heavy swo
Nansouty led his men in three deliberate charges, crushing
Russian cavalry back on their infantry, scattering the infan
itself, and taking eight guns.

These charges enabled Caffarelli's division, backed by a d
sion sent by Bernadotte, to cut the centre of Bagration's infan
The Frenchmen drove the larger part of the enemy towa
Pratzen, while the smaller part fought on at the end of the line.

The Allied cavalry, rallying, rode in to support Bagration, w

v found himself facing the bayonets of Suchet's infantry. The
strians and Russians might have had a chance, but they were
-generalled. A brilliantly combined French movement of
goons, cuirassiers, and infantry was too much for the enemy.
bayonet charge by Suchet's men put the finishing touch to the
tle, while a series of rapid light-cavalry attacks completed the
t and drove the enemy survivors towards Austerlitz. On
part of the field alone the Russians and Austrians lost about
0 men killed, 8000 prisoners, 27 cannons, and 2 standards.
llopers took the news to Napoleon.

Napoleon's right was having a hectic time. Davout's 10,000
n—tired after a hard march to get into position—were hold-
30,000 enemy led by Buxhöwden, who had assumed com-
nd of corps led by Doctorof and Kienmayer. That they did
d them was due to their own courage and to the enemy in-
lity to deploy in the narrow passes—which was nothing more
n Napoleon had foreseen.

Despite this advantage the pressure on the French troops was
nense. Soldiers of lesser calibre could not have held the
my. Napoleon, as always, was fully aware of the position,
l he ordered the Imperial Guard and some grenadiers to
eaten the flanks of the massive column attacking Davout. To
ken the enemy thrust further he sent two divisions of Soult's
ps marching to the rear of Buxhöwden's columns.[2]

n every battle there is a crisis. Now, at one o'clock in the
ernoon, Napoleon faced his crisis for Austerlitz. Near Pratzen,
ssian infantry, supported by the Russian Imperial Guard,
de a desperately fierce assault on the divisions led by Van-
nme and St Hilaire.

Napoleon, from his position of vantage, saw the enemy masses
ep on to his own lines. The odds against the French were
at. He knew his troops would hold for a time, but for how long
ore being swamped?

On his right he saw that the Russians were pressing Davout
d and threatening his rear. The artillery roared into such a
scendo that it seemed the Allied flanking movement on the
nch right must succeed. Then, heartened, he saw troops under
roc moving to support Soult and Davout. The right flank would
safe, after all.

Back at the centre repeated attacks by the Russian Chevalier
ards and cuirassiers of the Russian guard, brilliantly led and

[2] Just as Claudius Nero had done at the Metaurus.

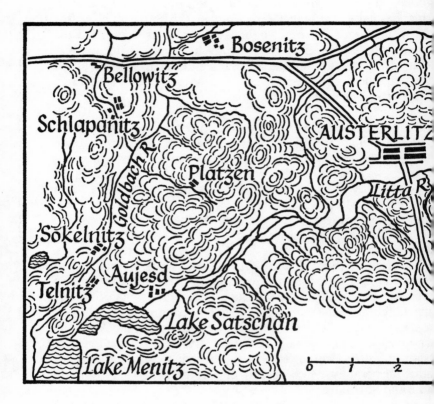

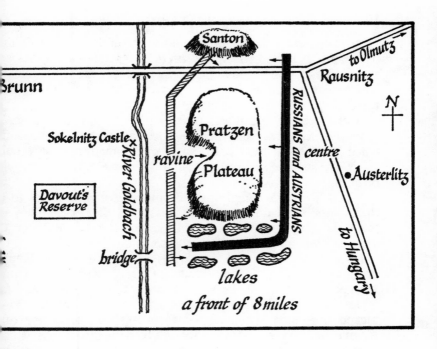

The area shown by the map was well wooded, rough,
rshy, and with wide, shallow lakes; Napoleon made full use of
ground for his own concealment and protection.

Many of Napoleon's officers wondered why he had abandoned
high ground—the Pratzen (or Platzen) plateau. He might
ve given battle on the plateau and repulsed the enemy, but his
ject was not merely to win a battle but to destroy the enemy
ny. He predicted, rightly, that the enemy would expect him to
ht a defensive battle. He intended a vigorous attack. Davout's
ps on the right held the ground between Satschan Lake and
elnitz; Lannes held the other flank, with Murat's horsemen
dy to exploit favourable cavalry country. The Santon was
avily armed with artillery. In the centre was Napoleon's strik-
; force—the corps of Bernadotte and Soult, the Imperial Guard
d the cavalry of the Guard. Napoleon allowed the Austrians
d Russians to commit themselves more and more in their
ack on his right, thus steadily weakening their centre, which
poleon attacked and pierced, thus placing himself on the flank
d rear of the main enemy thrust. The Allied left collapsed under
e attack.

vigorously pushed home, broke and scattered two of Vandamm
battalions. Napoleon saw one of these battalions lose its ea
standard and was bitterly disappointed. These were the men v
had earlier gained such spectacular success. Now they were
rified.

In vain senior and junior officers tried to stop the panic.
mob knocked down and trampled over at least one young off
when he stood in their path. Some of the men, seeing Napol
close by, shouted hoarsely, "*Vive l'Empereur!*", but they k
on going.

When his single remaining aide moved forward to try to s
them Napoleon said contemptuously, "Let them go." They w
the only Frenchmen that day to break ranks, and later tl
general, Vandamme, was inconsolable at the disgrace.

Now Napoleon acted decisively. He sent General Rapp
bring up the cavalry of the Imperial Guard. Rapp brought up
Mamelukes, of which he was Colonel, the *Grenadiers-à-Che*
under General Morland and the Chasseurs of the Guard—
picked horsemen. Then he led them against the flower of
Russian cavalry and drove them back with heavy loss. Russ
horsemen fell or were captured in droves. It was one of the m
bitterly contested cavalry fights in history.

Napoleon's confidence in his Guard cavalry was not *
placed, and eventually General Rapp, a strong, aggressive lea
returned to his emperor and saluted him with bloodstai
sword. "Sire," he said, "we have overthrown and destroyed
Russian Guard and taken their artillery."

"I saw it," Napoleon said. "Gallantly done. But you
wounded." He frowned at the deep sabre cut on Rapp's forehea

"A scratch, sire," the cavalryman said, and returned to
duty.

But General Morland, disdaining death as Napoleon deman
that his cavalry generals should, had found it on the field.
died under Russian sabres at the head of his grenadiers, one
the few senior French leaders to lose his life, though many w
wounded.

Count Apraxin, a young artillery officer captured by
chasseurs, was brought before Napoleon. "I wish I could d
Apraxin cried. "I am dishonoured! I have lost my battery!"

Napoleon had a horse brought for the count. "Be calm, yo
man," he said. "It is no disgrace to be conquered by a Frei
man."

e French were now successful on their centre and left.
y of the enemy, including all the reserves, were fleeing to-
s Austerlitz, harried and hurried on their way by artillery of
mperial Guard. The French artillery was used intelligently
effectively throughout the battle, as well it might be seeing
Napoleon himself was a master gunner.

urat and Lannes had the left completely in hand, and
leon trusted them to bring the battle here to an end. He
Bernadotte, with a large part of the Guard, to finish off the
y who had been driven off Pratzen plateau.

ith the climax of the battle approaching, Napoleon left the
ts to take part in the fight. He led Soult's corps, plus a force
valry, reserve artillery, and infantry remnants in an attack
e rear of the Russo-Austrian force near Telnitz and the lakes.

is hapless force of 30,000 men, still entangled in the defiles,
l itself attacked on three sides. Though tired out from in-
nt, day-long fighting, the men fought on bravely, but their
ion was hopeless and their suffering great. Their only way of
e was across frozen Menitz Lake. Thousands of men rushed
the ice with horses, artillery, and wagons.

e French gave them no respite. Artillery kept up a fire, and
shot fell on the ice and cracked it. With the weight of men,
s, and equipment, the ice soon broke and split into frag-
s. Thousands of Austrian and Russian soldiers fell into the
water, there to drown, though the French pulled many others
fety. It was an appalling spectacle, and it put an end to the
.

the 30,000 men who had gone into action with Buxhöwden
e morning only 2000 escaped. The rest were either dead or
ners.

four o'clock the battle was over and the guns were quiet.
nly disappointment from the French point of view was that
dotte had allowed the whole of the enemy right, which had
defeated by Lannes and Murat, to escape past his front and
towards Hungary. Napoleon was furious about this, for it
unded his maxim that a beaten enemy must be followed up
estroyed to prevent his rallying.

always after a great fight, the battlefield was a ghastly sight,
wounded soldiers suffered dreadfully on the frozen ground.
leon stayed on the field, personally helping some of the
ded. Surgeons and their orderlies were busy, but they could
ope to cope with the vast number of casualties. Working

parties were bringing in the dead and wounded and piling t gear.

As darkness fell on that winter night icy rain and mist d over the field, making it impossible to find all the wounded n Napoleon ordered that strict silence was to be observed, so calls for help could be heard. He himself was on the field v ten o'clock, by which time he had reached a small post-hous Posoritz, where he stayed the night.

Despite their suffering and hunger, the French troops v elated. It was different for the Russians and Austrians. T rout was complete. The Russo-Austrian army lost 12,000 ki and wounded, 30,000 prisoners including 20 generals, 46 s dards, 186 cannon, 400 artillery limbers, and all their wagons baggage. About 25,000 demoralized men survived the c strophe. The French lost 6800 men.

Napoleon's order of the day to his army was brief but suffici "Soldiers, I am content with you."

Legend has it that when William Pitt, Prime Ministe England, heard the news of Austerlitz he had the map of Eur on his wall rolled up so that he could not see it. The ges meant that Napoleon now controlled Europe. Pitt's death, s after, is believed to have been hastened by the shock of Au litz.

But if politicians hated Napoleon, generals strove to emu him. In one way or another he left an indelible stamp that pressed itself deeply on commanders who followed him. Per the most significant aspect of the battle of Austerlitz is that lington used Napoleon's own defensive-offensive tactics to de him at Waterloo.

CHAPTER SIXTEEN

————————◇◆◇————————

Prussian Collapse and
Prussian Reform

BRILLIANT military writer who died two years after Austerlitz, Dietrich von Bülow, said that battles of the future
uld be decided by tirailleur-fighting. Discipline and courage
re merely contributing factors; the mass and quantity of the
nbatants decided the issue. "A general must praise the men
order to make them worthy of praise," he said, echoing
poleon, of whom he was an admirer.

Some leaders did praise their men, but leaders and Govern-
nts forgot them once they were too old or unfit for fighting.
r instance, the only pension granted to the discharged German
eran was a licence to beg publicly.

Another great reformer was Georg von Behrenhorst (1733–
4), a former aide of Frederick. Behrenhorst wrote, in 1797:

The art of war calls for a vaster amount of knowledge and
more inborn talents than any of the other arts, in order to form
a system of mechanics which does not rest upon immutable
laws, but upon the unknown.

Von Behrenhorst saw farther than his contemporaries.

New inventions allow passing advantages, then they become
general, and then the whole thing reduces itself to mere bare
manslaughter, just as it was in the beginning. The art of fight-
ng *en masse*, because it necessarily frustrates itself by its own
development, cannot possibly belong to those steps of progress
which mankind is destined to make.

But the Prussians were slavishly content to follow Frederic[ ]
system, and were flattered, too, that the British had tended to co[ ]
it. Reide, in his *Military Discipline* of 1795, noted:

> A very great change has taken place within the last four [or]
> five years in the discipline of the British Army which is n[ow]
> entirely modelled on that of the Prussian, as established [by]
> Frederick the Great. The utility of that monarch's tactics h[as]
> long been known and in part adapted into our service.

Principles might remain constant, but practice does not, a[nd]
in 1806 Prussia, saturated with militarism, but now only ligh[tly]
veneered with modern military skill, was presumptuous enou[gh]
to challenge Napoleon and the French, although their rece[nt]
victory at Austerlitz had resounded throughout Europe as one [of]
the most brilliant battles in history. History would have wept [at]
the result.

Napoleon expected King Frederick William to retire behi[nd]
the Elbe and dispute its passage until his Russian allies cou[ld]
join him. He was surprised when he heard that the Prussians we[re]
concentrating west of the Elbe; this forward movement defeat[ed]
the Prussians from the beginning, and so completely that t[he]
Prussian army disintegrated.

The French advanced in three great columns into the roc[ky]
valleys that led from Franconia into Saxony—an army, when t[he]
cavalry and artillery of the Guard joined it, of 186,000 men, l[ed]
by martial masters—men like Davout, Murat, Ney, Lann[e]
Augereau, Bernadotte, and Lefebvre.

The Prussians changed plans repeatedly, exposed their mag[a]
zines, left their flanks invitingly open, and made many march[es]
by crossroads and byways in country for which the Prussi[an]
staff had not a single map. After many skirmishes came t[he]
historic clash at Jena.

Napoleon, who never made the mistake of underrating [an]
enemy—even the Prussians of 1806—addressed Lannes' cor[ps]
"Soldiers," he said, "the Prussian Army is turned as t[he]
Austrian was a year ago at Ulm.... Fear not its renown[ed]
cavalry; oppose to their charges firm squares and the bayonet."

In a terrible charge Murat and his cavalry arrived and swe[pt]
through the Prussians in a whirlwind of slaughter. No battle c[an]
show carnage more merciless and horrible than that surge of t[he]
heavy horsemen among the flying Prussians after Jena. Th[ey]
spared nothing in their path, and every one of those 15,000 lo[st]

ds was red with blood from point to hilt. And all the while French bandsmen played, while Prussians in their many urful uniforms scrambled for brief safety.

na is the classical pursuit of military history, and was strongly niscent of Alexander's pursuit of Darius after the battle of ela in 331 B.C. The only other pursuits which approach Jena fectiveness are Waterloo; Tel-el-Kebir, 1882; the final offen- in Palestine, 1918; the British pursuit of the Italians in North ca, 1940.

it Jena, sanguinary though it was, was not the major battle e campaign, even if it is the best remembered. Another action, ht near Auerstädt at the same time, broke up the main body russians and covered Marshal Davout with glory.

ith 28,750 men to face at least 66,000 Prussians, Davout set it his task with such characteristic attention to detail that he :ted 10,000 casualties on the Prussians, captured 3000 men 115 guns, but without numerical superiority could not bring it the chaos Murat had inflicted at Jena. The Prussian war hine was systematically broken.

it mistakes can drive home a lesson, and the long-term result ie disaster was that Prussia and Germany were never again epared for war. Their soldiers were never caught unready command nor their soldiers unfitted for combat. The German ies of 1813, of 1870, 1914, and 1939, and of today were the rings of the remaking of Prussia after the disasters of Jena Auerstädt.

ederick William III, more mortified than any of his subjects, d on Gerhard Johann David von Scharnhorst to reorganize Prussian Army. The creator of the new German military idea the pupil of an exceptional man, Count William, Prince of umburg-Lippe. As a British mercenary he had been made l-Marshal of Portugal, but the rôle of a British mercenary did suit him, so he returned to his own country. There he had an icial island built in the Steinhuder Lake and constructed a ess on it, which he called Wilhelmstein. In this fortress he ed his subjects and thought so much about the art of war that ormed a small military school there. This first military emy of modern times never took more than twelve pupils, were admitted without regard to birth or means. The Prince elf examined every candidate as to his suitability. In con- to other military schools, the boys there were not only ated into the secrets of one kind of fighting, but into military

matters and theory in general. Scharnhorst was accepted as
pupil in 1773 and became the prince's favourite student. Af
the death of his prince, Scharnhorst went into Hanoverian serv
as an ensign and became a remarkable artillery captain. (
returning from his first war he made the admission: "I ha
learnt nothing in this war. As a matter of fact no-one who h
systematically studied military science can learn much in war."

Scharnhorst, Gneisenau, and others—including Scharnhors
favourite pupil, Clausewitz—were men in the mould of Frederi
the Great. They realized that Prussia had to be reforged, and
do this they had to militarize the Prussian people. They first of
inspired the school-teachers of the country; the school-teache
from primary school to university, went to work with a will
the minds and emotions of the children and young people. Th
were infected with nationalism, filled with militaristic fervour a
a belief in 'Prussia's destiny'.

Scharnhorst pleaded for an increase of the army and a regu
militia. He wanted a special propaganda war newspaper to stim
late and arouse the nation and its soldiers.[1] He objected to t
prevalent idea that the talent of the general was the sole decidi
factor. A resolute nation could win even under mediocre leaders
if the nation had strength of will and high character.

"When the necessity of a war is once recognized by a natic
nothing further is needed than the resolution of the leader
conquer or die," he wrote, echoing the Spartans, the Athenia:
and the Romans.

After Jena, with so many officers failing and falling, Gneisen
so stood out as steady and competent that he was given grea
responsibility. In the following spring he was sent to take over o
of the few points which still held out behind Napoleon's lines
the little fortress of Kolberg on the sea-coast of Pomerania. F
brilliant defence of the place until the armistice won him uniq
popularity throughout the country.

Scharnhorst himself, Gneisenau, Clausewitz, Grolman, a
Boyen—both majors—were the inner circle of the reformers, a
like that of all reformers their way was hard.

Scharnhorst believed that the French had survived from a
triumphed against the attacks launched against them becau

[1] In later times propaganda war newspapers and magazines were comm
place in Prussia and Germany. In 1939–45 one of the most successful v
Signal, published in many foreign languages—including English—for circt
tion in the Channel Islands.

ey were able to conduct the war with the resources of the
le nation and in the last resort to sacrifice literally everything
e continuation of the struggle ".

it in France the reform had come from below. In Prussia it
to come from above, and the reformers' task was much more
iidable and complex. One cardinal principle of the new
sian system was localization. Each army corps was a little
y complete in infantry, cavalry, and artillery, recruited and
ianently stationed in a particular province. Each regiment
raised in and permanently connected with a town or group of
ges. Not that this adaptation of the old tribal system to
ern war was anything new, but the Prussians intensified it.
ade mobilization a simple business in the case of reservists.

:yond doubt, the most drastic, far-reaching, controversial,
unpopular edict was that comfort in war had to end. This
:y, copied from the French, foreshadowed the German Army
he future—indeed of all future armies—but it furiously
red Prussian officers at the time.

he reformers performed another major service to military
ency. They restored the artillery and engineers to their
:ful place of honour, for Scharnhorst and his colleagues were
interested in inter-service rivalries. They wanted to win any
in which Prussia might engage.

harnhorst also cleared out the scientific part of the secrecy
rtillery. "With the single exception of theology," he said,
re is no study which is so full of prejudices as artillery." He
ded schools for training artillery NCOs and ensigns and
ted the first artillery testing board. Every technical innovation
to be submitted to this board so that no general could dis-
rd it merely because it was new or inconvenient to him.

1942 a German writer (in *Signal*) said that Frederick's and
rnhorst's ideas have continued to live until our own day,
that no fundamental change has taken place in the sphere of
lery tactics since Frederick the Great. Only, the principles have
developed down to the last detail.

ne of Scharnhorst's greatest deeds was that he relieved sub-
nate commanders of their fear of assuming the responsibility
aking action. Another was to build up behind Napoleon's
a new secret army. Also, he had created an institution which,
mously enlarged, carried on the military school of Steinhuder
e in the Prussian Army. His creation was called the Great
eral Staff. The name was to be found elsewhere, but the

thing itself was not. In most other countries the 'general sta
was merely the association of individual army leaders plus so
additional senior officers too old for field commands. In contr
to this the Prussian creation was an independent organizati
with two great tasks—the pre-preparation for war and the tra
ing of a suitable younger generation of officers for the fut
General Staff.

In the academy and in the General Staff the officers once m
learned Hannibal's and Frederick's idea of destruction. Offic
were told—as Hitler was to tell them much later—that the histc
of the art of war proved that only those army leaders who h
trained and intelligent troops at their disposal (troops, that
whose training and good sense enabled them to distrust insti
on the field of battle) had been able to apply the idea of destr
tion. Instinct drove people together on a battlefield into one gr
mass, but logic kept them apart and made them obey the co
mands of the leaders.

Scharnhorst died from wounds received in the battle of Lütz
1813, but Gneisenau lived on to become the chief director
Prussian field strategy during these campaigns and during tl
of Waterloo, even though Blücher was the Prussian commander
the field. Clausewitz served on the staff of an army corps dur
this campaign.

Gneisenau carried on and perpetuated Scharnhorst's work
reorganization, while Clausewitz—an experienced practi
soldier and a voracious reader of military history—gave
Prussian Army, in his writings, a practical theory of war on wh
it acted for the next century. No military writer has been so deif
as has Clausewitz—and far beyond the borders of his o
country, for he has been translated into at least thirty languages.

CHAPTER SEVENTEEN

---◇◆◇---

Clausewitz, High Priest of
War; Wellington

RUSSIAN officers swore by Clausewitz's work. It was a point
of honour among them to insist that he was the best and most
knowledgeable writer on war; no officer would have dared to
differ from an opinion expressed by Clausewitz.

Clausewitz ranked the military profession supreme over all. It
was, he said, an intellectually determined activity of men. His
description of an army imbued with soldierly spirit is especially
illuminating, for in it we see the German Army of the future.

An army which retains its accustomed order under the most
devastating fire, which is never overcome by fear and fights for
every foot of the ground, which even in the chaos of defeat does
not lose its discipline or the respect for and confidence in its
leaders, an army which regards every effort as a means towards victory and not as a curse on its banners, which is
reminded of all these duties and virtues by the short catechism
of one single conception, the honour of its weapons—such an
army is imbued with the soldierly spirit.

Clausewitz's notes—for that is all they were—were published
in 1832 in book form, the year after his death.[1] Some of these notes
had been delivered as lectures or had been separately published before this, but the publication of them in book form—a 1000-page

---

[1] About the same time the Archduke Charles of Austria wrote a series of
military essays which were greatly admired and closely read by military
students of the last century.

tome under the title *On War*—crystallized his whole ma:
philosophy, and as a philosophy on war it remains unrivalled.

Thousands of German officers of all ranks appear almos
have made decisions, paramount and petty, with a copy
Clausewitz's book in their hands. It was largely his teaching wl
led Prussia and Germany, as a unity, into preparation for
conditional and absolute war and the determination to put
preparation into effect.

Whole generations of Prussian, German, and Austrian sold
were brought up on his book, and there were times when Cla
witz's ideas were used by other nations against the Germans,
times when these nations, by over-rigid adherence to Clausew
teachings, defeated themselves.

"War belongs to the province of social life," Clausewitz said.

State policy is the womb in which war is developed, in w
its outlines lie hidden in a rudimentary state, like the qual
of living creatures in their germs. . . .

War is the province of physical exertion and suffering
certain strength of body and mind is required, which prod
indifference to them. With these qualifications, under
guidance of simply a sound understanding, a man is a pr
instrument of war. If we go further in the demands which
makes on its votaries, then we find the powers of the un
standing predominating. War is the province of uncertai
three-fourths of those things upon which action in war mus
calculated are hidden more or less in the clouds of acute
certainty. Here above all a fine and penetrating mind is ne
sary. An average intellect may, at one time, perhaps hit u
this truth by accident; an extraordinary courage, at anot
may compensate for the lack of this tact; but in the majorit
cases the average result will always bring to light the defic
understanding. . . .

As long as his men, full of high courage, fight with zeal
spirit, it is seldom necessary for the Chief to show great en
or purpose in the pursuit of his object. But as soon as difficu
arise—and that must always be when great results are at s
—then things no longer move on by themselves like a v
oiled machine. The machine itself begins to offer resista
and to overcome this the commander must have great forc
will. . . .

The military virtue of an army is one of the most impor
moral powers in war, and where it is wanting we either se
place supplied by one of the others, such as the great su
ority of generalship or popular enthusiasm, or we find

:sults not commensurate with the efforts made ... the astonish-
ig successes of generals and their greatness in situations of
xtreme difficulty were only possible with armies possessing
ais virtue. This spirit can be generated from only two sources
nd only by these two conjointly. The first is a succession of
ampaigns and great victories; the other is an activity of the
Army carried sometimes to its highest pitch. Only by these does
ae soldier learn to know his powers. The more a general is in
he habit of demanding from his troops, the surer he will be
hat his demands will be answered.[2] The soldier is as proud of
vercoming toil as he is of surmounting danger. ...

We do not ask, how much does the resistance which the
vhole nation in arms is capable of making, cost that nation?
3ut we ask, what is the effect which such a resistance can pro-
luce?

War is nothing but a continuation of political intercourse,
vith a mixture of other means.... Is not war merely another
ind of writing and language for political thoughts?—It has
ertainly a grammar of its own, but its logic is not peculiar to
tself. ... In one word, the Art of War in its highest point of
iew is policy, but, no doubt, a policy which fights battles
nstead of writing notes. According to this view, to leave a
;reat military enterprise, or the plan for one, to a purely mili-
ary judgment and decision is a destinction which cannot be
.llowed, and is even prejudicial. ...

There is no human affair which stands so constantly and so
;enerally in close connection with chance as War. But to-
;ether with chance, the accidental, and along with it good luck,
)ccupies a great place in war. If we take a look at the sub-
ective nature of war ... it will appear to us still more like a
;ame. Primarily the element in which the operations of war
re carried on is danger. But which of all the moral qualities is
irst in danger? Courage. Now certainly courage is quite com-
)atible with prudent calculation, but still they are things of
quite a different kind, essentially different qualities of the mind.
.. From the outset there is a play of possibilities, probabilities,
;ood and bad luck, which spreads about with all the coarse and
ine threads of its web, and makes War of all branches of
auman activity the most like a gambling game.

While Clausewitz was evolving his philosophy, while Prussian
litarism had been undergoing a rethinking and Europe was
iding the knee to Napoleon, British arms were becoming active

History bears this out time and time again, for nearly all great generals have
n 'great demanders'.

in Iberia. Two commanders stood out here—John Moore
Wellington. Moore, a dedicated soldier, would have achie
great deeds had he lived. Carola Oman, one of his biograph
says that Moore had practically no fiction in his library. Mos
his books were connected with arms, and most were by foreig
—von Ehwald, Tielke, Sontag, de Rottenburg. He complai
of the lack of good books by British military men. Caesar
the "prime object of his admiration as a soldier".

Late in 1808 Napoleon, in Spain to plan the country's subj
tion, heard that the commander now pitted against him
Moore. "Moore is now the only general worthy to contend v
me," he said. "I shall move against him in person."

This was a remarkable compliment, for though Napo
rarely made the mistake of underestimating an opponent
equally rarely praised them and sometimes derided them, as
did Wellington. It is interesting that Napoleon and Moore v
such keen students of history. In appalling winter conditi
Moore was forced to retreat to Corunna, where he died
wounds.

From the British point of view the Peninsula War was an
standing example of enterprising, patient strategy—a policy ai
at wearing out the enemy rather than knocking him out. I
Turenne in 1675, Wellington in his first campaign broke up
opposition before it had chance to form. But Wellington
capable of a knock-out punch when the opportunity occurred.
showed great audacity in the Vimiero and Talavera campai
and in the storming of Ciudad Rodrigo and Badajoz.

Wellington was a fine tactician and an accurate judge of
materials he had to work with. He realized that his predecess
had given him a steady, solid army. Turenne-like, to protect
men and mystify his enemy he usually made full use of cover
ground—in fact, in his time, he was outstanding for this.
developed defensive-offensive tactics—that is, he induced
enemy to attack and then attacked him in return. His tac
demanded artillery dispersion, whereas Napoleon favoured c
centration.[3]

His greatest strength was that as far as humanly possible
command was all-embracing and supreme. He once said, ""

[3] Napoleon showed that at times sheer offensive power could succeed w
surprise or mobility might fail. At Friedland, in 1807, he used new arti
tactics—massed gunfire at a selected point, a sort of break-through policy
favoured by the Germans.

reason why I succeeded ... is because I was always on the
—I saw everything, and did everything myself." In essence
ington's command was Napoleonic.

s campaigns in Iberia cannot concern us here, for they added
to leadership though they added much to the reputation of
British soldier. Wellington's victories in Spain did not, in any
cause the French collapse. The continuous strain of the
less guerrilla warfare was more wearing on the French,
damaging to their morale, and caused more casualties and
s of equipment, weapons, and stores than their intermittent
t in battles. Wellington's forces were really only a stra-
detachment from the forces in Europe.

ellington's emotional impact on the British people was
nous, and his place in history is safe. Significantly, his
an campaigns are still a set subject for British Staff College
nts.

1814 Wellington brought his Peninsula campaigns to a close
he won Toulouse, and while not seeking to detract from the
merits which sustained him through so much arduous cam-
ing I think it is fair to say that the British Army won the
battles which had brought Wellington from Madrid across
yrenees into France.

is equally true to say, conversely, that Napoleon rather than
army won the astonishing series of French victories in the
aign of 1814. Vastly outnumbered by his enemies now con-
ng on France, Napoleon realized that he could not expect to
a military decision, so he aimed to dislocate the co-operation
en the Allied armies, and he exploited mobility more re-
ably than ever. He inflicted a series of defeats against them,
n five occasions attacked the enemy in the rear.

s strategy and tactical handling of his army were never more
ant. With small, poorly equipped forces he defeated Blücher,
k, and Sacken in turn. His victories at La Fothière,
mirail, Champaubert, Étoges, and Craonne were remark-
But while he fought at one point the Allies continued to
h and in the end their 300,000 men were too much for his
0, and finally Blücher defeated Napoleon at Laon.

terloo cannot find a place in this book, for, though
leon, Wellington, Blücher, Ney, Grouchy, Soult, Van-
e, d'Erlon, Kellermann, and others were present, the battle
ot distinguished by any brilliance of manoeuvre. Napoleon
oo much to fortune, and Fate caught up with him, but he

nearly mastered it, despite more setbacks—largely caused
subordinates—than most commanders have ever faced in a bat

Of the several reasons for Napoleon's failure at Waterloo
of the most important was the incompetence of Ney and Gro
—but then he himself had selected them for high commar
think it very likely that the lesson to be deduced—choose
fully those sub-commanders who are to have independenc
action—was not lost on succeeding great captains. Napo
also confounded one of his own maxims concerning conce
tion of forces in that he could have collected as many as 36
additional soldiers from secondary theatres; such added stre
could easily have decided the issue in his favour, especiall
June 14th, four days before Waterloo.

Waterloo was a particularly bloody combat, and it ma
the end of an epoch. Wellington's main triumph was that
defensive-offensive method was proved sound. Later Wellin
himself put the battle in true military perspective. Napoleor
said, "just moved off in the old style"—that is, in columns—
was "driven off in the old style"—by men in line. Wellin
had made his men into a precise firing body, and his tactics
typically English, his inheritance from the great comman
who had gone before him.

On the night of the battle Wellington said to Lord Fit
"I have never fought such a battle and I trust I shall never
such another." To his brother he wrote, "In all my life I
not experienced such anxiety for I must confess I have neve
fore been so close to defeat."[4]

With Napoleon fading from the scene as a great command
is particularly apposite at this point to quote from the elev
edition of the *Encyclopaedia Britannica*, 1910, which states
equivocally that

Among all the great captains of history Cromwell alone ca
compared to Napoleon. Both in their powers of organiz
and the mastery of the tactical potentialities of the weapo
their day were immeasurably ahead of their times, and
also understood to the full the strategic art of binding an
straining the independent will power of their opponents, a
of which Marlborough and Frederick, Wellington, Lee
Moltke do not seem ever even to have grasped the fringe.

[4] It is ironical to reflect that in 1799 Napoleon disbanded the French Ba
Corps, despite the valuable service it had rendered in its brief life of five
In 1815 it could well have saved him with its observation of Allied moveme

d, remember, Napoleon himself urged students of arms to
dy Cromwell and actually likened himself to Cromwell. How
ch of Cromwell's methods did he himself adapt for his own?

After 1815 the rest of the first half of the nineteenth century
s more important for military and quasi-military inventions
n for great battles or great generalship. In many countries
tish soldiers fought fierce, poorly publicized minor battles and
lured the rigours of long campaigns in terrible climates. True
their history, nearly always unruffled, they won most of
ir battles—sometimes in spite of their generals, who in this
: were among the most wooden-headed commanders in all
tory.

t is always possible to recognize a potential aggressor and to
etell a war if one looks far enough ahead. But in 1833 when
issians became the first to grasp the supreme potential im-
rtance of the railway in war nobody in Europe took any notice.
1833 F. W. Hakort wrote that a railway between Cologne and
nden and another between Mainz and Wesel would be of great
portance in defence of the Rhineland. C. E. Ponitz urged
ieral railway construction to protect Prussia against France,
stria, and Russia. Friedrich List pointed out that railways
ild raise Prussia into a very powerful state, and in that year,
33, before a single rail had been laid, he planned a network of
lways for Germany which is substantially that of today.
russia ", List wrote,

ould be made into a defensive bastion in the heart of Europe.
Speed of mobilization, the rapidity with which troops could be
noved from the centre of the country to the borders and the
other obvious advantages of interior lines of transport would
e of greater relative advantage to Germany than to any other
European country.

While Germany planned, Britain and other countries plodded
ng towards the spectacularly stupid debacle of the Crimean
r—a display of soldierly courage at its best and of leadership
its worst. The armies of Europe were rigidly professional at
s time, and most of them—the French Army was the only
able exception—were wedded to a pathetic directness which
s considered soldierly. The charge of the Light Brigade was a
nptom of this directness. Fortunately for the Allies, the
ssians were also extremely direct and had no more intelligent
tics than to march masses of men straight into cannon- and
sket-fire.

The war proved once again that the British line—the 'thin r
line' in this case—could still beat the column formation of
enemies and that British fire discipline was exemplary. About t
only tribute that can be paid to anybody's leadership is to say tl
the French attack on the Malakoff was better conceived and bet
executed than the British one on the Redan. I do not intend to
a party to any attempt to immortalize the names of any of t
inept generals who commanded during the war.

CHAPTER EIGHTEEN

The Battle of Solferino, 1859

FRED VAGTS in his *A History of Militarism* says: "On the whole the time following the Restoration of 1815 and closing with the Great War of 1914 was one of relative quiet. Be-n Waterloo and Marne stretched a dull period of tran-ity."

his is one of the most extraordinary statements ever made by istorian. This "dull period of tranquillity" saw these major —the Crimean, American Civil, Franco-Austrian, Prusso-trian, Franco-Prussian, Russo-Turkish, Spanish-American, ·, Russo-Japanese Wars. The host of minor wars—and not ybody would agree that all these *were* minor wars—include: Kaffir Wars; the Maori Wars; the Kandyan (Ceylon) War; 3urmese Wars; the Afghan Wars; three Chinese Wars; the Sikh s; the Austro-Sardinian War; the Indian Mutiny; the Ashanti s; the Egyptian and Sudan Wars; the Servo-Bulgarian War; Prusso-Danish War; the Sino-Japanese War; the Greco-:ish War; the Chilean War; the Boxer Rebellion; the Turco-an War; the Balkan War. I could list hundreds of actions h could be classed as battles. *A time of relative quiet, a ɔd of tranquillity!* How could this possibly be so in the great ury of empire-consolidating and of intense nationalism?

ne of the greatest, most significant, and most interesting es of the century was that of Solferino in 1859, fought be-n the French and the Austrians. Sanguinary, tragic, distress-violent, Solferino has been strangely neglected in military ies, perhaps because it is lost in time between the Crimean

War and the American Civil War, both of which have tended
push it out of sight.

Napoleon Bonaparte had been dead thirty-seven years wl
Solferino was fought, but he won the battle as assuredly as if
and not his nephew—Louis Napoleon—had been in comma
This requires some explanation and modification, and we v
find it in an account of the battle.

Since the fall of the Roman Empire there had never beer
time when Italy could be called a nation any more than a sta
of timber could be called a ship. This was true even in the days
the medieval magnificence of the city-states of Venice, Gen
Milan, Florence, Pisa, and Rome. But after that period It
became a field for intriguing dynasties and the wars of jeal
nations.

Napoleon—'the Corsican tyrant' many Italians called hin
turned out to be a counter-irritant and paradoxically a cleans
one. For a while at least Italy was rid of the Hapsburgs and
Bourbons, had the political divisions of the country reduced
three, and saw justice administered fairly and taxation app
tioned equitably. More than this, the Napoleonic occupat
gave the Italians a new consciousness of themselves as a race.

After 1815 the cruel, corrupt, and crazy princes climbed ba
on to their thrones, and the map was remade into the same
patchwork—with the difference that the spirit of freedom was
the air. After 1848 the Austrians came back to Italy and w
guilty of atrocities against the independent-minded Italians.
man found even with a rusty nail—"A potential weapon"—v
shot.

The Italians hoped for help from France, but Napoleon refu
it until the attempt on his life by the Italian Orsini in Paris
January 1858. The Emperor and Empress were virtually
touched, but 8 people were killed and 156 wounded by Orsii
bombs. Napoleon, often the target of would-be assassins, n
decided to unite with Italy against Austria, at least stron
enough to annul the hate of every assassin in Italy.

On New Year's Day 1859 Napoleon told the Austrian a
bassador, "I regret that our relations with your Government
not so good as they have been hitherto." In the diploma
language of the day this was tantamount to a declaration of w
but by tortuous diplomacy the Italian statesman Cavour indu
Austria to make the formal declaration of war—in April 1859.

Napoleon arrived in Genoa on May 12th to take command

own army, the Sardinian Army, and that of Piedmont, the
dom of his ally, King Victor Emmanuel. Napoleon Bonaparte
self had never had such a rapturous welcome; Genoa was
with delight and colour as decoratively uniformed French
ps poured into the city, their élan high and lusting for action,
d of the world's acknowledgment of them as the finest troops
xistence. Most of them professionals, they welcomed a return
he first of Napoleon's battlegrounds. The stately grenadiers
he Imperial Guard, the infantry élite of France, fresh from
luxurious quarters in Paris, roughed it on the dry bed of a
—and exalted in it. Napoleon had revived for them the
orm of the Old Guard of his uncle—huge bearskins, dark
coatees, white breeches, and gaiters.

om Algeria were hussars in light-blue tunics and baggy red
sers strapped over the foot. Algerian sharpshooters—or
:os, as they were called—were present in their fantastic uni-
of jacket and baggy knickerbockers of light blue, yellow
ngs, red sashes, and turbans. Indifferent to minor punish-
ts, death was the only sentence the Turcos respected, and even
ing-party had little terror for them. Slouching, irresponsible,
equally colourful Zouaves brought with them many hundreds
ets—monkeys, parrots, and dogs—a menagerie for each
alion. Most of the Zouaves were French, not African as
rally believed.

he Bersaglieri were the most picturesque men in the Pied-
tese Army—and some of the toughest soldiers of their time.
t men, selected for their strength, depth of chest, and agility,
were trained commando-style to make forced marches, to
rivers in full equipment, and to scale mountains impassable
dinary infantry. The idols of Italy in 1859, they wore a green
orm with a large round hat, pulled down over the right ear
with a plume of cock's feathers down the back.

o secret was made about the troop assemblies, but the
dreds of guns landed in Genoa were closely guarded, for
were new rifled guns, and the French were sensitive about
cy. As fast as possible the troops were pushed up to Pied-
t, which had already been invaded by the Austrians. At one
there was panic in case the Austrians reached Turin before
French could arrive, but rapid marching by the French over
Alpine passes and the procrastination of the Austrians com-
d to save Victor Emmanuel's capital.

ight days after Napoleon landed in Italy the first of a series

of battles was fought. At Montebello and at Palestro the Al|
armies beat the Austrians, who made a gallant but also unsucc
ful stand at Magenta. Then they retreated slowly to a str
position east of the Mincio river, their front covered by the ri
and their flanks guarded by forts at Mantua and Peschiera
Lake Garda.

The Allied armies, hampered by lack of transport—
Austrians had commandeered most of it—followed the Austri
and on June 23rd camped on both banks of the Chiese ri
fifteen miles west of the Mincio. At two that morning they
sumed their march, for Napoleon had been told that the Austri
were in positions east of the Mincio. In fact, they had recros
the river and by nightfall on the 23rd the leading Austr
columns were occupying ground on which the French had be
ordered to camp on the evening of the 24th. The Austr
Emperor, Francis Joseph, had planned to attack the Allies w
they were crossing the Chiese, but his information was as faulty
that of Napoleon.

The two armies were marching towards each other, their co
manders expecting battle in three or four days' time. In fact, t
were within hours of contact. The situation was grimly piqu
The Allies had 150,000 men and 400 guns; the Austrians 175,(
men and 500 guns. These two massive forces were moving in
dark along every road of a 12½-mile front.

The first touch of the encounter occurred when a detachm
of French cavalry saw, but were not alarmed by, a large hus
watching by the roadside. The horseman disappeared mom
tarily, jumped a ditch into the road, and charged the Fre
officer in command, sabre-slashing him twice. A volley from
French detachment brought the hussar down, and echoing i
the hills was the signal that the two armies had met. It was
electric moment.

This, then, was to be an encounter battle—a battle fought w
out a premeditated plan, without efficient reconnaissance, w
out proper dispositions. The French had cavalry forward, t
had pushed out scouts, they even made balloon ascents on
23rd, but nobody reported anything that might indicate a coun
offensive or an attack. This would never have happened
Bonaparte: he would have had his cavalry screen ranging fo
fifty, even a hundred miles ahead and on his flanks.

There is an odd notion that an encounter battle, becaus
nearly always devolves into a 'soldiers' battle', cannot illustr

eralship. On the contrary, an encounter battle by its very
ure challenges the training, discipline, and control of every
n involved, as well as command and response to command.
h a battle shows up an army in its true colours, for it then
st fall back on its moral reserves. The moral reserves of the
nch Army of 1859 were Napoleonic, and though Napoleon
was no great captain—he was, for instance, a dislodger of
mies rather than a destroyer—that day he showed signs of
poleonic skill and method.

though neither the Allies nor the Austrians had known a
tle was so imminent, many civilian inhabitants sensed it. Sol-
no, a natural battleground, had been the scene of many earlier
ts, and the ground-drum of hundreds of thousands of boots
. hooves and the rolling of guns and wagons spread ominously
r the still countryside. Experienced civilians packed a few
ntials and quickly headed south; others packed more than they
ld carry and ran in any direction—often into trouble. The
rly, the disabled, and many others stayed in their homes—
some died there.

Many villagers hid in cellars, vaults, wells, and even in trees,
ing there for twenty hours or more, without light or food,
il they could struggle out to gape at the death and devasta-
.

Austrian staff organization at this time was inferior to that of
French. The whole force was under the Emperor with his own
f, while the First Army, under Field-Marshal Count Wimp-
, and the Second Army, under General Count Schlick, a
alry general seventy years old, also had their own separate
fs.

he arrangement produced nothing but chaos. Imperial head-
rters still issued voluminous detailed orders for each corps,
the intervening army staffs, far from simplifying orders or
wing any initiative, succeeded only in inflicting further delays.
direction of several armies is only feasible when general
ctives take the place of orders; the French had long realized
, just as the Prussians were realizing it.

But all the necessary conditions for working such a system—
formity of training, methods, and doctrine, abstention from
rference in details by the supreme command—were lacking
he Austrian Army of 1859.

Nevertheless, Francis Joseph had made some salutary changes
administration, notably an order to the infantry to send their

heavy equipment and parade full-dress to the fortresses; greatly lightened the overburdened infantryman.

Despite the French superiority in organization the Austr were the first to react to the battle contact—largely bec they had more favourable terrain—and early on the mornin the 24th they occupied every vantage-point between Pozzole Solferino, Cavriana, and Guidizzolo. Their formidable arti spiked a line of low hills to form the centre of a front more twelve miles long. From their vantage-points on the hills Austrians swept the French with shells, case-shot, and gr shot. Dirt and dust mingled with the fumes of smoking guns shells.

The hill of Solferino, the key to the position, was a formid stronghold. It stood then—as it does now—at the head of a va network, so steep that the roads along them are locally kn as the Steps of Solferino. On the dividing spurs were strong s buildings, a church, a convent, a high-walled cemetery, an feudal tower—all commanding the approaches to the har The houses, built on terraced gardens, rose tier above tier or slope. Early in the day war arrived in Solferino, with the Austr occupying the place in force. It became a nest of minia fortresses which would have to be breached by cannon or ta by escalade. But, strong though it was, it had a grave tac disadvantage—the reverse side of the hill was so steep th could be descended by only one winding path.

If General Schlick, commanding at this point, had stu Napoleon's tactics at Austerlitz he would have allowed the Fr to occupy Solferino and other heights and would then have she them mercilessly from even higher flanking hills. As things tu out, this is what the French did to the Austrians.

Away from the hills spread the plain of Médole, with long of poplars marking the roads and with solid farmhouses stan like islands in a sea of vines, mulberry-trees, and standing c The plain was wonderful cavalry country, and in this arm Austrians excelled, but during the day they made no g charges, for one cavalry leader, Lauingen, panicked and with his splendid division from the field before the battle began.

The day was warm even before sunrise, giving promise of g heat later. The Austrians had been marching all night; the Fr had been on the move since before daybreak and had had not but coffee. Every man involved must have known as the sun c up that some real soldiering would be done that day.

Because of the length of the front we shall need to describe the
ttle sectionally.

Quite early the vanguard of Niel's corps, the Fourth met a
ong force of Austrian cavalry in front of Médole, but after a
rmish Niel drove them off and stormed Médole. He received a
ssage that MacMahon intended to move left to aid d'Hilliers,
o was in trouble to the north, and that the Austrians were
ninating every height. Would Niel also turn left to avoid caus-
a gap? Niel agreed, provided Canrobert, commanding the
ird Corps on the extreme right, guaranteed his flank. But Can-
bert was unable to assist Niel until late in the afternoon, for
poleon had ordered him to watch for 25,000 Austrians who
re said to be threatening the French right from Mantua. The
strians did not appear, but Canrobert was paralysed until
.M., and until then took no part in the battle. It was a major
torical lesson in the evils of faulty reconnaissance.

Niel found out that Wimpffen had brigades on all roads leading
Guidizzolo, and a whole division was making for the large
mhouse on Casa Nuova, about a mile out of Guidizzolo. This
m was surrounded by ditches, walls, hedges, and trees, its out-
ldings gave flanking fire, and Austrian engineers had improved
se natural advantages into a major strong-point.

Niel concentrated his 42 guns on the farm, but could make no
pression, and by noon, with fresh Austrians advancing, he
ew that only determined assault could take the place. After
avy shelling he unleashed his infantry, and in fierce hand-to-
nd fighting they took the farm, smashing down barricades and
ors and hunting Austrians from room to room. A detachment
engineers was put to work to loophole the walls facing the
strians, and the 6th Chasseurs were ordered in as a garrison to
ld or die.

Wimpffen's First Army made several counter-attacks on the
m and on Robecco—a hamlet captured by Niel south of the
mhouse—but despite great gallantry the Austrians could
t retake the positions. Still, the French suffered severely. One
ttalion, surrounded by Austrians, was retiring when the ensign
rrying the eagle was mortally wounded; an elderly sergeant
cked up the standard, but a shell took off his head; a captain
abbed the pole, but a shot smashed both him and the standard.
her men died to save the eagle, which after the battle was
nd under a mound of dead.

By modern standards the very carrying of a provocative target

during battle is suicidal enough, let alone certain-death atte
to save it, but the days of close-quarter fighting, though fad
were still alive, and the eagle served as a rallying point. More
this, the French Army of 1859 was still imbued with Napole
fervour about regimental eagles.

When the action started field hospitals were set up in fa
houses, convents, and churches, and sometimes even under t
A prominent black flag in those days marked the location of
aid posts or field ambulances, and both sides generally respe
them. Officers were always treated first, then non-commissio
officers, and finally privates. The doctors had no rest.
French surgeons had so many amputations and dressing
attend to that they fainted. Another became so exhausted
two soldiers had to steady his arms while he operated.

The canteen women moved about the field under enemy
and were often wounded as they went among the wounded me
give them water.

Early in the afternoon Niel's position was critical; his men
worn out with exertion, hunger, and heat, and his formations
broken and confused. Napoleon had filled the gap between
left and MacMahon's right with the cavalry of the Guard and
hussar regiments, which were ordered to charge so as to give
breathing-space. The charge was so spectacular and succes
that Niel restored order and even moved seven battalions aga
Guidizzolo. But this was too ambitious, and his men were be
back by withering fire.

MacMahon, meanwhile, had been forced to remain on
defensive facing Cassiano, and for several hours the fighting
his sector was confined to an artillery duel. To do Napo
justice, he had firmly grasped his uncle's idea that artillery
to be effective must be overwhelming and concentrated un
the direction of one commander. The French grouped their a
lery in masses; the Austrians fought their batteries independer
with the result that a single Austrian battery was in action aga
24 of the new French rifled guns. To distract the French g
ners and to enable the battery to withdraw, some Aust
horse-artillery batteries, supported by cavalry, made a demons
tion.

But their batteries came into action singly, and at 1700 ya
the French opened fire on the first battery and wrecked five ou
its six guns. As the second battery galloped up the French g
wiped it out. Then the French guns turned on the cavalry. T

00 of the cavalry and artillery horses in the action, which
1 only a few minutes.

raguey d'Hilliers' First Corps was hotly engaged around
rino. Napoleon told d'Hilliers early in the day to take the
;e, and slowly and painfully this tough general had by noon
the lower slopes of Solferino's cone-like hill, but the Austrians
; to the spurs and commanded the valleys. They broke up a
r French attack on the old tower, but French artillery
hed breaches through the convent and cemetery walls, and
ch infantry poured through them, to take the positions with
ayonet.

poleon now ordered the Chasseurs of the Guard to reinforce
irst Corps. They were formed up in the dense columns that
urvived in the French Army since the days of Bonaparte and,
 their colonel at their head, awaited the signal. The bugles
ded the charge, and the colonel shouted, "*Bataillon en avant
s de gymnastique! En avant, en avant!*"

'ive l'Empereur!*" shouted the Chasseurs. They were cheer-
onaparte had they only known it.

e whole mass pounded up the hill, the sun bright on their
d bayonets. Shells, musket fire, yells, and shrieks made a
tful din, and the Chasseurs dropped fast, but the survivors
ed the first houses, wavered under volley-fire, then in a wild
 swept the white-coated Austrian infantry and the Tyrolese
s before them. The attack was indirectly assisted by the
rians themselves, for, in accordance with an often fatal
ice of those days, one corps was being replaced by another
at narrow track at the height of the battle.

ery house, every garden, and every vineyard was a fortress,
he French had to take each by force.

 saw several small enclosures covered with bodies," a news-
r correspondent wrote. "I counted more than 200 in a small
"

 two o'clock, after repeated assaults, the French had
ered Solferino and threatened the Austrian centre.

l around Solferino and especially in the cemetery the ground
littered with broken weapons, helmets, shakos, mess-tins,
idge-boxes, belts, remnants of blood-stained clothing.

eanwhile some Voltigeurs of the Guard and other troops were
y forcing their way along the heights towards Cavriana—
ch élan and intelligence against Austrian doggedness and
at arms. On Monte Fontana the Turcos were put in to winkle

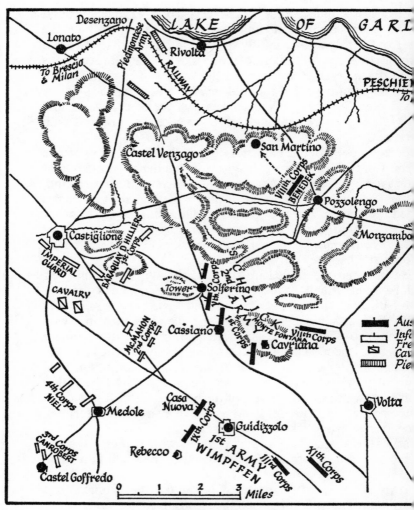

The Situation at 8 A.M.
From *Battles of the Nineteenth Century*
(Cassell, 1901).

OLFERINO

Solferino was a complex battle and a long one, beginning soon
ter sunrise and lasting until evening. From a church steeple at
astiglione Napoleon III saw the Austrians trying to divert the
tack on Solferino, the key to their position, by outflanking the
rench right, filling up the gap between the Second and Fourth
orps, and thus cutting the French army in two. Napoleon sent
ders to prevent his force from being divided. His plan, quite
ementary, was to carry Solferino at any cost, and then, by a
ank movement, to beat the enemy out of his positions at Cav-
ana. With heavy casualties, this plan he effected by 4 P.M.
ictor Emmanuel and his Piedmontese beat Benedek out of San
lartino. The French were so exhausted they made no attempt
t pursuit.

out the Austrians. Lovers of bayonet-fighting, the Africa
crawled, ran, and jumped from rock to rock and cover to cov
and, yelling like fiends, took the hill. But the Austrians, re
forced, retook it. The Turcos came back for more, captured t
hill, and were again dislodged. The sweating, battle-grim
Austrians, who had received no rations other than a double rou
of brandy, lay panting on the hill.

The hand-to-hand struggles were nightmares of frightfulne
with Austrians and Allies trampling one another under foot, ki
ing one another on piles of bloody corpses with butt, bayon
and sabre. Many a man, wounded or without weapon, used rock
his fists, and even his teeth on an opponent. Some picked
enemy soldiers and threw them into ravines.

By mid-morning the heat had been torrid; soon after noon
was fierce, and whole regiments, oppressed by fatigue, threw
their knapsacks so as to be able to move and fight more free
Every mound, crag, and height was the scene of a fight to tl
death. Very little chivalry showed itself that day. The Croats
the Austrian Army clubbed to death every wounded man the
encountered; the Algerian sharpshooters gave no quarter
wounded Austrians.

The French gunners now started to drag their guns up tl
heights, and when the horses could not move them they mar
handled the weapons. Even then there were too few artillerymer
so the Grenadiers of the Guard, normally so dignified, hauled th
guns to the crest and formed a chain to pass up cartridges an
shells. From these heights the French shelled the Austrians o
Monte Fontana.

Napoleon himself came up to inspire the men attacking Cav
riana, and he and his brilliantly uniformed escort instantly becam
a prime target. A colonel urged the Emperor to retire—"It is a
you they are aiming."

"Very well," Napoleon said—with a smile, according t
legend—"silence them and they will fire no longer."

A French officer is supposed to have written, "The expressio
gave us fresh vigour, and I know not how it was, but at a boun
we gained a hundred metres, and twenty minutes later we ha
taken Cavriana."

I think it very likely that Napoleon III had learned a lot abou
personal publicity from his uncle.

At times French troops showed enterprise worthy of thei
Revolutionary history. An Austrian cavalry regiment charge

.ch mounted skirmishers, but in doing so passed a battalion
hasseurs who were lying down in the standing corn. As the
rians rode by the Chasseurs stood and raked them, while
French batteries took the regiment in flank.

rtillery constantly changed position throughout the day,
horses, guns, and limbers pounding over dead and wounded,
erizing, pulping, and mutilating the already damaged bodies.
French grape-shot, effective at distances hitherto unknown,
:ted casualties even on distant Austrian reserves.

1e Austrian right was as busily engaged with the Sardinians
Piedmontese as the left and centre were with the French.
Sardinians were roughly handled. Some of their columns
: under practically point-blank grape-shot fire, and the men
: so shocked that they panicked; some ran two miles before
could be stopped. Finally, strongly reinforced, they made
ral more exhausting assaults, but General Benedek, a com-
der in the Blücher mould, fought them successfully all day.

battle is often separately known as the battle of San
tino.

1e proud Bersaglieri were badly battered here, and many a
1ered hat lay on the battlefield. Though they were to fight
1, the Bersaglieri never did fully recover from their mauling
1n Martino, and by the time of World War II, though still the
of the Italian Army, they were much inferior to the Bersag-
of 1859.

f the 25,000 Sardinians and Piedmontese engaged around
Martino and at Pozzolengo 179 officers and 4428 men were
d or wounded—evidence both of a hard fight and of inept
:rship.

1e Austrian Emperor had had his centre broken, but his left
: held its own against the French Fourth Corps, and his right
: on Lake Garda was still secure. He correctly saw that the
move was an all-out attack against Niel's tired men at Casa
va, and ordered Wimpffen to use three corps to 'crash
1gh' the French line and then roll it up. The Austrians fought
and in line wave after wave of them beat against the walls of
arm, still held by the 6th Chasseurs. Then a French lancer
1ent exploded from cover behind a belt of trees and speared
Austrian assault to destruction.

other assaults the Austrian infantry had time to form
re, and the cavalry attacks were easily beaten off, but the
ssity for halting and forming square had wasted too much

time, and the Casa Nuova defenders had strengthened their p‍
tions, Wimpffen believed the assault was hopeless, but Fra‍
Joseph made several furious and desperate attempts to bring
exhausted and beaten troops into action, and in the centre
Austrian rearguard held out for two hours in several success
positions against the attacks of MacMahon and the Guard.

Fighting was still continuing when a violent storm, soupy w
dust, broke up the battle and gave the Austrians cover while t‍
retreated east of the Mincio. The battle had raged for fift
hours.

The losses were: Allies, 14,415 killed and wounded and 2‍
missing (a total of 17,191); Austrians: 13,317 killed and wound
9220 missing (total 22,537). The Sardinians' share of the All
losses amounted to 5521. Two months later the total figure v
practically doubled by dead or those in hospitals from sickn‍
fever, sunstroke, or excessive exhaustion.

Napoleonic spirit and training, Napoleonic artillery the‍
Napoleonic trust in well-chosen marshals and generals—th
won Solferino. But what was the maximum time a nat
could live on a legend? In France's case just another eleven ye‍

It has been said that the American Civil War marked the
ginning of truly modern warfare. In the sense that more milit
inventions were used in this war than in previous wars this may
true, but then the same applies to every great war. Solferino v
the prime punctuation mark in warfare between 1815 and 19
It showed that set-piece chessboard battles were over, that the
of great-area battles had begun. But the war was short, and ‍
foreign countries had been quick enough to send skilled observ
to Northern Italy to study military developments. Significan
Prussia was one of the few; she had observers with both si‍
Their intelligent detailed reports to the General Staff were clos
studied and acted upon. It was no coincidence that seven ye
later Prussia decisively and completely defeated Austria i‍
mere seven weeks' war.

Solferino was fought at the height of the tourist season, ‍
though most visitors fled from the area some remained. One
these at the little town of Castiglione della Pieve, near which
battle started, was Henri Dunant, a Swiss. Dunant was so appa‍
by the sights and sounds and smells of Solferino that he beca‍
the founder of the Red Cross.

Dunant and the other civilians who exhausted themselves
their efforts to help the wounded had reason to be appalled.

first night injured men were brought in or struggled in by
1selves, but not until sunrise on the 25th did anybody discover
full horror of the battlefield, littered by dead, dying, and
nded men and animals and the battered and ghastly debris of

took three days and nights to bury the dead on the battle-
, but in such a wide area many bodies lay hidden in ditches
enches or under bushes or mounds of earth and were found
much later. Burials were perfunctory and not always
ient, so that limbs often protruded from the earth. Some
y wounded men, inevitably, were buried alive.

astiglione was the most important rescue centre, and over-
/ding in the place became "unspeakable", as Dunant was
rite. Mule carts came in at a jolting trot, so that the wounded
in the carts cried out continually in pain.

he number of convoys increased so much that the authorities,
ownspeople, and the able-bodied troops could not cope with
situation. There was food and water, but men died of hunger
thirst; there was plenty of lint, but not enough hands to dress
nds. Wounds were infected by flies, heat, and dust. On the
:s of churches lay Frenchmen and Slavs, Germans and
bs, Rumanians and Croats, Sardinians and Algerians. "Oaths,
es, and cries such as no words can describe resounded from
aulting," Dunant wrote.[1]

'ith faces black with flies that swarmed about their wounds
en gazed around them, wild-eyed and helpless. Others were
) more than a worm-ridden inextricable compound of coat
id shirt and flesh and blood.... A wretched man ... had had
s nose, lips, and chin taken off by a sabre cut ... a third, with
s skull gaping open, was dying, spitting out his brains on the
one floor ... at the entrance to the church was a Hungarian
ho never ceased to cry out ... a burst of grapeshot had
oughed into his back, which looked as if it had been fur-
•wed with steel claws, laying bare a great area of red, quiver-
g flesh. The rest of his swollen body was all black and green.
. Over against the wall, about 100 French non-commissioned
ficers and soldiers were stretched in two lines, almost touch-
g.... They were calm and peaceful.... They suffered with-
ıt complaint. They died humbly and quietly.

ut many died in desperate agony from untreatable wounds or
e having a limb amputated without anaesthetic. "In these

[1] In his famous book *A Memory of Solferino*.

Lombardy hospitals," Dunant wrote, "it could be seen a realized how dearly bought and how abundantly paid for is t commodity which men pompously call Glory!"

Dunant, a civilian, forged a new link in Military command recognition of the necessity for skilled and adequate medi services. He did not initiate Army medical services; doctors, o kind, had accompanied armies for centuries, and Florer Nightingale had already set a splendid example at Scutari in t Crimean War, but Dunant by the publicity he gave to the aft math of Solferino created a universal awareness of the need f proper medical services.

CHAPTER NINETEEN

Ten Tempestuous Years

*The American Civil War; Moltke introduces Technical War;
The Battle of Königgrätz; The French Collapse*

ISTORIANS of general history—and even many military
historians—have written that the American Civil War intro-
ed the conception of total war and of psychological warfare,
I they cite General Sherman's semi-punitive march from
anta to Savannah to prove the point.

'rue, Sherman was a ruthless, totalitarian general. "It is use-
to occupy Georgia," he reported,

ut the utter destruction of its roads, houses and people will
ripple their military resources. I can ... make Georgia howl.
.. We are not only fighting hostile armies, but hostile people,
nd must make old and young, rich and poor, feel the hard
and of war.

And the hard hand of war the South did feel. Sherman marched
• miles with an army of 62,000 men, all of them living off the
ntry. They cut a swath of destruction 50 miles wide, destroy-
railroads, arsenals, and other military objectives, putting
nmunications and industrial centres out of action, and seriously
naging Southern morale.

3ut there was nothing new about this. Sherman could point
nundreds of earlier generals who had been more ruthless than
to dozens of campaigns in which civilians suffered more
tely and for longer than the Southerners—during the Thirty
ars War, for example—to the British, who at that very time had
de a practice of burning down the villages of their enemies in
ia and elsewhere. Sherman's march was less devastating than

many made by Napoleon and various of his marshals, far
barbarous than those made by the Russians and Turks. To a
that Sherman 'invented' totalitarian war is irresponsible
betrays a lamentable lack of knowledge.

Still, Sherman proved that the indirect approach to the ene
economic and moral rear was decisive and far-reaching. Ge
Edmonds, the official historian of the First World War, said
was the operations of Sherman's grand army of the west whic
to the collapse of the Confederacy." These operations had a
found effect on the generals who studied it.

It is wrong to believe—as many people do—that the genera
the Civil War were inferior. Historians who have studied
Civil War rate high the standard of generalship. In fact, the
brought forth more really able commanders than any wa
history other than the Second World War—Sherman, McCle
Lee, Johnston, Meade, Jackson, Grant, to mention a few.

General Grant had something of Napoleon's make-up, as is
by his indirect approach, using several thrusting columns, ir
Vicksburg campaign—although he adopted this approach
after more direct approaches had failed. Unfortunately, he dic
learn as rapidly as Napoleon, and he suffered subsequent de
because of direct approaches.

The war also introduced an astonishing range of martia
novations or improvements. There was the repeating rifle-
Spencer initially—wire entanglements, land-mines and bo
traps, grenades and mortars, explosive bullets and flame-throv
submarines, naval mines and torpedoes, railroad artillery
volving gun-turrets, telescopic sights, trench periscopes. Rec
machine-gun—one of the very first—was introduced, an
1864 the South contemplated using 'stink-shells', although t
is no record that they were actually used.

Amphibious attacks and aerial observation came into
while sabotage was used so extensively that its techniques
not equalled until the Second World War. The Military Teleg
Service made a big difference to the war, and was in fact a n
weapon, particularly for Union forces. During the last year o
fighting the Service laid an average of 200 miles of wire a
General Grant, when Commander-in-Chief, kept day-by-day
trol over half a million men spread over an area of 800,000 sq
miles.

Railways offered tremendous opportunities to enterpr
generals. Time after time both sides moved troops to the scer

ttle by train. At one crucial period the Federals rushed 16,000
n a distance of 1200 miles in a week, an astonishing achieve-
nt for its time—and one that was carefully noted by the hand-
ked Prussian observers at the front.

The rifle made the defensive the stronger form of warfare; the
ensive became more difficult and more costly. And this, in
n, led to armies of greater size, for more men were needed to
kle a job. In 1864 the total Union forces were 683,000—an
mense army by any standards. The Confederates had only
5,000.

Tactical changes were much slower than technical ones because
tics were the responsibility of senior officers, most of whom
re old and violently opposed to change. They did not much
e technical improvements for that matter, but these were
vitable.

Change was most rapid in Prussia. In 1864, while the American
vil War was still in progress, the Prussian capture of the Danish
loubts of Duppel hinted at Prussia's frightening military
iciency. In 1866 the great battle of Königgrätz—or Sadowa as
is sometimes called—showed it off completely. Bismarck, the
inister-President, wanted a war with Austria and consulted von
oltke, possibly the greatest military brain Prussia or Germany
s produced, and as keen a student of military history as
poleon.

Moltke promised him victory—but only in a short war. Moltke
d his short war; technically it lasted seven weeks, but hostili-
s were limited to three weeks, fighting to seven days and to
e decisive battle.

A rare combination of realist-visionary, Moltke saw that the
w inventions would allow a war to be opened quickly and con-
ded quickly. He founded a Railway Department in the General
ff. In 1866 he had a Railway Corps, the first in Europe. 'Rail-
y troops' had been successful in the American Civil War, just
ished. Moltke also ordered ready-made mobilization plans,
pt up to date day by day, so that the Army could go into action
thin hours.

He showed how it was now possible for a commander-in-chief
remain many miles behind the lines yet intimately control
mplex troop movements by telegraph. At any moment a divi-
nal general could contact the C.-in-C. because the C.-in-C. was
vays in the one spot. No longer was there a frantic search by
llopers to find the man in charge. Moltke was one of the first

generals to organize battles from a large map. At the same
Moltke gave his subordinate commanders a lot of indivi
initiative.

The great battle-thinker, "the silent one in seven languag
as the Prussian General Staff called him, had many maxims,
perhaps the most important was "March separately, strike
gether."

Late in June 1886 he sent three main armies into Bohemia
the upper Elbe, where the Austrians were concentrating. Tota
220,000, they were led, respectively, by the Red Prince,
Crown Prince, who was Queen Victoria's son-in-law, and Ger
von Bittenfeld. These three armies left from separate points
marched towards different points. Moltke sat among his map
the offices of the General Staff, with his hand on the telegr
wire.

When the troops were marching towards the battlefield
King of Prussia began to doubt whether a victory could reall
won if an army were divided into so many parts, and these p
were transported along many routes to the battlefield. How c
he be certain that this disjointed and complicated machinery wc
join itself up again when it got there? The King sent Bismarc
Moltke to ask about the state of the operations. Bismarck c
back and merely said, "It is all right."

The Austrians tried hard to block all three armies, but
destructive needle-gun, the long lance of the plunging Uhl
and the slashing sabre of the cuirassiers cleared the way throu;
series of preliminary triumphs. The Austrians, though stron
cavalry, still had muzzle-loading firearms.

By June 29th all the Austrians with their Saxon allies
Hungarians—about 215,000 of them—had retired under
shelter of the guns of the fortress town of Königgrätz, on
left bank of the Upper Elbe. This united force was comman
by General Benedek, who had chosen his position well and
transformed the whole field into a natural fortress.

The battle took place on July 3rd along a front of five mile
the centre the Prussians pushed battery after battery into ac
and kept up heavy fire, but the Austrians had ranged the gro
better, and their fire was more effective.

Columns of Prussian infantry moved forward to storm
villages of Sadowa, Dohalitz, Dohalicka, and Benetek, wl
desperate hand-to-hand fighting occurred for the first time.
the mêlée here was nothing to the furious fight in Sad

d. The Austrians clung to their positions under shells and
ts, but by eleven o'clock they had been bayoneted out.

ng William wanted to storm frontally some entrenched
rian batteries on Lissa Heights, but Moltke abruptly counter-
led the royal order. A frontal charge against guns was not
sm to Moltke, but military stupidity.

'ter hideous bloodshed and frightful scenes the Crown Prince
d the Austrian right flank according to Moltke's plan. By
in the afternoon the Prussian line of attack resembled a huge
ae-like semicircle hemming in the masses of battered and
en Austrian troops. The nature of the ground had prevented
1 use of cavalry, but on the line of retreat to Königgrätz
al lance and sabre conflicts occurred. The Austrians were
d into full flight, pursued by cavalry, volleyed at by infantry,
ered with shells. By superior arms, superior numbers, and
rior strategy Prussia, at the cost of 10,000 casualties, had
a resounding victory. Austria lost 40,000 men, including
)0 prisoners, and 174 guns.

ederick the Great had taken seven years to humble Austria;
ke had needed only seven days to achieve the same result.

hile Bismarck schemed Moltke and von Roon carried on the
: of perfecting the military machine. With the help of the rail-
and the telegraph Moltke managed armies of a size hitherto
own. Not for Moltke any more than for Napoleon the con-
hat one soldier of his own race was worth three of any other
One man equalled one man, who merely cancelled each
: out. Therefore to win a battle a general needed a majority,
the bigger the majority the better. This was at a time when
French believed that quality outweighed quantity; one
chman was at least as good as one and a half Germans;
a small French army could defeat a big German army.

oltke became the great representative of the German school.
m was united the will of Napoleon with the mind of Scharn-
, and Clausewitz. He combined vast knowledge with great
ower. His pupil Count Schlieffen said in his memory:

This man of action, when he was called to do immortal
eds, was sixty-five years old. He was a man of the map and
e compasses and the pen. . . . He could not boast, as Napoleon
d, of having for nineteen years made a military promenade
rough Europe, but within six weeks he succeeded in en-
cling three proud armies. . . . He did not conquer, he
stroyed!

Without being so well acquainted with the battle of Canna Schlieffen, Moltke, through his critical study of the Napole campaigns, had arrived at Hannibalistic or, to be accurate, G ideas.

The Germans aimed at the annihilation or total disperseme the enemy's army. This was possible, however, as the exam of Epaminondas and Hannibal, Frederick the Great, Napo and Moltke proved, only when the attacker initiated a m battle with the object of falling upon the enemy's flank (encircling and destroying piecemeal.

Moltke calculated the distance that a marching army (took up on a road, and he arrived at the surprising figure of and a half or five miles. If he wanted to march a second corps along the same road and from the same place, the se corps could not start till the next day. It needed the rest o time to let the first corps pass and then to get started itself. M drew the conclusion that every army corps needed its own That is to say, the armies would march separately and only forces on the battlefield to strike the great blow. Translated Hannibal's way of thinking: "It is important to know in adv how am I going to place my army. If I know that, I can arr the march. All my available forces must be on the scene of a in time, the rest is determined by courage and luck!"

To translate such a seemingly simple idea into deeds he ne an exact knowledge of every detail of troop movement and apparently unessential thing. The troops had to know every m ment necessary for the manoeuvre, and Moltke needed to k to the second how much time the individual needed. An enorm amount of calculation was necessary to collate and work ou these thousands of small facts. Everything that can be don intelligence in the case of war should, according to Mol doctrine, be done before the battle. With Moltke begins modern era, the era of gigantic armies, the age of 'technical' fare. Napoleon III still believed that it was not necessary to any dispositions before the commencement of the figh Moltke, on the other hand, once the fighting had begun, m played the part of an observer on the battlefield. During Franco-Prussian War, at the battle of Sedan, Moltke did issue one single order to the troops engaged in the fighting. is probably the greatest staff triumph ever celebrated on the b field. He considered that the task of the commander-in-chief army had been carried out when the plan for the dispositic troops had been decided, even down to what might seem to the most trivial details.

When France declared war on July 19th, 1870 every French-n was wild with confidence. The French certainly had many vantages. They had the revolutionary Chassepot breech-load-; rifle with twice the range of the Prussian Dreyse needle-rifle. ey had the mitrailleuse, a machine-gun of 25 barrels, axis-uped, which was sighted to 1200 metres and could fire 125 nds a minute. France had a greater population, more money, l greater industrial output. Her army was one of veterans, o had fought in the Crimea, Italy, and Algeria. Napoleon III s to command in person the armies in the field and would win ck the old Rhine frontier, and his marshals were men like cMahon, Bazaine, and Canrobert.

But Prussia won because she intended to win, because the issian General Staff planned to win. Never had there been an ny staff like this. War had become the national industry of issia, and its officers were war-businessmen. They brought to ir trade a unique degree of efficiency. They used railways for r in a way the French had never dreamed of.

The old way of warfare was gone. The hallowed old combina-n of 'brilliant', usually intuitive leadership, high morale, and agnificent' cavalry charges was no match against a finely ganized mass army, superior in number and directed not by tinct but with cold-blooded competence.

Moltke reckoned correctly that the French would not be able bring more than 250,000 men against his 381,000 and that, be-ise of their railway communications, they would be compelled assemble their forces about Metz and Strasbourg—which meant it they were separated by the Vosges mountains. He assembled three armies behind the fortresses of the middle Rhine and inned to split the French Army.

The two main French armies remained separate in Alsace d Lorraine and allowed themselves to be beaten separately. oltke practised great enveloping manoeuvres because of his merical strength, and he succeeded in bottling up the larger rts of the French armies in Metz and Sedan.

With the coming of the breech-loading rifle the French doctrine d changed; it decreed that the way to win battles was to sit tight a good position, preferably on high ground, and destroy the emy by rapid fire. French military schools taught that the fensive was now the superior, though a cavalry charge was

occasionally permissible. The last great cavalry charge of hist
—that of General Galliffet's Chasseurs d'Afrique—took place
Sedan, and a single heavy volley was enough to shatter it.[1]

The German doctrine was that only attack could give r
results. It might be more costly, but the cost had to be paid.
attack was to assert from the outset the sense of power and
determination to win. This was reaffirming the doctrine of Mi
ades, Hannibal, Scipio, and others right up to Napoleon.

A few historians have said that Moltke's strategy was essentia
that of a direct approach. Liddell Hart says that Moltke relied
the sheer smashing power of a superior concentration of for
Theoretically his approach was indeed direct, but his object
was disguised. To say he had no guile is misleading and tends
malign the man, but his guile was that of method rather than
animal cunning.

Throughout the many battles of the Franco-Prussian V
German artillery played a great part. Efficient breech-load
served by competent crews, they played havoc with Fre
defences. The guns were never short of ammunition; Moltk
plans had seen to that. And every shell burst, unlike many of
French ones, which simply buried themselves. When Gern
staff officers rode through areas and towns and fortificati
devastated by artillery the lesson was not lost on them. "We wa
more and better guns," they said thoughtfully. "If the artill
preparation is heavy enough the infantry can simply take o
after the bombardment."

The Franco-Prussian War should have shown the trend
future wars to leaders of armies and leaders of nations. It v
inevitable that the French should copy the Prussian prototyp
because the vanquished usually reform themselves on the patt
of the victorious.

[1] The British charges at Omdurman and elsewhere after 1870 were he
and spectacular, but not great in the sense of being on a grand scale.

[2] Before 1871 was over a French parliamentarian demanded that the Fre
Army model itself on the Prussian. "The victory of Germany has been
victory of science and reason. Prussia is our best model. We need a mili
law closely copying the Prussian system."

————— ◆·◆ —————

CHAPTER TWENTY

The Not-so-Great War

*The German Spartan System; The French Roman System;
1900–18; Decline in the Art of War*

LLOWING the Franco-Prussian War there was a rapid im-
rovement in armaments. Most significant was the adoption of
l-bore magazine rifle and smokeless powder, first used on an
nsive scale in the Boer War. The attackers now no longer
ssarily had the initiative.

paramount lesson learned in many campaigns was that
pline was often more important than leadership, overwhelm-
numbers, or the development of arms. As usual, discipline
best exemplified by the British infantry. Standing fast under
y attack, they calmly and deliberately did what they were
, and in the end they triumphed—until the Boer War. For
h the same reasons the Americans won their Indian wars
their Cuban, Philippine, Nicaraguan, and other campaigns.

ow and then the cavalry had a chance to shine, as did the
ish horsemen in some of the battles against the dervishes in
Sudan and in parts of India and Persia. But if anybody noticed
cavalry units spent most of their time in scouting, manoeuvr-
and ceremonial parades nothing was said.

avalry was fading, but the highly irregular tactics of the Boer
emen gave British arms a rude shock during the war of 1899–
2. These ragged, ununiformed farmers, outnumbered and
unned, consistently defeated the best generals and regiments
ne British Army, the army which was so proud of its martial
rd. Some of the defeats were disastrous in their magnitude.

he secret of the Boers' success was twofold—mobility and
nificent shooting. "The Boers slink like curs behind rocks

and fire from cover," Louis Creswicke, a leading English
historian complained.

The Boers fought as had the Eastern horsemen of the Mid
Ages. They used their horses merely as a means of transport; t
did not fight on horseback, and they were always under cove
action. The British, brave in the old tradition, fought in the of
Horse and foot, loyal to their past, they charged valiantly a
vainly and died in their thousands. The infantry often floute
cardinal rule of war and charged up rocky hillsides.

A small number of defenders could lie well concealed alon
wide front. For instance, at Colenso 4500 Boers were spread al
a front of 13,500 yards. These thin, long fronts could not
pierced, and rifle frontal attacks could no longer succeed.

The German Official History crystallized the lessons of
Boar War:

> In South Africa the contest was not merely one between
> bullet and the bayonet, it was also between the soldier dri
> to machine-like movements and the man with the rifle work
> on his own initiative. Fortunate indeed is that army wh
> ranks . . . are controlled by natural, untrammelled, quicken
> common sense.

Machine-guns had been developing steadily, reaching a dea
peak of efficiency. Among them were the Gatling, the Gardr
Nordenfelt, Hotchkiss, Colt, Maxim, Lewis, Vickers.[1]

As early as 1902 the *Swiss Military Review* published an arti
by an unconventional French officer, Émile Mayer, in which
said:

> The next war will put face to face two human walls, alm
> in contact, only separated by the depth of danger, and t
> double wall will remain almost inert, in spite of the will
> either party to advance. Unable to succeed in front, one of th
> lines will try to outswing the other. The latter, in turn, v
> prolong its front, and it will be a competition to see who v
> be able to reach farthest. There will be no reason for the war
> stop. Exterior circumstances will bring the end of the pur
> defensive war of the future.

---

[1] In 1881 a London Volunteer Unit, the Rangers, somehow unoffici
acquired two early-pattern machine-guns for trial and practice. An offi
rebuke was not long in coming: "Report why you are in possession of
authorised weapons, which are entirely unsuitable for infantry use." This
more than thirty years before the machine-gun became the master of
battlefield.

ome years earlier M. Bloch, a Warsaw banker, had foretold
same thing and the Bloch-Mayer theory was proved by the
ning, mauling struggle in Manchuria between Japan and
sia in 1904.

rance and Germany had studied this war through observers
he spot, and while the Germans learned more than the French
1 sides missed the main conclusion—that the preponderance
rojectiles in defence must lead to trenches.

fter 1871 the French had discovered Clausewitz, and, as they
ight, they made his doctrines work for them. In 1908 Foch
iched Clausewitz at the French Staff College, where senior
ers were prepared for high command. But to teach Clause-
: without qualifications was misguided because his thoughts,
iy of them more idealistic and intellectual than practical,
been conditioned by the age in which he lived. His ideals
ld be re-established in another age, but not his methods. In
case, Clausewitz was obviously working for the Germans, not
French. The Germans understood his *philosophy*, but the
ich stifled their own independent thought by slavish devotion
is *theories*.

och and his colleagues, accepting new weapons—mainly
llery—without being aware of the limitations they imposed,
eved that they would add considerable momentum to attack.
Germans already knew, from their skilled observers in
ign wars, that heavy guns aided defence rather than attack.

iddell Hart cites the French staff officer. Colonel de Grandson as saying that "the French Army knows no other law but
offensive. All attacks are to be pushed to the extreme ... to
rge the enemy with the bayonet to destroy him. ... This result
only be obtained at the price of bloody sacrifice."

he French generals of the period preceding the Great War—
they included Foch—childishly believed that the infallible
ver to the bullet was high morale. This was why, they said,
French Army was unbeatable.

ed by de Grandmaison, the French advocates of the direct-
roach offensive formulated in 1912 what was known as Plan
II—an infamous piece of work. This plan called for an all-
attack against the German centre—a frontal and almost
le-front push. Yet the French strength was only barely equal
he German strength, and the Germans would be fighting from
r own fortified frontier zone. Such arrant imbecility is difficult
omprehend.

Defenders of the direct approach even quoted Napoleon
support of their foolishness, although Napoleon would ha
agreed with Churchill that the enemy alliance should be view
as a whole and that an attack in some other theatre of war wo
be equivalent to an attack on an enemy's strategic flank. T
Gallipoli campaign of 1915 was just such an attack.

Plan XVII played right into the Germans' hands, for they t
had a plan—the Schlieffen Plan, prepared by Graf von Schlief
in 1905. Schlieffen, Moltke's pupil and successor, was definit
inspired by both Cannae and Leuthen—Cannae by virtue of
grand envelopment tactics and Leuthen in regard to the mo
ments within this grand design.

At that time Schlieffen had 72 divisions available; he put 53
the right, 10 on the Verdun pivot, and only 9 on the left. As
French attacked in Lorraine and pressed back the German l
wing the massive German right wing would slam through Belgiu
hit the French in the back and knock them on their face.

Basically, by 1914 the German system was Spartan in type a
amounted to a wall of advancing men without any specific reser
The French system was Roman-type, a lighter front leading
heavy rear. The Germans, methodical as ever, based all on
elaborate plan backed by sheer force; the French, carrying th
individualism to extremes, pinned their faith to skill and to
tuitive ability to use ground and opportunity to best advanta
They thought they could easily outwit the "stodgy German".

Foch's appreciation of history was acutely limited. He saw lit
importance in the vital possibilities of the defensive-offensive
that is, to induce the enemy to exhaust themselves in a vain assa
and then to launch a violent counterstroke—although these tact
have paid greater dividends than any other in history. Foch p
claimed Napoleon as the grand master of war, but did not anal
his idol's masterpiece, Austerlitz, and did not make use of
lesson it taught. This in itself proves Foch's intellectual limi
tions.

France has produced more truly brilliant generals and milita
thinkers than any other country in history, so it is all the mo
surprising that between 1904 and 1918 she should have produc
generals so stodgy that they discounted the possible use of mo
vehicles in war.[2] They said that cars were too big and therefo

[2] Although General Galliéni was astute enough to commandeer 1200 Pa
taxis in September 1914 and used them to rush reinforcements to the battlefr
of the Marne.

de vulnerable targets, that they were slow and would break
vn and were therefore not so reliable as horses; that they could
y travel along a road, unlike cavalry which could travel any-
ere; that they made a noise and would therefore give away
itions to the enemy. The generals said much more in this vein.
velopments had come too fast for them.

Another prime architect of French near-defeat was General
nnal, a deep but dim-witted devotee of Napoleonic strategy.
had imbibed so much military history that he won the reputa-
a as the leading strategist of his day. But Bonnal was a copyist,
apable of applying Napoleonic theory to changed practical
ditions, and his plan—likened by General Fuller to "the Jena
n is elephantiasis"—to counter any stroke by the Germans
unworkable.

Had Schlieffen's plan been acted upon the French must have
n defeated early in the war, but Moltke 'the younger' (the
at Moltke's nephew) botched it by adding more and more
isions to the left, and by making it safe he destroyed the great
n, with the indirect result of the battle of the Marne, September
4, a decisive conflict and turning-point, for with the German
of the battle the war developed into a siege, as Bloch and
yer had foreseen.

As early as January 7th, 1915, Lord Kitchener wrote to Sir
n French: "The German lines in France may be looked upon
a fortress that cannot be carried by assault ... with the result
t ... operations [may] proceed elsewhere."

But Kitchener's warning was unheeded. From the beginning
conflict of 1914–18 was a fearful war, the bloodiest in history.
vas the war of the machine-gun, and the Germans excelled in
use. Over and over again the British and French charged the
man lines, nearly always to be repulsed. The Germans, who
uld have known better, charged the British and French
hine-guns with the same result. There was a little give and
e, but year after year the position was virtually one of stale-
te. And all the time the big guns thundered, blowing many
usands of men to pieces. Many might have survived had they
been so grossly overweighted with equipment. In the end
ut one man in every three had no known grave. Many were
ply lost in the bottomless mud which the artillery and the rain
created. The predictions of the prophets had come true. In
trenches men fought with bombs, bayonets, boots, shovels,
axes, and even bottles. Many trenches became graves.

The casualties were stupendous, greater than ever before
perienced. On the first day of the first battle of Ypres the Br
lost 40,000 men. Statistics beggared the imagination, but
generals knew nothing else other than bombardment and fro
attacks.

Great masses and heavy artillery led to no proportiona
decisive results—and never will do so. It is incomprehensible
most leaders of the Great War could not understand that
dominance acquired by artillery and machine-guns would
warfare to the point of bloody stalemate.

The Germans, eager for a break-through, used poison
Some gas was designed to suffocate, some to blister. The first
caught in it died dreadful deaths.

Scharnhorst had once advised officers "not to be caught
their own enterprise", and had German tacticians heeded
they would not have used gas, for the prevailing winds on
Western Front were westerlies, making the use of gas much r
favourable for the Allies than for the Germans. They were l
with their own petard.

Wellington's line of Torres Vedras in 1810 pointed the wa
the trench warfare of 1915–18. But the German invaders had
advantage Wellington had not enjoyed—that of living in the r
fertile lands of France and Belgium. Also, Wellington alway
mained strictly on the defensive; to win all he had to do wa
hold his own. But the Allies in 1915–18 ran the risk of losing
they could not drive the Germans from France and Belgium
did the invaders unless they could pierce the defenders' li
Therefore the deadlock was involuntary and continuous as
side struggled to drive the other out. Neither side won more
local and temporary success on the Western Front until 1918.

On the Eastern Front in 1914 Ludendorff showed that he
learned from Frederick about the 'interior lines' form of indi
approach. As Hindenburg's Chief of Staff he made the da
move of withdrawing nearly all his troops from one front
rushing them into action against the flanks of General S
sonov's army, practically destroying it—a manoeuvre Ture
would have applauded.

Ludendorff was responsible, too, for one of the more cap
pieces of generalship when he competently withdrew part of
German forces to the Hindenburg Line in the spring of 1917.
anticipated a renewed Franco-British attack on the Somme
had a new trench line prepared from Lens to Reims via No

devastated the area behind his original positions and then thdrew to the newer, shorter line. This manoeuvre, though fensive, threw out of gear the Allied spring offensive and gained rmany a year's respite. This operation was so much like ellington's at Torres Vedras that it is difficult to resist the nclusion that Ludendorff—an intellectual and educated soldier was influenced by it.

Study of the war from the standpoint of my analysis would be itless. Generalship was obstinate, criminally stupid, ridicusly rigid, almost totally unenterprising, pathetically feeble, d absolutely inhuman. It is only charitable to concede that the nerals had to do their best in a type of warfare into which y were forced and of which they had no personal experience. e lessons of 1914–18 were sharp ones, and later leaders profited them and, indeed, are still profiting.

After much study the only leaders to whom I can attribute any mprehension, enterprise, or evidence of profound military nking were Fuller, who was so outspoken that he made emies; Elles, victor of the tank battle of Cambrai, November 17; Salmond, commander of the RAF in the field in 1918; onash, the brilliant Australian Jew, who probably would have cceeded Haig; Currie, the enterprising Canadian; Allenby and auvel, whose work in Palestine was classical in its planning and ecution; Liman von Sanders, Commander-in-Chief of the rkish forces in the Gallipoli peninsula; Mustafa Kemal, who three separate occasions proved his genius during the Galoli campaign; von Hutier, victor against the Russians in the ttle of Riga, 1917; and Ludendorff, occasionally.

Perhaps the greatest—and least known—of them all was lonel (later General) von Lettow-Varbeck, the German military mmander in East Africa, who was the only German Commander remain undefeated throughout the war. No fewer than 120 lied generals were sent against him; he mastered all.

Throughout the war no senior French commander showed any tstanding ability. Foch was no more than mediocre. Gallieni, ven the opportunity, could have shown brilliance.

It is no coincidence that all these commanders were ardent sciples of the doctrine of surprise and mobility. What Fieldarshal Wavell said of Allenby in a biographical study applies all of them. "The soft modern doctrine of safety first, which so ten marks the decline of business, of Governments, of armies, nations, found no place in Allenby's creed." The term

'surprise' comprises general and tactical surprise, and 'mobi[
includes, of course, boldness, and rapidity of decision and act
These modern leaders were the moral successors of Cyrus,
founder of the Persian Empire and victor at Thymbra, 546 i
of Miltiades at Marathon; of Epaminondas—the victor
Leuctra, 371 B.C.; Gustavus, Frederick, Napoleon, and L
Roberts, whose advance against the Boer leader Cronje in 1
was an almost classic example of the complete strategic surp
of an enemy.

Apart from the few senior commanders mentioned, the lea
generals of the Great War seemed bent on breaking every lin
the chain of command, for they ignored or flouted every princ
propounded throughout the centuries. For instance, it is an
matic—as Liddell Hart has pointed out—that a comman
should never renew an attack along the same line or in the sa
form once it has been repulsed. The Great War commanders
just this—many times. Many great captains, historians, ph
sophers, and observers have called the waging of war an 'art
'science'. In the Great War this art or science degenerated in
trade—butchery. From a scientific point of view the whole unh
shambles was disgraceful.

Towards the end the German offensive of March 1918 wa
splendid conception that deserved to succeed, but Ludend
spread his strength according to the enemy's strength and did
concentrate it against the weakest resistance—thereby confou
ing one of his own principles. He further violated it when, a
breaking the Allied line south of the Somme, he persisted
attacking a powerfully resistant section of the line at Arras. W
it was too late he sent reinforcements to the place of least re
tance. He had made a fracture at the point where the British a
French armies joined, and the French had told Haig that if C
man progress continued here they would have to pull back Fre
reserves to cover Paris. Ludendorff could have wrenched t
fracture wide open, but he gave no weight to his effort here.
the end he had driven three solid wedges into the Allied lines,
achieved no great damage and left the Germans themselves w
open to counter-attacks.

A few farsighted people, including Winston Churchill, s
early in the war that some new development was need
Churchill, then First Lord of the Admiralty, wrote an histc
letter to the Prime Minister, Herbert Asquith, which read
part:

The present war has revolutionised theories about the field fire. The power of the rifle is so great that 100 yards is held fficient to stop any rush and in order to lessen the severity of tillery fire trenches are often dug on the reverse slope of sitions, or a short distance in the rear of villages, woods or her obstacles. The consequence is that the war has become a ort-range instead of a long-range war as was expected, and posing trenches get ever closer together, for mutual safety om each other's fire.

The question to be solved is not, therefore, the long attack er a carefully prepared glacis of former times, but the actual tting across 100 or 200 yards of open space and wire en-nglements. All this was apparent more than two months ago, it no steps have been taken and no preparations made.

It would be quite easy in a short time to fit up a number of eam tractors, with small armoured shelters, in which men and achine guns could be placed. Used at night, they would not affected by artillery fire to any extent. The caterpillar system uld enable trenches to be crossed quite easily and the weight the machine would destory all wire entanglements.

Forty or fifty of these engines, prepared secretly and brought to positions at nightfall, could advance quite certainly into e enemy's trenches with their machine-gun fire, and with enades thrown out of the top. They would make so many ints d'appui for the British supporting infantry to rush for-ard and rally on them. They can then move forward to attack e second line of trenches.

The World Crisis Churchill wrote:

Accusing as I do without exception all the great Allied fensives of 1915, 1916 and 1917 as needless and wrongly nceived operations of infinite costs, I am bound to reply to e question, "What else could be done?"

And I answer it, pointing to the Battle of Cambrai [in iich tanks were successfully used] "*This* could have been ne." This in many variants in better and larger forms, ought have been done, and would have been done if only the nerals had not been content to fight machine-guns with the easts of gallant men and think that was waging war.

radoxically, the nation to make the most use of tanks and anization generally in later years and to achieve the most them was that which had suffered most *from* them— nany. In the next Great War German tanks and armoured of the highly efficient Panzer Corps overran country after try, often without being forced to fight, so great was the

intimidation-power and surprise of the tank. It was now no ⟨
bersome, creeping caterpillar, but a surging, speeding battle
on land.

The only surprising thing about the tank is that anybody sh
have been surprised that it had arrived and that it was so effec
The tank was nothing more than a compact, mechanized, ⟨
ernized version of the ancient phalanx. Both had the s
characteristics—they were armoured, relentless, practically irr
tible, frightening, mobile.

I can imagine that Miltiades, Hannibal, Alexander, Ca⟨
Scipio, and the others must at times have thought, "I wish I
armour on wheels and some way of making it go forward
tinuously." *Continuously.* This is the key word. Every ⟨
commander of every age has longed and striven for *contin*
attack, for while ever he maintains momentum he is winning.

CHAPTER TWENTY-ONE

The Germans apply History;
the Prelude to Alamein

THE moment the Great War ended the world started to prepare for another war—not consciously, perhaps, but in-
itably. And when the Treaty of Versailles—that monumental
isbegotten masterpiece—was signed preparation became more
finite, at least with the Germans.
Clausewitz had written:

> The military power must be destroyed, that is, reduced to
> such a state as not to be able to prosecute the war. . . . The
> country must be conquered, for out of the country a new
> military force may be formed. But even when these things are
> done, the war, that is, the hostile feeling and action of hostile
> agencies, cannot be considered as ended as long as the will of
> the enemy is not subdued also.

No Allied statesman who took part in the treaty negotiations
derstood Clausewitz; nor did they appreciate the profound
fluence he had on German military thought. The Allies did *not*
stroy Germany's military power; they did *not* conquer Ger-
any; they had *not* subdued the enemy's will. The conclusion
awn by the Germans who then commanded and who later were
command was obvious: *We were not beaten.*
Clausewitz even had a principle for them to fall back on: "The
al decision of a whole war is not always regarded as absolute.
e conquered state sees in it only a passing evil, which may be
paired in after times by means of political combinations."

The lengths to which Germany went in her preparations f war have been discussed in detail elsewhere[1] and do not ne elaboration here. It is enough to know that all her preparatio were based on Clausewitz's theory, Moltke's organization, a Frederick's intention, a meaty compound further thickened ingredients supplied by statesmen, strategists, and tacticians fro Arminius to Hindenburg.

From the point of view of leadership one of the few notal wars between 1918 and 1939 was the Kurdistan campaign of A Vice-Marshal Sir John Salmond. Salmond, who showed gre enterprise during the great battles of 1918, was the first Briti air officer to command a joint Army-RAF expedition. Comi after the stagnant military thinking of 1914–18, his campaign w remarkable for its initiative and sense of adventure, but did n receive the publicity it deserved.

The Kurdistan campaign was a small war, but it was a jewel a campaign. Cutting loose from his bases, as Grant had done his 1863 Vicksburg campaign, Salmond sent his infantry colum deep into the fastnesses of Kurdistan to stop Turkish infiltrati into the territory of Mosul and to squash the Turkish-inspir Kurd rebellion.

It had become increasingly difficult for a commander in t field to commit himself and his forces to an action purely on l own initiative, but this is precisely what Salmond did. It was decision Napoleonic in its arbitrariness, and its execution was keeping with all the best tenets of the great captains. For the fir time in history Salmond used aircraft to transport troops to t battle area, and he used them, too, to drop great amounts of su plies and to evacuate wounded.

His most important contribution to command was to show th even in modern war audacity paid dividends and that surpri could be achieved. Right from the beginning he had a mor supremacy over his enemy.

In 1918 Salmond had not wanted to make peace with t Germans; he felt that not enough of them had been killed. Th is, he was in accord with Clausewitz. Even while Salmond w conducting his remarkable campaign in Iraq the Germans we recovering.

One of the prime architects of Germany's military recovery w von Seeckt, the Scharnhorst of the twentieth century. Schar horst had built up a secret army without Napoleon's knowir

[1] Not least in the present author's *Jackboot, the Story of the German Soldi*

ıt it. Using Scharnhorst's methods, von Seeckt built up such
ırmy without the Allies knowing about it, a classic example
equeathed skill.

fell to Adolf Hitler to use this army. Now it is a common
ake to regard Hitler as a mere megalomaniac, an insane-
tician. Hitler was a military commander, the supreme leader
he largest armies in history. Despite his many vices and
ngs, Hitler was a student of history, an enterprising com-
der, and at times an astute one. More importantly, he was
rely Frederician in military outlook. Probably he knew as
h about Frederick's campaigns as any German university
essor specializing in Prussian history.

ccording to Hitler, technical inventions did not change
egy. "Has anything changed since the battle of Cannae?"
sked.

id the invention of gunpowder in the Middle Ages change the
ws of strategy? I am sceptical as to the value of technical in-
entions. No technical novelty has ever permanently revolu-
onized warfare. Each technical advance is followed by
1other which cancels out its effects. Certainly the technique of
arfare advances and it will create many more novelties until
1e maximum of destruction is reached. But all this can pro-
ıce only a temporary superiority.[2]

e also said:

I do not play at war.... There is only one most favourable
ıoment.... I shall not miss it. Let us not play at being heroes,
ıt let us destroy the enemy.... My motto is: Destroy him by
l and any means.

1 1935 Hitler was reported to have said:

If I were going to attack an opponent I should act quite
fferently from Mussolini. I should not negotiate for months
eforehand and make lengthy preparations, but ... I should
ıddenly ... hurl myself upon the enemy.

his is perfectly logical, if we accept the premise that a nation
ts a war to win. If the aim of war is more permanent peace,
the sooner it is over the better. The idea of declaring war and
1g the potential enemy even an hour to prepare himself for
ılow is ridiculous.

ermany had the great advantage of a realistic testing-ground:

[2] Quoted by Hermann Rauschning in *The Voice of Destruction*.

during the two and a half years of the Spanish Civil War she s
about 50,000 specialist officers and men to try out new Germ
equipment under war conditions.

Very few British officers after the First World War bothe
to read German military books, but German officers certai
read British military books, and to good effect. One outstand
German commander not too proud to learn from the British w
General Heinz Guderian. He became deeply interested in armc
through reading English books and articles on tanks and th
tactics—by Liddell Hart and Fuller, among others. He also re
de Gaulle's ideas for armour, and he could see that throu
mechanized mobility the enemy's command could be complet
paralysed by a blow sudden and swift enough to smash his fro
Guderian was a well-read general; he knew that Arminius, G
tavus, Turenne, Marlborough, Frederick, and above all
Spartan generals, such as Cleomenes, Leonidas, Pausania
Agis, and Agesilaus, and also Napoleon, Sherman, some of
Southern generals of the American Civil War, and Moltke k
used mobility as a psychological weapon. Guderian plann
'ultimate' mobility—to confuse, distract, dismay, and finally
terrify. He wanted a war-strike so fast that no enemy operat
on conventional methods could possibly keep track of what w
happening on their front, flanks, or rear. And he achieved
Largely owing to Guderian the North-west Europe campaign
1940 was one of the most successful in history.

Since the nineteen-twenties the Japanese Army Staff also l
been studying the history of war. Previously they had kno
little about it, but, applying themselves to its study as assiduou
as they worked at copying Western industrial methods, tl
translated into Japanese Clausewitz and many other milit.
writers and set about imbibing foreign philosophy and practi
The generals saw their nation as a great military country in
German mould, but they set their sights too high—nothing l
than the most ambitious scheme of military conquest yet kno
—and they blatantly copied the Germans in practically ev
detail, even to trying to imitate the goose-step.

Their initial stroke—on Pearl Harbor—a copy of the Na
attacks on Warsaw, Rotterdam, and elsewhere—was bold a
successful. But the Japanese had not read history deeply enou
One bold, violent military stroke is just like one bold, viol
blow on the nose; it makes the recipient angry. As the Germa

³ Regent to King Pleistarchus, not Pausanias, second Spartan king.

w, an attack must be sustained, followed up by one sledge-
mer blow after another. For many reasons the Japanese were
pable of delivering these blows against their major enemy,
United States.

enerally, the Germans and Japanese were the only ones to
w any sense of 'future' in warfare, by both their material and
c psychological approach to it. By their bombing of Pearl
bor the Japanese showed that they had a true Arminius-like
reciation of the purpose of warfare. Their attack has been
lled 'treacherous', 'vicious', 'cunning', 'foul', and many
r things. Vicious and cunning it was, for war largely depends
oth, but treacherous it was not. War is not a game played to
s like cricket or football. It would have been absurd for the
anese to give notice of their intentions and so let their prey
pe.[4]

: was difficult to select a battle from the second Great War of
lern times to illustrate facets of the sequence of leadership. So
ly great and successful campaigns or battles occurred: the
man capture of Fort Eben-Emael, their overrunning of
ope, their capture of Greece and Crete, and their great battles
ie early days of the war with Russia, such as Vyazma-Briansk
)ctober 1941, their magnificent defence of Monte Cassino in
3–44.

he Australians' defence and retaking of New Guinea; their
arkable defence of Tobruk and their campaign in Syria;
American battles in the Pacific, such as those for Tarawa or
nawa or Iwo Jima. The battle of Alamein, of Tunisia, of
ly, Anzio; Kohima; the D-day landings and the battle for
mandy; "the Battle of the Bulge". The many German-
sian battles on the Eastern Front, of which Stalingrad is the
ie example. In the end, for reasons which I hope will become
arent, I chose the battle of Alamein, October-November
2.

owever, as we have seen, no great battle has occurred with-
preliminaries, and in the case of Alamein the preliminaries
e protracted and complex. We must go back to Wavell, who
manded the British forces in the Middle East 1939–41, to
erstand the situation which came to exist in October 1942.

The author should point out that he has a healthy dislike for the Japanese
a loathing for their treatment of their prisoners. He could never forgive
for the way they ill-treated and murdered Army nursing sisters they
ired. As an infantryman he fought against the Japanese and has no respect
hem as men, but he considers them efficient soldiers.

One day Wavell's capabilities as a general will be appreciat
He was the first British commander in the Second World W
to understand the lessons of the German campaigns in Pola
and France and to apply them to desert fighting. He was the fi
British commander efficiently to co-ordinate British land, a
and sea forces in a single campaign. Most outstandingly he weld
an army of several nationalities into a first-rate fighting for
and with it in 1940 won some of the cheapest victories in Brit
military history.

Wavell's army won these campaigns because it was super
in leadership and in the quality of its fighting troops. In eve
other respect the enemy was vastly superior, although he hims
gave a different picture in an order to his army:

> In everything but numbers we are superior to the enemy. '
> are more highly trained; we shoot straighter; we have bet
> weapons and equipment. Above all, we have stouter hea
> and greater traditions, and we are fighting in a worthier cause.

It was a good order, but it was too flat, too self-conscious
especially when delivered to the Australians and New Zealand
who formed the infantry fighting backbone of his army. Wav
was a close student of Allenby, whom he admired tremendou
—enough to write a biography of him. During two years
Palestine he learned many of Allenby's methods of comma
observed his handling of the polyglot British army and
methods of maintaining discipline and morale. "He saw a m
tary mind of real magnitude ... resort to ancient stratagems
war and receive and destroy an enemy."[5]

Wavell also learned from Allenby that a commander could
the most out of his subordinates if he gave them freedom of acti
to the limit of their abilities. Wavell, who lectured and wr
about soldiers and soldiering more than most other gener
have done, likened the relationship between the general and
army to that between a horse and a rider. "The horse (the arr
should be cared for (training and maintenance) in the stable a
he were worth £500. But he should be ridden in the field as if
were not worth half-a-crown."

Wavell, in 1939, felt it was a mistake for the British Army
spend its time studying the characteristics of foreign soldiers,
in this he was wrong and was merely echoing the narrow se
ments of third-rate generals, to which group Wavell did *not*

[5] H. A. de Weerd, *Famous British Generals.*

g. He changed his mind, for two years later it was largely his
dy of Italian military morale in North Africa which induced
 to launch his pursuit-offensive against the retreating Italians.
Many military critics believed it was impossible to surprise an
my on a bare coastal plain,[6] but Wavell saw—and was probably
first British general to see—that the desert could be used like
sea to ship men and equipment to any decisive point—if a
mander had adequate mechanical equipment and absolute
stery of the air.

His preparation for his big attack against the Italians in Decem-
1940 amounted to an elaborate feint, and he used as a model
nby's Gaza manoeuvre of November 1917. Using camouflage
ginatively, he built dummy emplacements, a fake aerodrome,
 a great counterfeit tank park in such positions as to lead the
ians to expect a conventional frontal attack on Sidi Barrani.
fact, Wavell's force struck from the south-west, and surprise
 complete.

he few months that followed were history-making. In one of
 most brilliantly bold operations of war Wavell sent the 7th
noured Division cross-country to cut off the retreat of General
lera's forces south of Benghazi. They caught the column and
ght and bluffed it into surrender—112 tanks, 216 guns, 1500
:ks, and 20,000 men. All this was blitzkrieg pattern, even if it
 not accomplished with blitzkrieg speed.

Because of his victories Wavell became, overnight, "the most
ous British general", but Wavell himself would have ad-
ted—he was of the most honest, forthright soldiers ever—
t Allenby was at his shoulder during his campaigns.

t is no slight on Wavell to say that the Italian commander,
ziani, helped the British victories. Graziani was still imbued
 First World War philosophy—that is, he fought battles
territory instead of trying to destroy his enemy's army.

'oor Wavell. Rommel retook Libya, and Wavell was suddenly
sferred to the command of India. It is wrong to judge a com-
der by the extent or number of his victories. Wavell certainly
 some disasters—but at a time when nobody else could have
e any better.

But Chauvel, under Allenby's command, achieved it on a bare plain with
Australians at Beersheba in 1917.

———◇•◇———

CHAPTER TWENTY-TWO

Montgomery and Rommel;
A Return to the
'Personality' General

has become a cliché that the North African desert is a paradise
or the tactician and a nightmare for the quartermaster. It is
atively easy here to lead armies, much more difficult to feed
:m even in static positions, but much of the warfare was now
pbile and armoured, and the British, though they had pioneered
ık warfare, were now inferior to the Germans. A tactical device
actised by Rommel had much to do with one defeat after
other inflicted on the British. When counter-attacked he would
:m a hidden screen of strong, efficient anti-tank artillery and
' to lure British tanks into fire from short range.

Right through to Alamein the Axis methods were sound
ough and reflected the sober and reasoned German approach to
evious experience and to history. They would make several
:ll-spaced probing attacks to find a weak spot. But, in any
:ack, the moment the leading tanks were knocked out the
:ack would become static. The Germans had long since learned
at to drive against stiff resistance was sheer suicide. The British
ıd the Americans learned from the German methods.

After Wavell's transfer to India the British Eighth Army
ffered several serious and assorted setbacks. One of them, the
:ath of Lieutenant-General W. H. E. Gott when his transport
rcraft was shot down, brought about Churchill's appointment
' General B. L. Montgomery as commander of the Eighth Army,

under General Alexander as Commander-in-Chief, Middle E
The Italians and Germans were at El Alamein, the Arm
fortunes were at their lowest ebb, and everything hung in
balance—or so it appeared.

When an historian praises a contemporary figure he runs
risk of being accused of being blinded by that figure's persona
and reputation, so I must here make clear that I am no bl
disciple of Field-Marshal Montgomery. In some ways he n
have been insufferable. One can be forgiven for thinking of l
as conceited, dictatorial, immoderate in his statements, h
handed in his actions, and lacking in discretion.

But after giving all proper credit to O'Connor, Wavell, Aucl
leck, Cunningham, and Ritchie, generals upon whose four
tions his victory was laid, I still think that he was the outstanc
senior Allied general of the Second World War, although infe
to Gustavus, Turenne, and Napoleon.

Montgomery had always been a capable soldier, but after
death of his wife in 1937 he studied war as never before, not c
delving into military history but probing the psychology of c
mand in large armies.

But when he took over the Eighth Army in 1942 the Germ
could not have been particularly perturbed. Rommel, "the De
Fox", was at this time the best-known general in the world;
British and Commonwealth troops in the Middle East regar
him with a sort of veneration. Even the Australians, noted
their irreverent, caustic, and loudly voiced opinions of gener
conceded that Rommel was "a good bloke". Possibly by a c
bination of accident and design Rommel had become a lege
If you were up against Rommel you had little chance of winn
—this is what most soldiers thought, despite the way Morshe;
Australians had kept him out of Tobruk. The Rommel comp
was the German's not-so-secret weapon, and his personality
felt as much as had been that of Hannibal or Caesar, Welling
or Napoleon.

Montgomery's first battle was to outshine Rommel, and as
was public relations conscious and as he had a natural abilit
project himself—as had Hannibal, Caesar, Charles Mar
Charlemagne, Condé, Napoleon and most of his marsh
Allenby in Palestine, and Orde Wingate in Burma—this was
too difficult for him to *want* to do.

Nevertheless, under modern conditions of war it is difficult
a commander to project his personality and to use it as a driv

.[1] He has advantages that generals of other ages had not, as radio and high-speed transport, but his men are much numerous and they are generally scattered over a great . Also, the commander has so much 'office work' to do that innot hope to move around among his troops and be seen by ally every man as were generals of other eras.

ontgomery's success in becoming a 'character' was out-ling. The only Allied leaders who had comparable success ng the Second World War were Orde Wingate, "Blood and ," Patton, and, to a lesser extent, "Tiny" Freyberg. Others senhower, MacArthur, Blamey, Wavell, Slim, to name a —had personalities strong enough to be felt at some distance, hey were not 'characters'. The make-up of the German and ian soldiers and of the German and Russian armies and ical structures made it impossible for any of their generals 'characters', but Rommel came nearest to being one in the nan Army and Zhukov in the Russian. Nearly every German ral had a powerful personality—an inheritance of command Frederick.

orrelli Barnett says of Montgomery's public-relations activi-in his book *The Desert Generals*: "All this would have been oundly distasteful, even had it been necessary, to any man abnormally vain." But distasteful to whom? To more odox generals perhaps. To Mr Barnett assuredly. But not to ens of thousands of men who made up the Eighth Army—they were the men whose reactions counted.

oldiers love a character, whether he happens to be their platoon commander, C.O., or commander-in-chief. Mont-ery was a genuine character, a born exhibitionist with a sense e dramatic and with tremendous confidence in himself. Such n can be inspiring.

ot necessary? It was vitally necessary for Montgomery to ect his personality, to make a splash. Barnett, *inter alia*, dly and justifiably condemns orthodoxy and its dreadful ts and then rebukes the one man who most successfully broke from it.[2] From a purely practical point of view drastic action

lsewhere during the Second World War the 'personality cult' was less suc-d. In 1944 Marshal of the RAF Lord Tedder advised the Supreme nander, General Eisenhower, to get rid of Montgomery, and Eisenhower early did so.
ome of Barnett's dislike of Montgomery may be due to the impression in order is a basis for discussion. Neither Montgomery nor any other captain would tolerate such an attitude towards an order.

was necessary: in the previous six months prior to Alam H
the Army had suffered more than 100,000 casualties.

Montgomery cleverly built up his own personality. He ado
the Australian slouch hat, covered with various hat badges.
wore it square on his head, as no Australian ever did, but it
the desired effect. Later he exchanged the hat for black ber
the Royal Tank Regiment, and on it wore their cap badge as
as his own badge of rank.

His habits disturbed many of his officers, they even distre
some. He neither drank nor smoked; he prayed and qu
scripture. He disliked needless noise, and before conferer
which he was apt to call at inconvenient times, he set aside
minute periods for coughing. His inspection trips were w
wind-like, and he had his nickname, "Monty", painted on
personal reconnaissance tank.

Yet Montgomery was no mere martinet and could be tole
—especially when he knew he had to be. If this appears to
back-handed compliment it is not meant to be; the abilit
show tolerance and latitude when it is not inwardly felt is a ta
that only gifted commanders possess. When Montgomery
visited the New Zealanders he said to General Freyberg,
notice your soldiers don't salute." Freyburg replied, "Wav
them, sir, and they'll wave back." Montgomery tried it—ar
worked.

Yet the picture of Montgomery as a hell-for-leather, impet
general is false. He spoke with bravado but acted with caut
"I am proud to be with you," he told his army. "You have n
this army what it is. You have made its name a household w
... You and I will see this thing through together." He sp
playfully about "hitting the enemy for six right out of Afr
and piously referred to "the Lord Mighty in Battle", as Crom
had often done. But generally the picture was of Napoleon
his "*Mes enfants*" all over again.

A German staff officer, von Mellenthin, noted: "the figh
efficiency of the British improved vastly under the new leader
and, for the first time, Eighth Army had a commander who re
made his presence felt throughout the whole force."

In fact, his first order made the Army sit up and take notice
said that all withdrawal plans were to be burnt. "We will f
the enemy where we now stand; there will be no withdrawal
no surrender. We stay here alive or we stay here dead."
words were Montgomery's, but the instructions came from A

der. This was immaterial; Montgomery was the man on the
ɔt, and within a few weeks everybody in the Eighth Army knew
n.

One historian has written that Montgomery introduced some-
ng new into British military history—army *esprit de corps*.
here has been regimental *esprit de corps* before but not a
rit that distinguished a whole army." The Eighth Army was
leed unique in the Second World War, but it is too much to
im that Montgomery introduced army *esprit de corps*. This
s at least as old as Marlborough. "Monty" had several things
common with "Corporal John"; one was that both were aged
:y-four at the time of their most famous victories.

Montgomery had the best group of subordinate commanders
ce Napoleon selected his marshals. In de Guingand Mont-
mery had a Chief of Staff as able as Napoleon's Berthier.
nong his armoured and infantry commanders were Gatehouse,
msden, Briggs, Horrocks, Leese, Morshead, Wimberley, Tuker,
d Freyberg.

His programme of training was so severe that an American
icer is supposed to have said, "Montgomery put an army that
s already supposed to be veteran through a physical condition-
; programme equal to that of the commandos." The historians
10 have criticized Montgomery as a general have perhaps not
dized that his methods were more French and Napoleonic than
itish, or perhaps, knowing this, they resented it. I will discuss
ɔntgomery's Napoleonic make-up at greater length after an
:ount of the battle.

On the other side of the Alamein position was one of history's
ɔst formidable soldiers, even if he was not quite the wizard
it legend has made him out to be. Vibrant in Erwin Rommel
s the whole spirit, theory, and practice of hundreds of years
German military craft.

"Let it be quite clear," Rommel once told his officers, "that
:re is no such thing as 'Direction Front', but only 'Direction
iemy'!" In this he crystallized the creed of every great German
neral since Arminius and especially of Frederick and those who
ormed the Prussian Army after Jena.

"The final decision of any struggle if the enemy attacks will
ɔbably rest with the Panzers and motorized units behind the
e. Where this decision is reached is immaterial. A battle is won
ien the enemy is destroyed. Remember one thing—every indi-
lual position must hold...." This too was Frederician. The

infantry must stand firm while the cavalry dealt the *coup grâce*.

Long before Alamein, Rommel had said, "Whoever has t greatest mobility, through efficient motorization and efficient lir of supply, can compel his opponent to act according to I wishes." It was his misfortune at Alamein that because of shorta of petrol he did not possess enough of any of these three p requisites.

Rommel was one of the few generals of the Second World W to exercise personal control over a battle; the Germans said was too often in his command vehicle and too frequently abse from his headquarters. He gave practically all his orders radio as the occasion demanded.

Montgomery regarded Rommel with respect but not with aw he had a tendency to repeat his tactics, and that was proof th he was human and vulnerable. For his part, Rommel had an op mind about Montgomery.

Montgomery took over a 40-mile line that extended from t Qattâra Depression north to El Alamein. Its main features we Himeimat, Deir El Munassib, Ruweisat Ridge, the Hill of Jes (the so-called Double 24 feature), and Thompson's Post near the Mediterranean.

The most important general feature of this position was its u attackable flanks, a position strongly reminiscent of Miltiade front at Marathon.

On the British side were some concrete pill-boxes, with e tensive wire entanglements and minefields, covered by well-cc cealed artillery. On his first visit to the front Montgomery saw t strategic importance—as his predecessor, Auchinleck, had do —of Alam Halfa, an undefended ridge of high ground in the re of the Alamein position. Montgomery reasoned that Romm would make Alam Halfa his main objective, and he prepared a elaborate trap for the German armour. More than this, he I false maps fall into Rommel's hands—maps which showed th a soft and sandy approach to Alam Halfa was firm ground. In t defensive battle which Montgomery fought here between Augu 30th and September 7th, 1942, Rommel, for whom the battle w a desperate gamble, did everything that Montgomery wanted hi to.

Rommel had some bad luck, however. General von Bismarc commander of the 21st Panzer Division, was killed by a min and the Afrika Korps commander, General Nehring, was severe

nded. Rommel himself was so sick that he had to leave his
mand truck, a disaster for the Germans because Rommel was
her Charles XII—though a much more stable one—in that
epended more on personal observation and decision than on
econceived plan.

he victory at Alam Halfa was a fine spur to the Eighth Army's
ale, as Montgomery had known it would be.

he Germans lost 49 tanks, 55 guns, 395 vehicles, and 2910
; the British casualties amounted to 1750 men and 67 tanks,
ough only half of these were total losses.

his battle over, Montgomery turned his attention to assault.
n study, Montgomery noticed that whenever Ritchie, his pre-
ssor, fought a battle of confusion against Rommel the Eighth
ry was beaten. Montgomery wanted a simple plan with a
le intention: once action was joined the initiative must never
lowed to pass to the enemy.

evertheless, Alamein was not the simple slam-bang-bust-
ugh battle that many people suppose, but a complex opera-
of many phases and movements, and not the least of Mont-
ery's achievements was his masterly handling of the com-
ities.

lontgomery's plan aimed at maximum surprise and deception.
4th Indian Division would feint at Ruweisat Ridge, the 44th
50th would feint near Deir El Munassib, and the 7th
oured south of Himeimat. The Australians would pin down
e divisions along the coast. The real attack would come in the
h at Tel el Eisa, where infantry and engineers would create a
for the Armoured Corps—a specially formed striking force.
ificantly, Montgomery was deliberately striking at the
gest part of the German front, but the Germans were ex-
ing the main assault at Ruweisat Ridge, farther south.

o strike in the north was common sense, because a break-
ugh here would automatically cut off the enemy troops to the
h; a break-through on the south would merely force them
c on their lines of communication.

lontgomery, too, had learned from Allenby's deception at
a in 1917. Montgomery formed a truck park in the rear of
oreak-through point. Each day German scout planes watched
raining area of the 10th Armoured Corps far behind the lines,
each night squadrons of tanks disguised as trucks were moved
the truck park and an equal number of trucks were with-
vn. Until the invasion of Normandy the preparations for

Alamein comprised the most elaborate fake undertaken w
dummy huts, tanks, vehicles, dumps, gun-emplacements, wa
tanks, and even a fake pipeline. The blow was being readied.

The Axis line at Alamein was very strong, with minefields f
miles deep in places, but the overall defences were not nearly de
enough if a British attack in strength was anticipated—and t
must have been the case. Still, the guns were well sited, and ta
had been dug in to serve as strong-points, a sign that Rommel v
on the defensive and was not contemplating an attack.

In his forward minefields alone—"the Devil's Gardens"
Germans called them—Rommel had used 500,000 mines, p
great quantities of captured British bombs and shells made i
mines were of German, Italian, French, and Egyptian ma
facture, all with their own peculiarities. The most notorious v
the German Teller, a difficult one to deal with. Most mines w
intended to cripple tanks, but the S-mine was aimed at infant
men. When a soldier trod on the horns of the S-mine a cha
shot a cylinder into the air about stomach-high, where it bu
with a spread of shrapnel bullets. Trip-wires were connected w
S-mines and with the large aircraft bombs, which when explod
killed men in scores.

Across the trap-strewn desert the British infantry would ha
to walk, accepting casualties. However, on Montgomery's or
a special school was set up where methods of mine-detection a
-lifting were evolved so efficiently that mines could be dealt w
even by night. To explode mines harmlessly, a small number
Matilda tanks was fitted with "the Scorpion"—a contrapt
of whirling chains.

The situation, with unattackable flanks and both sides w
powerful defences, was piquantly, even alarmingly similar to
static lines of 1914–18, and everybody knew that battle on a la
scale was inevitable.

"War is a simple thing," Montgomery said, "the ABC
modern war is common sense." And he showed his own comm
sense by insisting that every man was to know the plan
Alamein. I think it likely that the men in the ranks knew m
about the plan of battle than any other private soldiers in hist
engaged in a major fight. His decision to make his plans genera
known proved that he had studied his Australian and N
Zealand fighting-men, for they above all others have alwa
fought even better when they were 'in the picture'.

It also proved that he had studied Rommel, for he was n

up' on his opponent. The British forces knew what they
e doing right from the start; the Germans and Italians had to
t for a succession of orders and were never fully informed
ut their commander's intentions.

1 September Rommel flew to Berlin, leaving von Stumme in
mand of the Afrika Korps. Stumme divided his armour,
ling some of it south so that if the British stab came where
ected Stumme could crush it by bringing his armour together
great jaws.

n October 23rd, with Rommel still absent, the Allied forces
prised 220,476 men, 939 tanks fit for action, 892 guns, 1451
-tank guns, and 530 aircraft. The Axis had 108,000 men, ining 53,736 Germans, 548 tanks, 1063 anti-tank guns, 350
raft. Another 18,000 Germans landed just before and during
battle, while another 77,000 Italians were in the rear areas.
itgomery had physical superiority.

a the days of Turenne and Cromwell, of Marlborough and
oleon, no commander would have considered giving or
pting battle voluntarily unless he had first managed, by art
ubterfuge, to gain numerical superiority. In modern war
erals had acquired the unprofessional habit of engaging battle
rdless of their prospects—in short, they gambled. Mont-
ery was no gambler, though he was prepared to take cal-
ted risks.

CHAPTER TWENTY-THREE

———◆•◆———

Alamein, a Battle won,
a Pursuit lost;
Napoleon—Montgomery

)N the eve of battle Montgomery issued a famous order:

When I assumed command of the Eighth Army I said that the
mandate was to destroy Rommel and his army, and that it
would be done as soon as we were ready. We are ready now.
The battle which is now about to begin will be one of the
decisive battles of history. It will be the turning-point of the war.

This was unequivocal, pure Cromwellian stuff. There was no
phole such as "*If every man does his duty* we will win
ough". Even Napoleon never claimed that he was about to
t one of the decisive battles of history. But, Montgomery
ed, twelve days of bitter fighting lay ahead.

A bombardment gives warning of an imminent attack, but
ntgomery did not make the mistake of the generals of the
t World War. At the battles of the Somme and Third Ypres
bombardments lasted several days, and though they did much
erial and moral damage, the Germans were able to reinforce
to reorganize. At Alamein Montgomery limited his initial
bardment to thirty minutes. At 11.30 P.M. on Friday, October
l, the British artillery barrage—450 guns on a six-mile front—
ck the Axis positions, and so began the battle which some
orians have called a "generals' battle", while others have

labelled it a "soldiers' battle". Few victories in history wer
much dependent both on a commander's capabilities and sold
skill.

The artillery battered the command-posts and cut commun
tions. Under cover of this bombardment, which stunned ever
veteran Germans by its violence, infantry and engineer pa
advanced half an hour later to clear mines and barriers, so
infantry could advance in strength. The RAF was vastly sup
to the Luftwaffe, and its fighters and bombers made a susta
and heavy attack on Axis positions.

After that, except for ten minutes' rest each hour to cool
gun, the guns fired for five and a half hours—600 rounds
gun. And they had orders that if they came under fire thems
they must not pause or take cover.

The extraordinary aspect of the battle is that infantry
engineers—*men*—were used to clear laborious tracks thr
minefields for *armour*. No army had previously faced su
complex and dangerous mine-lifting and 'de-lousing' task,
no doubt the lessons learned at Alamein will one day be p
use by future commanders. The task took twelve days.
enough armoured minesweepers been used they could well
cleared the way in as many hours. The British Tank Corps
invented minesweepers in 1917 and had used them most
tively. Montgomery had no minesweepers, so he used men,
somebody bungled badly in not providing him with mineswee
especially as it was well known that the Axis were using min
hundreds of thousands.

This infantry-leading-armour pattern of attack was ent
that of the French attack of 1916–17 when the infantry capt
enemy trenches and put ramps across them so that the s
Renault tanks could follow up and cross them.

Despite really tough opposition the Australians secured
of their final objective by 5.30 A.M. and the New Zealanders
of theirs. The Axis outpost troops fought magnificently,
owing to the smashed network of communications, comm
was practically paralysed.

On October 24th von Stumme died of a heart-attack. Ritter
Thoma took over and desperately tried to concentrate his arr
for the enemy break-through attack he knew must come. Ron
overshadowed von Thoma as Montgomery overshadowed
generals, yet without von Thoma Rommel might not have
so successful, for this tall, courageous man, wounded tw

ies, was one of the great masters of tank-warfare—perhaps
e greatest master. He had fought in Spain, Poland, Russia,
d France and was as able a tactician as ever Germany sent to
r.

Perhaps had Rommel himself been present from the beginning
. battle might have had a different twist, but not a different
ding. Napoleon, I think, would have recognized a break-
ough as inevitable and would have prepared accordingly—that
he would have lined the corridor along which the British
ust must pass and raked it as it ran the gauntlet. Or he would
ve pulled back earlier and allowed the British to beat the air.
lly an inspirational, opportunist general could have had a
ance of stopping Montgomery's attack dead—and then only
th his army's morale equal to that of the Eighth Army.

On October 25th Rommel, who had been in hospital, took off
North Africa, at Hitler's urgent request, and that evening was
command again. He learned from von Thoma of the desperate
ortage of petrol and of ammunition. Casualties in men and
chines had been very high, but the Axis defence was still for-
dable, and at one time Montgomery was forced to assume a
mporary defensive. Up till the evening of the 25th Axis losses
re no more than 3700, very much less than the British losses.

Fighting was spirited and sustained, for rarely have two armies
en so well matched in battle discipline. On the 7th, in one epic
ht within the main battle, 300 riflemen, gunners, and sappers—
m, respectively, the 2nd Battalion Rifle Brigade, 76th Anti-
nk Regiment, and 7th field Squadron—became a garrison
tpost at a position known as "Snipe" and were isolated during
determined German-Italian counter attack. In quivering desert
at they resisted with such spirit and became such a nuisance
Rommel that an all-out effort was made to wipe out the post.
one of those mistakes that can so easily happen in the heat of
ttle, other British tank units also tried to wipe it out.

The Axis tanks made repeated attempts to crush the post, and
times came within 100 yards before they were hit and wrecked
the defenders' 6-pounders. The action gained such fame that
Committee of Investigation was set up to examine it critically.
e committee concluded that the minimum number of tanks
rnt and totally destroyed was 32—21 German and 11 Italian
plus 5 self-propelled guns. Perhaps another 20 tanks had been
ocked out but dragged away by the enemy. Other miscel-
eous vehicles had also been destroyed. British losses were 72

riflemen and gunners killed or wounded. This remarkable
fence divorced from the major action going on around it,
remarkably reminiscent of the defence of Rorke's Drift in
Zulu War of 1879, and was one of Rommel's major setback
Alamein.

Tradition made possible the magnificent stand at "Snipe
tradition sown at Crécy and Agincourt, nourished at Blenhe
Quebec, and Waterloo, in the defence of Lucknow in 1857
and Kandahar in 1880, and brought to flower at Le Cateau
1914 and elsewhere. The link of leadership in junior ranks ne
showed itself more clearly than at "Snipe", where the sei
officer, Lieutenant-Colonel V. B. Turner of the Rifle Briga
won the V.C.

I accept the risk of being accused of bias when I say tha
believe that only British, Australian, New Zealand, or ot
German troops could have held out at "Snipe". French tro
certainly could not have done so, for the Napoleonic legend
spirit had crumbled to dust in 1871.[1]

With the intelligent leading of his senior officers and the
lantry of the soldiers, Montgomery imposed on Rommel a t
of battle to which he was not accustomed and in which he wc
probably react faultily. If Montgomery strengthened one linl
the chain of command which is stronger than the others, this i
By a combination of means he imposed his will on his oppor
—and he has left a clear pattern to be followed in the future.

"As long as you can make a German commander dance to y
tune, you have nothing to fear; but once you allow the initia
to pass into his hands you are liable to have plenty of troub
Montgomery said. I hope future British commanders will rem
ber this; for the time will come when they will have a chanc
test this tenet against German leaders.

At last, on the 29th, Rommel began to make preparations
withdrawal to Fuka—a decision he should have made days
fore. But while he made these advance preparations he reali
that Montgomery had switched his main thrust along the cc
road. This thrust was savage and bloody and was carried out

[1] Men of the Free French garrison of Bir Hacheim defended this for
magnificently in May and June 1942, but it *did* fall. "Snipe" and Ro:
Drift did not. General Koenig, commander of Bir Hacheim, so favo
evacuation that he refused to accept supplies. To answer those apologists
the French who point to successful defences carried out by the French For
Legion, it is only necessary to say that Germans predominated in the Legi
ranks.

already battle-scarred and casualty-depleted Australians.
mel reinforced his positions across the road, especially at
npson's Post, where some of the most violent fighting of the
e battle took place.

ontgomery, at his H.Q. beside the Mediterranean, studied
mel's tactics, which showed obviously that Rommel knew
nain threat was along the road. Accordingly at 11 A.M. on
!9th Montgomery changed his own plan. He would make
nal blow not along the road, after all, but six miles south of
d break Rommel's powerful defences on the Rahman Track.
rtheless, the Australians would resume their road-axis attack
ep Rommel distracted.

ieir attack was so savage, so typically Australian, that
mel reacted exactly as Montgomery wanted him to. He
v in everything he could spare—and much that he could not
—to hold the northern pocket. The Australians had obsessed
t Tobruk; they obsessed him again now.

ommel began to lose the battle the moment he attempted his
ring-ram counter-offensives, for his armour was as much at
nercy of the British anti-tank guns as British armour was to
ans.

e tried four times to throw back the Australian infantry and
sh tanks, and the pocket was an inferno of dust, heat, noise,
:ombat. But, as everywhere along the line, Montgomery had
en the right men for the right place, and, as General Alex-
r said, the Australians "fought the enemy to a standstill".
· suffered 22 per cent of the British casualties in the battle.

> lead the final assault, on November 2nd Operation Super-
;e, Montgomery chose Freyberg, who evolved an artillery
aration of an intensity not seen since 1918. A total of 360
from five divisions were put under command of just one
g commander, Major-General S. C. E. Weir, the New
ind artillery commander. This centralized control of artillery
been called 'revolutionary'. It was as old as Mahomet, from
n Gustavus learned how to use it, from whom Napoleon
inherited gunnery ideas. In a way it was a return to 1914–
vith the infantry advancing behind a creeping barrage, the
s in which would fall 12 to 25 yards apart. But this was a
ing barrage in depth—four curtains of it at least—and it
preceded by a heavy aerial bombardment. It lasted four and
f hours, and 15,000 shells were fired.

iis old-fashioned attack was the prelude to a dashing thrust

by the 9th Armoured Brigade (Brigadier J. Currie), 123 ta
many of them in battered condition; few were fully efficient
cause of heavy enemy fire, mines, and accidents 29 failed to a
at the starting-line on time. It was a desperate venture, and e
man knew it. Freyberg had told them that Montgomery was
pared to accept 100 per cent casualties, a psychological spu
old as leadership itself.

The attack by the 9th Armoured Brigade—the 3rd Hus
the Wiltshire Yeomanry, and the Warwickshire Yeoman
might better be termed a charge, for the spirit which perva
the men who made it and the dash with which it was mou
and sustained were entirely cavalry in character. The spirit o
Scots Greys, of the Death and Glory Boys, of thousands of I
dead dragoons, hussars, and lancers rode with the 9th Briga
its charge. This is no mere romanticism. In 1942 the men
served in armoured units still thought of themselves as 'cav'
were very conscious of the cavalry spirit. Tradition brought
tory to the 9th Armoured. Colourful Currie himself was a pro
of the Royal Horse Artillery, and two of his C.O.s were ma
of hounds.

Currie stood upright on the outside of his tank, some
manders sat on top behind the turret, the others, with
turrets open, stood up with head and shoulders outside. Penr
flying, the tanks carried all before them, crushing enemy sol
bewildered and dazed by the barrage, rolling inevitably
dead and wounded. But as night brightened into dawn the t
became silhouetted and the German gunners and infantry
back savagely. Tank after tank was knocked out and casua
mounted. The whole cold, dusty dawn was a thunderous, vic
scream of noise, and into it the Hussars and Yeomanry d
Currie, always erect, charged right in among the enemy guns,
in places the enemy were surprised and battered into early de
at point-blank range.

But a counter-attack column of the 21st Panzer Division c
up in the dust and did great damage to the brigade, as did p
88's sited farther back or on a flank. In some of the fierce act
only two or three tanks in a British squadron survived. The
Armoured Brigade was supposed to appear about this time o
heels of the 9th, but it did not arrive. Nevertheless, the
remaining tanks of the 9th extricated themselves and, with al
discipline of fine cavalry, re-formed and continued the fight.
3rd Hussars had started the battle with 35 tanks; they now h

elve officers of the regiment had been killed and only 4
nained alive and unwounded. The Wiltshires lost practically
ry tank. The brigade's total tank losses for the whole night's
eration were 103, and their casualties in men were well over
per cent.

But within 100 yards of their burnt-out tanks were 35 wrecked
emy guns, some entangled with the tanks which had knocked
m out. The gun crews had been shot down at their posts, just
cavalry had sabred gunners in a thousand earlier actions. The
gade had taken 300 prisoners, and could have taken many
re had infantry been available to collect them.

Freyberg said: "It was a grim and gallant battle right in the
emy gun-line. Although the 9th Brigade did not reach its
ective and had heavy casualties the action was a success as the
emy gun-line was smashed." Montgomery told the brigade's
vivors that their exploit had ensured the success of the opera-
n.

It had also ensured the brigade a place in history, for their
ion was unique—a cavalry-style tank charge against emplaced
1s. In fact, it was the ultimate in cavalry actions. The slow
ocess of evolution that had begun at the end of the sixth century
en horsemen were first equipped with spurs completed its cycle
Alamein.

It may be argued, as Freyberg admitted, that armour was
d incorrectly in this battle, but as an instance of evolutional
filment it was superb. Nevertheless, the charge proved that
nour cannot attack concealed or semi-concealed guns in a
od position, such as behind a crest, and hope to succeed. Tanks,
ether British or German, could no more advance against
ll-manned anti-tank guns than cavalry could against machine-
1s.

Rommel himself came to the conclusion that in general "there
ittle chance of success in a tank attack over country where the
emy has been able to take up defensive positions." The anti-
k gun and the mine dominated the battle of Alamein, and be-
ase of them the defenders were in a much stronger position
n the attackers.

It is not possible to win battles with tanks unless they have close
ti-tank support, as the Russians learned from the Germans on
: Eastern Front. The Germans repeatedly smashed Russian
nour, not with tanks alone, but with tanks aided by mobile
k-attack guns.

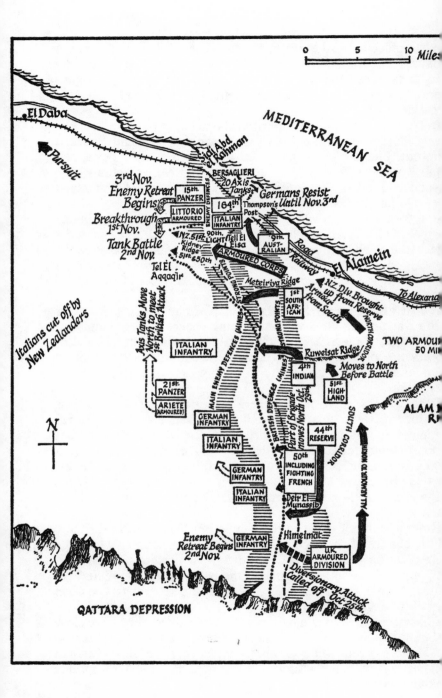

he German mistake was in waiting for the inevitable British
isive after the defeat of the German attack on Alam el Halfa,
ust 31st–September 7th. Montgomery's front, stretched be-
n virtually unattackable flanks, was what all commanders
: striven to achieve.

he British decision to make the main blow in the north was
:ly the execution of an ancient principle: Cut the enemy off
i his communications and supplies. Alamein was reminis-
of Leuthen in that Montgomery was, in a sense, delivering
nk attack, and if successful he could roll up the enemy line.
nade a thrust along the northern road, and when he realized
Rommel was reacting to this thrust he changed the axis of his
kthrough southward, where it would hit the Italians.

The charge by the 9th Brigade was the prelude to a mu larger battle, Tel el Aqqaqir, a tank duel on a divisional sc with both sides supported by intense artillery and anti-tank and by air action. In this vital battle, over and over British ta ran out of ammunition, and 'ammo trucks' drove out across shell-swept battlefield to supply them. Montgomery's arm fought the panzers and the Italian tanks to a standstill; by the of the day Rommel's tank strength had fallen by 117, of which were German. But though British artillery destroyed ma enemy batteries and the British tanks outclassed Rommel's, Axis tanks nevertheless brought their enemies to a halt a stopped all penetration; but Rommel knew the battle was lost. T Afrika Korps had only 35 serviceable tanks left, von Thoma I been captured, and the supply position was, as Rommel wro "absolutely desperate".

He was not yet beaten; perhaps he did not yet realize that was out-generalled. Rommel has been called the supreme opp tunist general, but Montgomery had a mind twice as agile. knew how to exploit success and had the rare courage—s only in genuinely great captains—to press on with a new act before waiting to see the result of the one before. He did this n Before the Tel el Aqqaqir battle was well under way Montgom decided to strike southward from what was known as "the N Zealand funnel"—a corridor driven into the Axis lines. T minor and completely successful operations were made, t widening the funnel and giving new ground for further explo tion. This day was the beginning of the end for Rommel, and abandoned any idea of a counter-attack. All he could hope to was to build some kind of barrier behind which he could w draw in good order, though in this he was hindered by air r after air raid.

But on that eleventh day of battle very few men in the Eig Army could foresee a decisive victory. Montgomery still exu confidence, but his officers were far too exhausted to soak up of it. Troops were scarce, and already base areas and hospi had been scoured for men fit for action. Montgomery had war everybody that the battle would be vicious and unremitting twelve days. One day to go.

That night Montgomery had enough evidence to show t Rommel was on the verge of a general retirement, and reasoned that his opponent would plan a stand on the scarp n Fuka. He gave instant orders for further exploitation—a lar

el through which he could launch the New Zealanders and
7th Armoured Division in a great south-north sweep in an
npt to cut off the enemy's retreat. This decision was a
iant conception and, again, reveals a first-class military brain.
is ability to come to a decision, to give instant effect to it,
ttgomery was equalled only by Alexander the Great,
erick, and Napoleon among the really great commanders.
attack on the night of November 3rd and the fights on
ember 4th ended the battle—twelve days after it had begun.
ttgomery's forecast had been right.

ommel was already withdrawing, but Hitler told him on
ember 3rd "not to yield a yard of ground". Rommel sent his
C. to Hitler to say that to stand fast meant annihilation. This
ited in Field-Marshal Kesselring's arrival at Rommel's H.Q.
November 4th. According to Rommel, he reaffirmed Hitler's
sion, but Kesselring was to write that he advised Rommel to
re Hitler and accepted full responsibility for a retreat.
imel, to save what he could of his army, ordered withdrawal.

asualty figures vary. According to Alexander between
ber 23rd and November 7th the Axis armies lost 10,000
d, 15,000 wounded, and about 30,000 prisoners.

arnett quotes German losses at 180 tanks, 1000 dead and
prisoners, the Italians losses at 1000 dead and 16,000
ners.

ital British casualties were 13,600 killed, wounded, or miss-
–and missing usually meant dead.

he German retreat from Alamein was magnificently con-
ed. Montgomery had won the battle, but he can be accused
aving lost the pursuit. He was hesitant in getting it started
over-cautious in the actual movement. He must have known
the Axis defences were smashed, that they had little armour
were running out of petrol, yet Rommel was able to with-
v much of his force. By re-grouping for pursuit on November
Montgomery gave Rommel eighteen vital hours during which
Axis troops never stopped moving.

ommel, though in great difficulties from lack of everything,
his command together by the strength of his own personality
by the innate steadiness of his men. He fought some splendid
guard actions, and when he couldn't fight he bluffed. That he
able to hold Montgomery down to such a slow rate of ad-
e despite British numerical and material superiority attested
is ability. Montgomery had, at times, 450 tanks to Rommel's

50, yet he took three months to reach Tripoli from Alame
Montgomery, the established-front, semi-static-battle general, v
no pursuit general.

C. E. Lucas Phillips, another defender of Montgomery a
author of an admirable book about the battle, *Alamein*, sta
that the "German divisions had been reduced to skeletons" a
that "the Italians had been broken to bits", and on the followi
page claims that the "resounding victory" was the beginning
"the no less victorious pursuit". There is no victory in a purs
which could average only thirty miles a day for the first sixte
days against a "skeleton" and "broken to bits" enemy. This
the only point of Lucas Phillips' assessment of Alamein with whi
I disagree.

The withdrawal was Rommel's victory. It was as compet
as that of Moore to Corunna in 1808–9, of the Russian re
guard actions under Rosen during the Russian retreat in 18
and similar actions under Ney when the French, in turn, we
retreating. It was as well co-ordinated as the British retreat fro
Mons in 1914. But, most of all, it was startlingly similar to t
intriguing series of rearguard actions fought by the Confedera
General Johnston when he held Sherman down in his march fro
Chattanooga to Atlanta to an advance of a mere hundred mil
in seventy-two days. Clever enough not to remain too long
one position, Johnston invariably took precautions to secure h
retreat—just as Rommel did. And, in final praise, let it be sa
Xenophon would have been proud of Rommel.

I have said that Montgomery was Napoleonic in many way
Anybody who has analysed the writings of both men will ha
seen the marked similarities in style and in personal evaluatio
Also, Montgomery closely followed some of Napoleon's stronge
maxims.

"I see only one thing—the enemy's main army", Napoleo
said. Montgomery followed this precept. On the northern flai
his troops surrounded a large force of Germans, but Montgome
refused to be drawn into a decisive action at that point. He co
tinued to concentrate his spearhead against the German mai
force—the panzer divisions.

Montgomery was positively imbued with the following Nap
leonic maxims:

"Glory and military honour is the first duty a general shoul
consider when he is going to fight; the safety and preservation c

men is secondary; but this very boldness and tenacity ensures
safety and economy of life."
Nothing is more important in war than unity in command;
s ... there should be but one army acting on one line and
by one chief."
In war the leader alone understands the importance of
ain things, and he may alone, of his own will and superior
dom, conquer and overcome all difficulties."[2]
In battle ... art is shown in directing fire from many quarters
one point; when the fight is once begun, a leader skilful enough
ring to bear on one point an unexpected mass of artillery is
e to carry the day."

The first quality of a commander is a cool head," Napoleon
te. And Montgomery echoed, "Never worry."
After the war Montgomery said: "I call high morale the
atest single factor in war. A high morale is based on discipline,
-respect and confidence of the soldier in his commanders, in
weapons and in himself. Without high morale no success can
achieved."[3] Napoleon had said this before him, as had a dozen
er great captains or military writers over the centuries, for the
in of command is a living thing.

De Gaulle, in 1934, in *The Army of the Future*, showed his profound
reciation of this point: "In order to secure distinguishing characteristics
military formations the leaders must stamp their own images on them.
y must be allowed the right to do that."
True, but the victor in nearly every case has been superior in weapons.

CHAPTER TWENTY-FOUR

❖❖

Full Circle and the Future

ɔʀ a few days each century destiny dominates a battlefield—I
use the term in its widest sense to include, as it now must,
itehall, the Pentagon, and the Kremlin. On these few days
 judgment, discretion, education, outlook, and authority of
nmanders, which depend mostly on the intellectual and moral
exes acquired during their whole career, are tested by fire.
ʾeace is merely the incubation period of war; the type of war
hot' or 'cold'—makes no difference. In practice the war is
ally won by the nation and the commanders who most deter-
nedly prepare for it in peace.[1] The defeat of the Germans in 1945
ɛs not invalidate this principle. They won everywhere during
 early years of the war. They lost in the end for a variety of
sons, chief of which were the aerial devastation of the German
neland, overwhelming Allied numerical and material superi-
ty, the drain of fighting on several fronts at once, Hitler's
erference with his generals, and the generals' failure to stand
for their own military principles.

The British appreciation of the scientific aspects of war is
ɔwn by the three-month course at the Royal Military College of
ence at Shrivenham, now attended by all British officers before
ir year's training at the Staff College. The commandant of
 college, Major-General R. W. Ewbank, wrote in 1964:

Whether we like it or not, the Army today lives, moves and
has its being in a scientific environment, and one which is becoming more so every year. I believe that an officer today,

[1] "If you want peace, prepare for war." Roman proverb.

whatever his arm, cannot but increase his efficiency—and means his ability to lead men in battle as well as to equip prepare them for battle—if he makes a real effort to tr understand what is going on in the world around him.

It is even more encouraging to find a senior lecturer at college writing:

> If there are lessons from history we must know them; if t are lessons from science we must know these, too ... there basic foundation of knowledge drawn from many fields w is a common requirement for all of us.

Such statements, coming from key officers, are encourag for science can improve the accuracy of predictions about future. It takes about ten years to bring a new weapon sys into service, so planners must predict at a range of fif years and upward. The environment of a nuclear battle will be vastly different from all previous military experie It will call for greater dispersion, but at the same time n more rapid effective command and control. Consequently, c manders must have or must develop an imaginative adjustr for the future.

However, some generals still want to fight a war with stra and tactics more suitable for the weapons and methods of te twenty years or even half a century before. It is the leader can adapt himself most rapidly to change who wins battles; th why it is wrong to give high command to an elderly soldier. man is so rigid in thought as an old soldier, and the few ex tions, such as Turenne and Blücher, only prove the point younger senior officers are the most effective ones. Most Gov ments now realize this and put their Service chiefs out to gra a comparatively early age.[2]

A purely professional environment is extremely danger and the higher the rank of the commander and the longer length of service the greater the danger. He becomes rigid in look and develops an inability to appreciate anybody e opinion; this happened to several German and Japanese gene to Hitler, and to Douglas MacArthur. MacArthur's frame of n became so very dangerous that the President had to remove from command.

[2] Had young and vital Captain John Moore of the 32nd Regiment bee command at Cawnpore in 1857 instead of doddering, indecisive Ge Wheeler there would have been no frightful massacre.

radoxically, many professional soldiers of all ranks know
little about war, even if they are well informed about the
anism of armies.[3] There is still an impression—fortunately it
ling—that a general automatically knows all there is to know
that it would be offensive to a senior officer to expect him to
rgo serious training. Somehow or other, by his very elevation
igh rank he is supposed to become imbued with profound
vledge.

Britain, at least, high-ranking officers no longer merely
ificate and are not confined within a purely professional
onment. It is encouraging to find that their education has
lar injections of information not directly connected with war-
but of vital concern to an officer whose interests must be
al and catholic.

igadiers who attended a representative course heard lectures
he following subjects: The Far East and Malaysia; The
nomic Future of Britain and the Commonwealth in its World
ng; Britain and the United States; the Future of Australia
New Zealand; Russian Foreign Policy; People and Power in
Middle East; 'Victory' or Co-existence?: The American
nma; Crisis in Africa; The Congo Impasse and the Com-
ist Threat to Tanzania; Problems of Western Europe.

ourses of this kind are held in the United States and in the
'O countries, with the result that senior officers become much
widely informed, and hence their minds stay more elastic.
tal elasticity is vital, for the modern commander has multiple
ests; battle is not his sole existence and end.

en so, soldiers are profoundly conservative and more prone
sist change than the members of any other profession. Even
great military innovators were slow in bringing in their in-
tions. Hundreds of military disasters or near disasters and
leaths of millions of soldiers can be laid at the feet of con-
tism, but the military hierarchy has never been permanently
l of it.

ne of the earliest examples of conservatism concerned the
an defensive system, which under the Emperor Augustus
no central reserve—always a paramount and fundamental
ssity. Nearly 300 years elapsed before Diocletian, during the
ten years of the third century A.D., partly remedied this by
lishing the *comitatenses*—a field army under the direct com-
l of the emperor. Even then Roman tactics remained wedded

n observation made also by Liddell Hart, in *Thoughts on War.*

to the belief that infantry was the decisive arm, and not until
was the cavalry able to prove itself the decisive arm—at the b
of Mursa, the first victory won in the West by newly raised Ro
heavy cavalry.

It would be frustrating to list the many examples of mili
conservatism. It was the morass of helplessness and hopeless
in which 24,000 British soldiers died of illness and exposur
the Crimea.

It was the pig-headedness before the 1914–18 war when 1
leaders, especially the British, refused to see the potential us
aircraft and mechanization in battle. It was the wall aga
which the tank pioneers beat their heads in vain for years. It
the criminal stupidity which sent human bodies charging aga
sheets of machine-gun bullets.

Even some of those who say most emphatically that the mi
now dominates the battlefield, persist as obstinately as other
their belief in close-quarter action. Tank soldiers—I have spo
to many of them—persist in their determination to rush at
enemy and deal with him at close quarters, which is as brai
as it is gallant.

The need for younger generals with more flexible mind
creases in urgency proportionately to the increase in speed
destructiveness of modern warfare. The capable comma
needs to be aware of the need for physical and mental fitne
modern war, especially guerrilla warfare, places increasing s
on the body and mind of the soldier.

Primarily, any general who aspires to be a great captain o
future must decide on his attitude towards destruction.
approach commanders have towards war, and in particular to
lengths they may justifiably go to bring an enemy to his kr
has its progressive chain. It is true that in the history of war 1
are always commanders who wage it with less ferocity
others. According to the accident of the existence of such
the behaviour of commanders and armies fluctuates from wa
war, but generally the trend is towards greater barbarity
greater destructiveness, even if most armies have succeede
curbing indiscriminate rape and plunder. As commanders
found greater power in their hands they have naturally used
power, and nearly always under the guise of 'military neces
At Agincourt Henry V ordered all prisoners to be killed, but
was an almost innocuous act compared with the sack of Ma
burg in 1631, when more than 40,000 people perished. And

s a minor atrocity compared with the destruction of Warsaw or
:sden or Hiroshima.

3y their intensive bombing of Germany, carried out without
·ning and with complete disregard for the life and property of
₁-combatants, the British, Americans, and Russians fulfilled
:he letter Clausewitz's philosophy of defeat and total destruc-
₁. Superb irony.

:hey also obeyed a maxim propounded by Lenin, who said
t the "soundest strategy in war is to postpone operations
il the moral disintegration of the enemy renders the delivery
the mortal blow both possible and easy." America was not
owing this maxim when she struck her mortal blow against
·an.

:he evolution of weapons has had much to do with the
uence of leadership. Thousands of years ago David showed
t with a missile a soldier could deliver a fatal blow without
ing a chance of receiving one. Gradually the expert archer im-
ved on this principle. The breech-loading rifle added to the
ge of the blow and the probability of a hit, and the machine-
₁ made hitting a near certainty, without seriously increasing
·osure.

:he trouble is that war has not yet recovered from the state of
₁vulsive evolution into which firearms threw it. Thousands of
es of muskets, rifles, and guns have come and gone. The sword
l lance had been nothing more than extension of the human
bs, but firearms possessed characteristics quite independent of
skill and bravery of the soldier.

·rogressively their range, rate of fire, stopping power, penetrat-
effect, quantity of ammunition required, and so on governed
choice of formations, place and time of combat. The volume
fire increased. In his later battles Napoleon usually began by
ncing the whole of the enemy's artillery by means of his massed
llery fire: he aimed at having 4 guns for each 1000 men. Many
·r commanders tried to follow this principle, with varying
cess.

:ombatant armies fought, usually, at greater distance from
h other, and troops, under dangerous fire, had to take cover.
₂ commander found observation and control much more
icult. Two things happened simultaneously: technical ability
l knowledge became more important; the commander's direct
ion on the man who was carrying out his orders decreased from
r to war, battle to battle.

Astute generals, realizing that they could not be seen by
their men at any one time, deliberately set out to infuse gr
esprit de corps, and at appropriate times and places tl
appeared in person, and often dramatically. Condé, Hoc
Napoleon, Rommel, and Montgomery were generals of t
type.

Moltke was the high priest of technical ability and knowled
Before the war of 1870, by studying the French railway syste
Moltke was able to forecast with absolute accuracy the direct
of Napoleon III's advance, the distribution of his forces, and
extent of the front they would occupy. Moltke was grii
materialistic, and by 1914 material elements began to reach
wards the ultimate.

The power of weapons reduced warfare pretty much to a mat
of mathematics. Vast and complex calculations and numeri
specialists to make them were required before a commander co
indulge in the luxury of what some called martial inspiration,
was nothing more than painful deliberation. He had to weigh
detailed proposals of his assistants, and when, after all the p
liminary staff work was completed—and it could take month
all he saw of the battle itself was its plotting on a map. There v
no longer much scope for genius or even for individualism, exc
under a few unconventional and enterprising generals.

It was once possible to choose between two kinds of strateg
those of annihilation and exhaustion. It is now highly improba
that a major *conventional* war could last long enough to exha
a nation by famine or in any other way, so that again history
turned full circle, and battles of annihilation, as practised
ancient times, will once more confront the world. The o
difference is that not only armies but whole communities will
annihilated, thanks to the conscription of science into the rank
combatants, for David's sling-shot has become a long-dista
nuclear missile.

The delivery of blows without exposure is the very essence
missile fighting and is the true source of modern military pov
In this respect the Polaris missile—fired from under water b
submarine which cannot be tracked—can hardly be bettered
a defensive-offensive weapon. Should intercontinental balli
missile warfare develop the aim will be largely Napoleonic
theory—to knock out the enemy's 'artillery' before he has mi
chance to use it.

The significant point is how the missile will be delivered—i

·livered. I have already pointed out that most great victories
: been won by the strategy of indirect approach. But sur-
ngly the direct approach has always been the accepted form
:rategy. Many a general has adopted the indirect as a last,
erate resource. When it worked, as it so often did—even
1 the general concerned had been previously militarily
kened—he apparently did not realize its significance. The
t consistently successful leaders, facing a powerful enemy,
ly attacked him directly; Alexander is the only exception.
lborough made only one direct attack—and paid for it.
ar erred several times—and also paid for his errors.

competent commander should do anything rather than com-
himself to a direct approach. He will cut loose from his com-
ications—as Hannibal, Genghiz Khan, Napoleon, Grant,
man, von Lettow-Vorbeck, and Salmond did—he will cross
rts, mountains, and swamps and suffer the inevitable hard-
s. A direct approach causes a stalemate which becomes more
luble war by war, if only because such an approach con-
lates and stabilizes the enemy on his own base. Far from
g caught off balance, he is ready to fight.[4]

eneral "Stonewall" Jackson's motto during the American
I War was "Mystify, mislead, and surprise"—the du
sclin theory. As a strategical and tactical principle it is un-
lled for present-day warfare. The power of striking like 'a
from the blue' has the greatest possible value, as Colonel
derson observed in his book published in 1905. "The first
ght, and the last, of the great general is to outwit his adversary
to strike where he is least expected."

:om the time of Waterloo there has existed the belief that
riority in numbers is decisive—and increasingly decisive. This
dangerously false doctrine. There is only one major factor in
y's war—surprise backed by continuous action. The victor
he next great war is the side which strikes first—without
aration of war, without even a hint that it is about to strike.
is the true and ultimate nature of war, and it amounts to
lysis by destruction. But—surprise is becoming increasingly
:ult to achieve.

ne major problem—that of supply—which bedevilled com-
ders more and more as warfare became increasingly complex,

he art of the indirect approach can only be mastered and its full scope
eciated by study of and reflection upon the whole history of war. Liddell
The Strategy of Indirect Approach.

has been largely solved, but the scope and extravagance of solution may be the undoing of the nation which has m noticeably mastered it—the USA.

The Americans' success in solving the problems of sup followed directly on their experiences in the Civil War, with la lessons from other wars. But this success has had a hamper effect on the US armies, which use a vast amount of transp to carry iced drinks, comic books, hot-water bottles, over cc fortable bedding, and an array of 'amenities' which would ma the ancient commanders roar with laughter—and their soldi too. During the Korean War the roads were cluttered with n essential transport which became a danger to the fighting troo The nation which can most nearly reproduce Spartanism in army in peace as well as in war will be best prepared to meet challenges of the future. An army which places too much str on its material comforts and in which the men are merely look forward to their retirement pension does not deserve the name army.

It is significant that in the American Army for every 18,0 men in the forward zone there are another 50,000 in the r areas of the theatre of war; the Russian Army needs only t behind the forward zone to support one in the zone. An Am can-type division needs 600–800 tons of supplies a day; a Sov type division 150 tons.

Despite scientific and technological improvements, by a curi paradoxical reaction machine warfare has reached the st; where leadership in the real sense is again paramount. Fire l caught up with movement, but never again could a front beco static in the sense of 1914–18 because there is no front, or, to l it another way, it is a 360-degree front with a depth extending the homes of the soldiers at home. Speed has reached such a mactic pitch that leaders of all ranks will have to make decisi and implement them in minutes or seconds.

The quality of audacity is fostered by subsidized 'advent training' in deserts, mountains, and even in Arctic regions. T is an enlightened aspect of Army planning.

The added responsibility which faces more junior officers war does not mean that the High Command or the General S is out of a job. On the contrary, never has planning and fc thought been so necessary. For now war, though undeclared, perpetual, and the General Staff must have its plans ready to minute. Prussian war plans, as evolved by Moltke, were elabor

far-reaching, but in comparison with today's requirements
are crude.

some circumstances, following the necessity for dispersion,
try warfare could easily assume a form of 'regular guerrilla'
ing. The infantry would always give way to opposing mech-
d columns, then would return when the armour had moved
At the same time enemy rear areas and bases would be
ar-attacked. This combination could easily exhaust mech-
d forces before they could reach their decisive strategic
tives.

hink it very likely that nuclear warfare, instead of leading to
intensive mechanized warfare, would bring about a type of
n in which infantry would again predominate, if only be-
the complicated and expensive war engines of all types are
ully dependent on complex supply services, which would
inly be thrown out of gear by base-area nuclear-attack.

e are going to need a type of really tough light infantry after
tyle of General Moore's creation. Between 1939 and 1945 the
nans and Russians produced infantry that could march 30–
iles a day, and were so reliable that they often arrived at an
tive before long motorized columns which had left the
rture point at the same time. Paratroops will be needed too,
gh much more in non-European theatres of war, such as in
, where air and radar cover will be more scattered.

ture wars—at least those fought on this planet—seem bound
ideological. Wars have for so long been fought for territory
we tend to forget that in various eras wars have been fought
attempt to impose a religion or a political system on an
y people. In the twentieth century we have come full circle.
ideological wars require ideological armies—and such armies
ot created overnight. Iron Curtain and Asiatic countries have
close attention to psychological and political problems of
ing and future armies. Because of the very democratic prin-
s they seek to defend, the Western countries lag far behind in
trinating and disciplining their troops to the iron standards
red.

would be difficult to overemphasize the importance and
t of guerrilla warfare, which is in itself a type of indirect
gic and tactical approach, especially in Vietnam. Ever
1945, without cessation, it has been taking place in one
try or another—in Palestine, Greece, Cyprus, Cuba, Malaya,
nam, Laos, Borneo, Algeria, Kenya, to mention just a few

theatres of operation. Between 1945 and 1965 no fewer than
wars occurred.[5] More than a quarter of the world is subject to
threatened by guerrilla warfare. Occasionally, there has bee
more or less conventional action, of which the Korean W
was the prime example. The world is confronted with two va
different weapons threatening its peace—the megaton hydro,
bomb and a nail in a piece of wood buried in a rice paddy.
remarkable contrast. There will be more guerrilla warfare, m
more, because the fearsome deterrents leave combatant Pow
no stronger form of war, as President Kennedy pointed c
Should conventional warfare break out there would be an ev
present and increasing risk of its getting out of hand to the pc
where nuclear weapons might be used. Nuclear weapons, howev
are virtually useless in guerrilla warfare.

Some races are natural guerrilla fighters; some countries ha
natural guerrilla terrain. In some places guerrilla warfare has
come a way of life, as in Vietnam, where Americans expect it
continue until the end of the century and possibly beyond th
They say that only an all-out war with massive forces on be
sides would bring about an earlier decision. We may well fi
that guerrilla warfare is 'conventional' warfare and that warf
formerly regarded as conventional is now unorthodox.

For armies of the more conventional Western or Westerniz
countries the mission is obvious: their soldiers must learn
master the guerrilla and to evolve counter-guerrilla tactics. To
this they must know the enemy intimately, his character a
mentality, his methods, tactics, techniques, strengths, weakness
They must themselves be versatile, enterprising, and tough. Mc
than that, as Lieut.-Colonel T. G. Greene, editor of the Unit
States Marine Corps Journal points out, "to beat the guerri
means to fight not in the sharp black and white of formal comb
but in a grey, fuzzy obscurity where politics affects tactics a
economics influence strategy. The soldier must fuse with t
statesman, the private turn politician." This is the doctrine
Clausewitz all over again—that war is a continuation of politi
The foundation of the United Nations, of the North Atlan
Treaty Organization, and of the South-East Asia Treaty Orga
zation are just such continuations.

It is not possible for the Western countries to give too mu
attention to counter-guerrilla training; we shall be living wi
guerrilla warfare for many years. The British have learned muc

[5] In the 5560 years to 1965 a total of 14,531 wars occurred—2·6 a year.

only the United States seems to have found the correct mental
roach to the problem, and even here the Marine Corps has
ved the best techniques. The Americans realize that they
aselves cannot become guerrillas—not unless they intend to
: in California or New England. Guerrillas have to blend with
local population; they must look, speak, act, and think like
ves of the troubled area. Neither the British in Borneo nor the
ericans in Vietnam can do this.

areer politicians, whose interference in war reached unhappy
hts between 1939 and 1945, will not have time to interfere in
ear warfare. A president, a prime minister, or a dictator
ut give the order to press the button, but after that he must
 out of the way. A commander's initiative will again be-
e almost absolute, in the Caesarian-Gustavian-Napoleonic

say this despite the sophistication of computer controls, which
 the Americans say—leaves practically nothing to chance or
uman error. In the new Combat Operations Centre of the
th American Air Defence Command built deep inside
yenne Mountain, Colorado, and opened in April 1966, are
ewer than 13 computers and a vast amount of other complex
pment. By simply pressing buttons, NORAD officers can
tronically scan the entire North American continent and its
unt approaches. A single operations panel can call up 12 mil-
 pieces of computerized information. But beyond the elec-
ic logic of the computers there is always a human brain which
t make the final decisions. The United States and Russia are
ıged in a race for the armed domination of space, a state of
rs that is almost unnoticed by the world at large. Already
two nations are doing a good deal of spying from unmanned
llites.

espite all scientific advance, and perhaps in part because of it,
ership is turning full circle.

he great commander will restore personal contact with his
. His armies are bigger, but he has the means to travel around
ı. He could not hope to do this during battle, except on
f occasions, any more than the great commanders of the past
so. But he must do so beforehand and with great assiduity
 dedication. In any case, while senior commanders must
ain with their maps and telephones and computers in rela-
 safety there should be field generals capable of once again
ing from the front and prepared also to head the casualty lists

as in the days of old and as so many German generals did d
1939–45.

The commander's personality must be developed again
"developed as a Law", as de Gaulle advised in *The Army o
Future*.

> To exercise imagination, judgment and decision, not in a
> tain direction, but for their own sake and with no other
> than to make them strong and free, will be the philosop
> training of leaders. The real school of leadership is ge
> culture. . . . Through it the mind learns to . . . educate itseł
> level where the whole can be appreciated without prejudi
> the shades of difference within it. There has been no illust
> captain who did not possess taste and feeling for the her
> of the human mind. At the root of Alexander's victories
> will always find Aristotle.

No poetic hyperbole this, for Aristotle was the young
ander's tutor for three years. And how many people know
Xenophon and Socrates were close friends? Did *philoso*
teachings make such great *soldiers*?

So has the chain been formed, so will it be lengthened, b
brotherhood of men with a hunger for glory and a taste for m
immortality. But remember this—those who will win
strongest links will be those most willing and able to s
lessons from the womb of time by an analysis of the birthpar
the past and to father their application to the present—whe
the present might be.

Appendix: Sun Tzŭ

———◇◆◇———

THE reader has encountered many military maxims and proverbs throughout this book. He may be interested to read a few of those propounded by Sun Tzŭ 2500 years ago and to reflect on the similarity between them and the maxims and practice of much more recent times:

It is a military axiom not to advance uphill against the enemy, nor to oppose him when he comes downhill.

An army should be always ready but never used.

Attacking does not merely consist in assaulting walled cities or striking at an army in battle array; it must include the art of assailing the enemy's mental equilibrium.

Attack is the secret of defence; defence is the planning of an attack.

The commander stands for the virtues of wisdom, sincerity, benevolence, courage, and strictness. [The five cardinal virtues of the Chinese are humanity or benevolence, uprightness of mind, self-respect or self-control, wisdom, sincerity or good faith.]

To secure ourselves against defeat lies in our own hands, but the opportunity of defeating the enemy is provided by the enemy himself.

If you know the enemy and know yourself you need not fear the result of a hundred battles. If you know yourself but not the enemy for every victory gained you will suffer a defeat.

To fight and conquer in all your battles is not supreme excellence; supreme excellence consists in breaking the enemy's resistance without fighting.

Without harmony in the State no military expedition can be undertaken; without harmony in the army no battle array can be formed.

Avoid what is strong and strike at what is weak ... the soldier works out his victory in relation to the foe whom he is facing. ... He who can modify his tactics in relation to his opponent and thereby succeed in winning may be called a heaven-sent captain.

With a superior force, make for easy ground; with an inferior one, make for difficult ground.

Do not repeat the tactics that have gained you one victory, but let your methods be regulated by the infinite variety of circumstances.

Only the side that gets more men will win.

Bibliography

ETT, CORRELLI: *The Desert Generals* (William Kimber, 1960).
s of the 19th Century (Cassell, 7 vols, 1900).
ES, NORMAN: *The Byzantine Empire* (Oxford University Press, 5).
ELL, CHARLES: *Arms and Armour in Antiquity and the Middle es* (Reeves and Turner, 1874).
E, LIEUT.-COLONEL ALFRED H.: *The Art of War on Land* thuen, 1944).
CHILL, WINSTON S.: *The World Crisis* (Odhams, 1919).
SEWITZ, KARL VON: *Vom Kriege* (*On War*), German edition of 0.
E, STEPHEN: *Great Battles of the World* (Bell and Sons, 1901).
SY, SIR EDWARD: *The Fifteen Decisive Battles of The World* cmillan, 1902).
, EDMUND: *Trench Warfare* (United Newspapers, 1915).
ON, COLONEL G. T.: *A History of Cavalry* (Macmillan, 1913).
E, COLONEL T. A.: *Gustavus Adolphus* (Houghton Mifflin, 1895).
NT, J. HENRI: *A Memory of Solferino* (Cassell, 1947).
MAJOR H. G.: *Historical Illustrations to Field Service Regulations, Operation, 1929* (Sifton Praed, 1930).
, CAPTAIN C.: *The Art of War* (Oxford University Press, 1961).
R, J. A.: *Military Manners and Customs* (Chatto and Windus, 5).
R, MAJOR-GENERAL J. F. C.: *The Conduct of War 1789–1961* e and Spottiswoode, 1961).
—— *Decisive Battles of the Western World* (3 vols, Eyre and ttiswoode, 1954–56).
—— *Armament and History* (Eyre and Spottiswoode, 1946).
—— "Machine Warfare" (*The Infantry Journal*, Washington, 3).
NER, S. R.: *History of the Great Civil War, 1642–49* (2 vols, gmans, 1886–89).
LE, GENERAL DE: *The Army of the Future* (1934).
RT, JACQUES DE: *Essai général de tactique* (2 vols, 1775).
EN, HARRY: *The Civil War* (New American Library, 1961).
TTLE, T. B.: *Dictionary of Battles* (Swan Sonnenschein, 1904).
CAPTAIN SIR B. H. LIDDELL: *Thoughts on War* (Faber and er, 1944).

HART, GEORGE H.: *Great Soldiers* (Grant Richards, 1911).

HENDERSON, COLONEL G. F. R.: *The Science of War* (Long 1905).

HENRY, PROFESSOR L. E.: *Napoleon's War Maxims* (Gale and Po 1899).

JACKSON, ROBERT: *Formation, Discipline and Economy of A* (Military Library, 1845).

JAMES, CHARLES: *Military Dictionary* (Military Library, 1810).

LAFFIN, JOHN: *Digger: Story of the Australian Soldier* (Cassell, 1
————— *Scotland the Brave: Story of the Scottish Soldier* (Ca 1963).
————— *The Face of War* (Abelard-Schuman, 1963).
————— *Swifter Than Eagles: Biography of Marshal of the R Sir John Salmond* (Blackwood, 1964).
————— *Jackboot: Story of the German Soldier* (Cassell, 1965)

MORLEY, JOHN: *Oliver Cromwell* (Macmillan, 1900).

NICOLAI, DR G. F.: *The Biology of War* (Dent, 1919).

PARKER, BARRETT (editor): *Famous British Generals* (Nicholson Watson, 1951).

PHILLIPS, C. E. LUCAS: *Alamein* (Heinemann, 1962).

PORTWAY, LIEUT.-COLONEL DONALD: *Military Science To-day* (O University Press, 1940).

REIDE, THOMAS: *Military Discipline* (Military Library, 1795).

ROGNIAT, H.: *Sur l'art de la Guerre* (1817).

ROSE, J. HOLLAND: *The Indecisiveness of Modern War* (Bell, 19?

SHEPPARD, MAJOR E. W.: *The Study of Military History* (Gale Polden, 1953).

STOCQUELER, J. H.: *The Military Encyclopædia* (W. H. Allen, 18?

TILLOTSON, J.: *Stories of the Wars, 1574–1658* (Ward Lock, 1899

VAGTS, ALFRED: *A History of Militarism* (Hollis and Carter, 196
Wars of the 19th Century (Cambridge University Press, 1914).

WAVELL, FIELD-MARSHAL EARL: *Soldiers and Soldiering* (Jon Cape, 1953).
————— *The Good Soldier* (Macmillan, 1948).
————— *Allenby: Soldier and Statesman* (Harrap, 1946).

WHITMAN, CAPTAIN J. E. A.: *How Wars Are Fought* (Oxford U sity Press, 1941).

Other reference works are mentioned in the text.

I have also referred to various issues of the *Army Quarterl British Army Review*, the *Royal United Services Institution Jo the *Swiss Military Review*, and other foreign official Service maga

Index

--------◇◆◇--------

2/05'